Additional Praise for *Currency Trading and Intermarket Analysis*

"Ashraf Laïdi shows his deep and broad knowledge of the currency markets in this book. As one of the most prolific analysts on the Forex markets, Laïdi outlines the historical linkage of monetary policy, world finance, and currency markets into a readable primer for any student of the global markets."

—Ginger Szala, Publisher/Editorial Director, Futures Magazine Group

"*Barron's* readers often ask if there is a book to explain to them how markets really work. After plowing through textbooks and graduate studies, it took three-plus decades of covering markets to learn that academics live in a different world than the day-to-day markets. Ashraf Laïdi has produced a work that is accessible to the layperson but at the same time provides a sophisticated view of all markets—commodities, precious metals, credit, and equities—and how they interact with the biggest market of all, currencies. If only I had this book when I started out!"

—Randall W. Forsyth, Editor, Barron's Online

"A very detailed book with an important flow of information and specific details related to some well-known periods of the USD changes. It should clearly please beginners seeking a better understanding of FX movements over the last decades. For sophisticated investors, they will appreciate discovering the new angles introduced in dissecting the major developments in currencies."

—Hamid Bousba, Director, Senior Portfolio Counsellor,
Citi Private Bank, Citibank (Switzerland)

Currency Trading and Intermarket Analysis

Founded in 1807, John Wiley & Sons is the oldest independent publishing company in the United States. With offices in North America, Europe, Australia and Asia, Wiley is globally committed to developing and marketing print and electronic products and services for our customers' professional and personal knowledge and understanding.

The Wiley Trading series features books by traders who have survived the market's ever changing temperament and have prospered—some by reinventing systems, others by getting back to basics. Whether a novice trader, professional or somewhere in-between, these books will provide the advice and strategies needed to prosper today and well into the future.

For a list of available titles, please visit our Web site at www.Wiley Finance.com.

Currency Trading and Intermarket Analysis

How to Profit from the Shifting Currents in Global Markets

ASHRAF LAÏDI

WILEY

John Wiley & Sons, Inc.

Published by John Wiley & Sons, Inc., Hoboken, New Jersey.
Published simultaneously in Canada.

For general information on our other products and services or for technical support, please contact our Customer Care Department within the United States at (800) 762-2974, outside the United States at (317) 572-3993 or fax (317) 572-4002.

Wiley also publishes its books in a variety of electronic formats. Some content that appears in print may not be available in electronic books. For more information about Wiley products, visit our web site at www.wiley.com.

Library of Congress Cataloging-in-Publication Data:

Laidi, Ashraf.
    Currency trading and intermarket analysis : how to profit from the shifting currents in global markets / Ashraf Laidi.
        p. cm. – (Wiley trading series)
    Includes bibliographical references and index.
    ISBN 978-0-470-22623-0 (cloth)
    1. Foreign exchange market.   2. Foreign exchange futures.   3. Investment analysis.
I. Title.
    HG3851.L315 2009
    332.4'5–dc22

                                                            2008032245

Printed in the United States of America.

10 9 8 7 6 5 4 3 2

To my parents Ahmed & Aisha Laïdi

Contents

Foreword

On the day of my birth, "Good Friday" March 31st, 1961, the Dow Jones Industrial Average was sitting at 678.5. The dollar was still anchored to gold, exchangeable at $35 an ounce. Interest rates were regulated and low, the economy was strong and steady in the fifteen years after the end of World War II.

The "Bretton Woods" global currency system of fixed exchange rates was in place and there was relative stability in the pre-Vietnam, pre-hippie years.

Ten years later, the next, and only, time my birthday would fall on "Good Friday," such stability was no longer assured. A few short months later, the stability fostered by the 1944 "Bretton Woods Accord" would be shattered when President Richard Nixon abandoned the gold standard on August 15, 1971.

I was ten years old and don't remember the event. I only remember the ramifications.

Within a matter of months, I recall that inflation became a national issue. As a young boy growing up in blue collar Buffalo, New York, I was perplexed as to why, so suddenly, food and energy costs were rising in a way that hurt my family's finances.

My father never made that much money to begin with, so the incipient inflation that would rage another 10 years, hurt us in ways I never understood.

We began crossing the "PeaceBridge," a span that connected Buffalo to the edge of Canada and bought groceries in another country where they were cheaper.

Shortly thereafter came the first of two oil shocks, wage and price controls, "Whip Inflation Now" buttons, and an economy so ragged and uneven we left a dying town for the presumed land of milk and honey, California.

But even there, another oil shock hit in 1979, gas lines were long and mean, social unrest set in, my first car loan, $2,000 for a tan 4-door, 1979 Chevy Nova (a babe magnet if ever there was one) cost me $20^1/_2$ percent in interest.

The economic calm of my birth year had turned to chaos and nearly ruinous chaos, at that.

Much of it came amid a radical departure from the "sound money" principles that drove our economy in the post-War years.

After twenty years of relative calm, from 1981 to 2001, again we find ourselves in a similar predicament, though with different root causes. The dollar, until recently, was falling precipitously as this latest credit crisis dramatically weakened the U.S. economy. A combustible mix of financial engineering and excess leverage has cost us dearly.

Among the fixes that may one day be necessary may be a more formal, global foreign exchange regime. While I am not necessarily a fan of returning to the "gold standard," I do understand and personally appreciate the need for a more stable global monetary system that contains and restrains some of the more animal spirits of markets gone wild.

It is my fervent hope that in the ensuing months and years we will find new and better ways to limit the damage that financial market panics have wrought, particularly the one of most recent vintage, which I believe has the capacity to entirely destabilize the world economy.

We need a much more enlightened, coordinated, and concerted global policy response to the financial market meltdown we are now enduring. Part of it may include a reform of our currency trading system. The currency markets are the biggest and most liquid markets in the world. And even though in a free-floating exchange rate system, a country's currency, rather than its interest rates or its real economy, acts as the "shock absorber" during times of stress. That shock absorber is being tested today.

Hopefully it will survive the test. Nearly half a century into my life, I am hoping that my ten-year-old daughter and my other two children do not have to face the wrenching dislocations I did some thirty-seven years ago, and will instead enjoy the serene calm that existed on the day of my birth, not the chaos that erupted just after my tenth birthday.

Ron Insana

Preface

As the weakness in the U.S. dollar becomes a prolonged trend in the foreign exchange market and the euro assumes an increasingly credible position in global exchanges, currencies are no longer a topic restricted to economists or bank traders. With the multiyear bull markets in stocks, bonds, and real estate having largely concluded their upward run, global investors remain on a continuous quest for yield. In the United States, individual investors have more than quadrupled their holdings of non-U.S. stocks between 1996 and 2007, elevating their awareness of foreign economies and currencies to new heights. Meanwhile, the multitude of banks and brokerage houses offering currency trading services for investors has increasingly integrated foreign exchange into investor portfolios worldwide.

Academics and market professionals have done their bit in producing literature about the mechanics of foreign exchange markets and the theories underpinning them. But relatively little is written on how to explore the practical intermarket relationships that shape currencies via interest rates, equities, and commodities. Most investors have come across the notion of interest rates' impact on foreign exchange rates, but have yet to grasp the situations when interest rates and central bank policy are displaced by shifting risk appetite and economic growth. While central banks aim to manage expectations in bond and currency markets, they tend to misread such risks as asset price inflation and financial market contagion, leaving professional and institutional investors wrong-footed. Integrating commodities into the mix, record-breaking prices have significantly driven the foreign exchange market, raising the need for investors to determine the currencies most responsive to price developments in energy, metals, food, and agricultural raw materials. And given the plethora of media types generating constant financial market information and advice, investors need to separate noise from sound market and economic signals.

This book aims at placing readers ahead of the pack in assessing shifts in economic and market dynamics so as to better predict central bank policy changes and make profitable decisions in currency markets accordingly. It also strives to build an understanding of market risk appetite and to highlight the currency implications of the changes in risk-driven flows. While the book's central theme is the foreign exchange market, it exposes the intermarket intricacies shaping currencies via equity, bond, and commodity markets. Noneconomic/market considerations, such as geopolitical events, are also addressed in detail to explain the changing trends in low- and high-yielding currencies.

The intended readership comprises those requiring a comprehensive breakdown of the intermarket forces driving foreign exchange rates. Anyone wishing to learn how to anticipate changes in central bank policies and their market consequences will find value in the chapters about yield curves and the Federal Reserve. In addition to those trading currencies for themselves, a bank, or a corporate treasury, traders of interest rate and equity indexes may also benefit from the unified approach in the book. Economists, students, and market reporters seeking a comprehensive analysis of the real-life interrelationships between currencies, equities, interest rates, and commodities will find here a unique analysis of tried and tested market patterns.

Chapter 1 starts with a historical investigation of the relationship between gold and the U.S. dollar, before introducing a gold-based approach to valuing the major currencies and determining their secular strengths and weaknesses throughout the past decades. The chapter also touches upon the role of gold relative to other commodities as a preview for Chapter 8, which is devoted to commodities supercycles.

Chapter 2 offers detailed analysis of the economic and geopolitical events shaping oil and the U.S. dollar since the 1971 collapse of the Bretton Woods currency system. The major shifts in oil diplomacy and U.S. monetary policy are carefully addressed, providing incisive examination into the evolving powers of oil-producing nations and their impact on the world economy.

Chapters 3 and 4 contain an original approach in ranking the major foreign exchange rates between 1999 and 2007 in relative and absolute terms, while citing the fundamental forces underpinning currency performances. A wide range of variables are tackled, such as national and world GDP growth, interest rates, capital flows, external balances, risk appetite, and commodity and equity markets.

Chapter 5 devotes substantive analysis to the role of carry trades in shaping risk appetite via low- and high-yielding currencies. An area of the financial market that is seldom understood by academics but regularly tackled in trading circles, risk appetite is addressed with demonstrable examples of major shifts in volatility, corporate spreads, and currency futures.

Chapter 6 picks up where several books on currencies left off in considering interest rates. The chapter exposes the relationship between

short- and longer-term interest rates and how it is best applied to anticipate vital shifts in central bank decisions and turning points in economic
growth. The relationship between oil and gold is also used as a complement
to improve the forecasting of these important cyclical shifts.

Chapter 7 highlights the widening budget and current account deficits
of the United States and the changing patterns of capital flows financing
these imbalances. Central bank currency reserves are analyzed in regions
such as the oil-producing nations, while assessing the evolution of power
between the dollar and the euro.

Chapter 8 examines the latest commodity boom with a breakdown by
individual commodity group and the implication for currencies. In addition to assessing the performance of commodity currencies, this chapter
evaluates the cyclical pattern between commodities and equities and the
implications for monetary and hard assets.

Chapter 9 introduces diverse currency themes ranging from the historical relationship between U.S. politics and the dollar, to the cyclical evolution of commodities relative to equities. The chapter revisits the U.S. yield
curve and interest rate cycles, while including the USD/JPY exchange rate
as an additional element in confirming tightening interest rate cycles.

Currency markets have increased in size and speed and so has their impact on the global financial scene. Attaining a solid grasp of these markets
is no longer limited to figuring out interest rate and growth differentials.
Currency Trading and Intermarket Analysis offers comprehensive tools
to maneuver through macroeconomic and financial market nuances with
the objective of making profitable decisions in foreign exchange markets.

Acknowledgments

I would first like to express my gratitude to Kevin Commins of John Wiley & Sons, who turned my aspiration of authoring a book into a reality. His command of the markets as well as his flexibility to work through the multi-themed dynamics of this book have proven invaluable for this project. I owe exceptional debt to my editor Emilie Herman, whose patience and understanding of my unfathomable time constraints were vital in maintaining mobility to the book and its frequent revisions. And thanks also to Meg Freeborn and Laura Walsh of Wiley.

My sincere thanks to Patrick Kempf, whose research prowess and resourcefulness exceeded expectations of quality and expediency regardless of what part of the world he happened to have been in. I also thank Eric Chang and Colin Cieszynski for always providing me the help I needed at short notice.

Many thanks to Vassili Serebriakov, Vicki Schmelzer, and Mohannad Aama, whose suggestions, feedback, and thought-provoking conversations helped raise vital questions on the divergence between the economy and the markets. A heartfelt thanks to Sarah Mitwalli for her support.

My gratitude to Ron Insana, Peter Garnham, and Alan Abelson for their incisive coverage of the markets and constant challenging of the conventional ways of analysis and assessment. I extend my gratitude to John Murphy, whose 1991 work on intermarket analysis revolutionized the all-encompassing approach toward financial markets and the global economy. A special thanks to Drs. Scheherazade Rehman and Hossein Askari for conveying their wealth of academic and practical expertise in international finance and economics in such an enthusiastic, professional, and inviting manner.

My love and heartfelt gratitude to my parents and sister, Ahmed, Aisha, and Adila, for their love and unconditional support.

Currency Trading and Intermarket Analysis

CHAPTER 1

Gold and
the Dollar

The relationship between gold and the dollar has long mirrored the decades-old battle between real tangible assets and financial assets. Traditionally the dollar has been the representative currency in any analysis of gold, due to its sustained role as the world's reserve currency and the preferred means of exchange and invoicing transactions. The creation of the euro in 1999 and its subsequent ascent as a credible and strengthening currency has certainly started to challenge the dollar's leading position among world currencies, but the euro has yet to dethrone the greenback from its dominating perch. Nonetheless, the probability of such occurrence has been gradually on the rise and may fully materialize as early as 2015.

Considering the 400-year historical connection between gold and paper currencies, the 100 years of dollar dominance, and the role of gold in initiating the present world currency order, it is appropriate to begin this book with the evolution of the relationship between gold, the dollar, and other currencies. Aside from examining the eventual trend between gold and the greenback, this chapter sheds light on how currency market participants can absorb the price developments in gold vis-à-vis currencies and equities in order to gain a better grasp of the cyclical shifts underpinning markets and economics.

During the final third of the nineteenth century, most countries abandoned the silver standard in favor of a gold-based currency standard. These moves were largely triggered by Germany's receipt of a war indemnity from France in gold following the Franco-Prussian war, prompting Germany to unload silver on its trading partners. As Germany adopted the deutsche mark, backing it with a strict gold standard, most nations followed suit and opted for the metal. But the merits of the gold standard were in doubt after the British economy began to slump in the 1880s.

The gold exchange standard ultimately saw its demise in the 1920s when World War I disrupted trade flows and the free movement of gold. In 1931, massive gold withdrawals from London banks triggered Britain's abandonment of the gold standard, and three years later the United States introduced the U.S. Gold Reserve Act under President Roosevelt's New Deal. The Act reset the value of gold at $35 per ounce from $20.67 per ounce and ended the legal ownership of gold coins and bullion by citizens for over 20 years.

END OF BRETTON WOODS SYSTEM MARKS GOLD'S TAKEOFF

The Bretton Woods Agreement of 1944 launched the first system of convertible currencies and fixed exchange rates, requiring participating nations to maintain the value of their currency within a narrow margin against the U.S. dollar and a corresponding gold rate of $35 per gold ounce. But the U.S. dollar began to lose value in the 1950s and 1960s, due to surging U.S. capital outflows aimed at Europe's postwar recovery, as well as an expanding global supply of U.S. dollars, which made it increasingly difficult for the United States to convert dollars into gold on demand at a fixed exchange rate.

The surge of the Eurodollar market in the late 1960s—where international banks held U.S. dollars outside the United States—coupled with the escalating costs of the Vietnam War led to the near depletion of U.S. gold reserves and a devaluation of the U.S. dollar relative to gold. At the same time, the United States kept on printing more dollars for which there was no gold backing. This persisted as long as the world was willing to accept those dollars with little question. But when France demanded in the late 1960s that the U.S. fulfill its promise to pay one ounce of gold for each $35 it delivered to the U.S. Treasury, a shortage of gold began to ensue relative to a widening supply of dollars. On August 15, 1971, Nixon shut down the gold window, refusing to pay out any of the remaining 280 million ounces of gold. Figure 1.1 shows the inverse relationship between gold and the dollar since the fall of Bretton Woods.

A series of dollar devaluations in the early 1970s eventually led to the end of the Bretton Woods system of fixed exchange rates, paving the way for a long-drawn-out decline in the dollar. This triggered a rapid ascent in the dollar value of two of the world's most vital commodities, metals

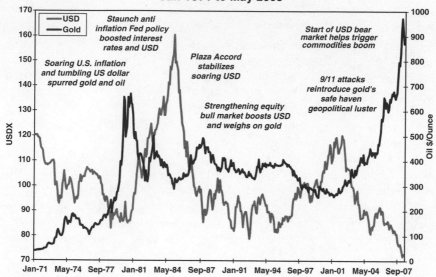

FIGURE 1.1 Gold prices generally move in inverse relation to the U.S. dollar as they compete over inflation risk, geopolitical uncertainty, and time value of money.

and oil. Oil producers holding the surplus of devalued U.S. dollars had no choice but to purchase gold in the marketplace, driving both the fuel and the metals higher and further dragging down the value of the dollar. A series of devaluations in 1972 culminated in the end of the Bretton Woods system in February 1973. The dollar became freely traded and freely sold.

From January 1971 to February 1973, the dollar dropped 26.0 percent against the yen, 4.0 percent against the British pound, and 17 percent against the deutsche mark. And from 1971 to 1980, the dollar lost 30 percent of its value in trade-weighted terms against a basket of currencies (deutsche mark, Japanese yen, British pound, Canadian dollar, Swiss franc, and Swedish krone).

FED TIGHTENING AND FX INTERVENTIONS REIN IN GOLD RALLY

A series of geopolitical events coupled with rising U.S. inflation increased gold prices more than fivefold in the later 1970s as financial markets sought refuge in the security of the precious metal from the eroding value of paper money. The falling dollar was exacerbated by OPEC's price hikes, which added fuel to the inflation fire. Surging social unrest in 1978 led to the 1979 hostage crisis at the U.S. Embassy in Tehran, which culminated in the over-throwing of the Shah and the Iranian Revolution. Oil prices nearly tripled between 1979 and 1980, and gold's last major surge spiked before start-ing a 20-year period of hibernation. The Soviet invasion and occupation of Afghanistan in December 1979 raised fears of renewed tensions between the United States and the Soviet Union, further destabilizing the security outlook in the region. In just three weeks, gold jumped from $520 to $835 per ounce. But what later ensued was a testament to the importance of economics over geopolitics in the behavior of gold.

In autumn 1979, U.S. inflation hit a 32-year high of 13 percent, despite double-digit interest rates. In October the Federal Reserve, under the new leadership of Paul Volcker, made the historical decision to shift monetary policy toward the targeting of money supply, away from the targeting in-terest rates. This meant that the Fed would manage monetary policy so as to lower monetary aggregates, with interest rates acting as a secondary element. The two years of ultratight monetarism saw interest rates hit 20 percent in 1981, leaving international investors little choice but to seek the high-yielding greenback as a way to offset double-digit inflation. Figure 1.2

FIGURE 1.2 Deteriorating geopolitics of the 1970s propelled gold prices up on the back of soaring inflation before Fed's tight monetarism headed off 20-year bear market in gold.
Source: U.S. Geological Survey.

shows U.S. inflation was more than halved in 1982, dragging gold down with it. In the first half of the 1980s, the dollar index jumped 50 percent while gold tumbled by the same amount to hit a six-year low.

CENTRAL BANKS' GOLD SALE AGREEMENTS

In 1997–1999, several central banks from Western Europe sold substantial amounts of their gold in an uncoordinated manner, with the principal aim of realizing substantial capital gains in the gold holdings they had purchased several decades earlier. Those gains helped beef up national budgets and state finances. The 11 European nations that first joined the Eurozone had to abide by strict fiscal conditions requiring that budget deficits not exceed 3 percent of GDP. The gold sales helped erode the value of the metal by 25 percent between 1995 and 1998, and lifted the U.S. dollar against the Japanese yen and deutsche mark by 84 percent and 36 percent respectively.

Central bank gold sales were particularly punishing for the precious metal in 1999 as both the Bank of England and Swiss National Bank stepped up their selling. In May 1999, gold's decline began after the announcement from the UK Treasury that it planned to sell 415 tons of gold. The announcement triggered a massive wave of producers' hedging activity and front-running speculation. A month later, the Swiss National Bank (SNB) decided that gold was no longer an integral part of monetary policy making and announced the sale of half of its 2,590 tons of gold reserves over the next five or six years. The central banks' announcements led to a 13 percent fall in gold to $252 per ounce, the lowest level in 20 years. Without any systematic limits on volume and frequency of the sales and no coordination, central banks were free to dump gold at their own choosing, creating sharp declines in the metal, and rapid moves in currency markets.

The resulting price action in gold ultimately paved the way for the first central bank agreement on gold sales, which provided the framework for subsequent gold sales by the Swiss National Bank, the European Central Bank (ECB), and 13 European national central banks. Under the agreement, the SNB sold 1,170 tons, which accounted for the bulk of the total 2,000 tons in sales by all participating central banks. As gold prices accelerated their fall, the European central banks sought to boost confidence in the metal and stabilize the plummeting value of their newly created euro currency by establishing the Washington Agreement on Gold. On September 26, 1999, 15 central banks (the ECB plus the 11 founding members of the Eurozone, Sweden, Switzerland, and the United Kingdom) announced a collective cap on their gold sales at around 400 tonnes per year over the next five years.

When the Washington Agreement on Gold expired in 2004, a new agreement was reached for the 2004–2009 period, called the Central Bank Agreement on Gold. The new arrangement raised the amount of annual gold sales to 500 tonnes from 400 tonnes set in the original agreement. The higher threshold of gold sales would help stabilize the value of the U.S. dollar, after the currency had lost 22 percent between 1999 and 2004 and the metal rallied 60 percent over the same period. As of 2007, central banks held nearly 20 percent of the worlds' aboveground gold stocks as a reserve asset, with individual nations holding approximately 10 percent of their reserves in the metal.

GOLD-USD INVERSE RELATION

One of the most widely known relationships in currency markets is perhaps the inverse relation between the U.S. dollar (USD) and the value of gold. This relationship stems mainly from the fact that gold serves as an inflation hedge through its metal value, while the U.S. dollar holds its value via the interest rate commanded by it. As the dollar's exchange value falls, it takes more dollars to buy gold, therefore lifting the value of gold. Conversely, when the dollar's exchange value rises, it takes fewer dollars to buy gold, thereby dragging down the dollar price of gold. Unlike currencies, government bonds, and corporate stocks—all of which are determined by demand and supply as well as the issuing power of central banks and corporations—gold is largely dependent on demand and supply and is therefore immune to shifts in monetary and corporate policies and the new issuance of equity, debt, and currency.

While gold's distinction from fiat currencies maintains an inverse relation with currencies other than the U.S. dollar, the negative correlation remains most striking against the U.S. dollar due to the currency's dominance in central bank currency reserves. Figure 1.1 showed the inverse relationship between gold and the dollar from 1970 to 2008. Figure 1.3 illustrates the highly inverse relationship between gold and the dollar between January 1999 and May 2008, highlighting a −0.84 correlation.

RECENT EXCEPTIONS TO THE INVERSE RULE

As with all close relationships between two assets, the USD-gold relationship has not been without its temporary periods of decoupling. The most

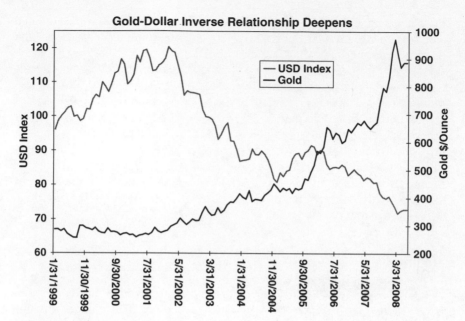

Gold-Dollar Inverse Relationship Deepens

FIGURE 1.3 Monthly correlation between gold and U.S. dollar index from January 1999 to May 2008 ran as high as −0.84, with a slight break in the relationship in 2005.

striking break in the relation occurred between April and December 2005 when both gold and the dollar appreciated. Figure 1.4 shows that the correlation had run as high as 0.66, showing a remarkably strong positive relationship. The explanation for this unusual correlation relates to developments pertaining to gold, the dollar, and the euro.

Gold was in the midst of a secular bull market that had started in 2001 and gathered strength in 2002 with the peak and the subsequent decline in the dollar. The rally was further intensified by the 2005 revaluation of China's currency, which enabled it to step up appetite for gold and other commodities.

The dollar's role in the temporary break in the USD-gold inverse relationship owed to the two-year campaign of U.S. interest rate increases (from June 2004 to June 2006), which lifted U.S. short-term interest rates above their Eurozone counterpart in the fourth quarter of 2004 for the first time in three years. As the U.S. interest rate advantage over the Eurozone was further widened by the Fed's 2005 rate hikes, the U.S. dollar strengthened against the euro, especially as the European Central Bank maintained rates at a historic low of 2.0 percent.

Also contributing to the dollar's 2005 recovery was a temporary tax break granted by the Bush administration to U.S. multinationals, allowing them to repatriate their profits from their overseas subsidiaries. The

FIGURE 1.4 The gold-U.S. dollar relationship became positive in 2005 due to higher U.S. interest rates, temporary U.S. tax incentives, and political Eurozone uncertainty, while gold rallied on strong Chinese demand.

Homeland Investment Act, designed to improve job creation, slashed the tax on multinationals' overseas profits from 35 percent to 5.25 percent. U.S. multinationals rushed to take advantage of the substantial tax break and repatriated an estimated $600 billion, prompting a surge of inflows into U.S. dollars from euros, especially in the second half of the year. Unsurprisingly, the temporary inflows of 2005 gave the dollar its best annual performance against the euro since 1999.

Since the euro makes up 58 percent of the dollar index, it is worth mentioning one factor specific to the Eurozone behind the euro's 2005 decline against the dollar and other major currencies. France's rejection of a proposed European Union Constitution dealt a blow to confidence in the European Union and the future of its currency, particularly because France is the second-largest economy of the Eurozone.

USING GOLD TO IDENTIFY CURRENCY LEADERS AND LAGGARDS

Assessing the performance of currencies against the value of gold enables a transparent examination of the strength of a nation's currency, without the influence of dynamics in other currencies and their economies. A rising euro against the U.S. dollar, for instance, may not necessarily be a reflection of improved fundamentals in the Eurozone but of deteriorating fundamentals, technicals, and/or sentiment in the U.S. dollar. Meanwhile, the euro could be selling off against the Japanese yen and be little changed against the British pound—a different performance from that against the dollar. Charting the euro against gold would allow for a secular view of the euro, which is not influenced by factors specific to individual currencies. Unlike currencies, which are largely influenced by interest rate movements resulting from economic policies and capital flows, gold is mainly a reflection of supply and demand, and not a direct result of any particular central bank actions.

Charting several currencies against the price of gold presents a broader view of currencies against a neutral asset such as gold, enabling a less biased look at the currency in question. Figure 1.5a shows the percentage increase in the value of gold against the aussie (Australian dollar, AUD), loonie (Canadian dollar, CAD), euro (EUR), and kiwi (New Zealand dollar, NZD) from January 2001 to May 2008. All charts show an uptrend, reflecting gold's appreciation against all currencies since 2001. The graph with the least appreciation throughout most of the eight-year period is against the loonie, showing that gold grew the least against the Canadian currency. Nonetheless, at the end of the period, gold ended up 90.5 percent against the aussie versus 123 percent against the loonie, meaning gold's appreciation was the least against the Australian dollar. This suggests that the Aussie was the best-performing currency in the group. The weaker increase in gold against the AUD, CAD, and NZD reflected the broad rally in those currencies due to their dependence on rising commodities as well as high interest rates prevailing throughout the period.

Similarly, Figure 1.5b measures gold against the U.S. dollar, Swiss franc (CHF), Japanese yen (JPY), and British pound (GBP) over the same period. Note how gold's performance against these currencies was mostly higher than its performance in Figure 1.5a, suggesting these currencies have underperformed the AUD, CAD, EUR, and NZD. Thus, with gold showing the highest percentage increase against the USD and the lowest percentage increase against the AUD, we can conclude that playing the AUD/USD currency pair (buying AUD and selling USD) would have produced the highest rate of return if held between January 2001 and May 2008. Indeed, opportunities in foreign exchange markets are not limited solely to trading currencies against the USD, but also in those pairs involving non-USD currencies. Charting gold against different currencies over a three- or six-month period enables a truer assessment of individual currencies than comparing them against the dollar or the euro. This way, traders can not only determine the secular performance of currencies but may also rank them

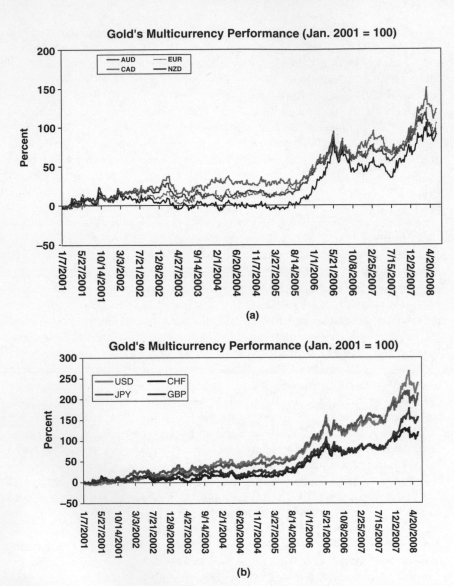

FIGURE 1.5 Measuring gold in various currencies enables more secular assessment of those currencies and better determination of strongest and weakest players.

in order of strength and be better able to buy the strongest against the weakest.

Figure 1.6 shows a more recent performance of gold against AUD, GBP, JPY, and USD, measuring currencies between January 2007 and May 2008. The aussie was the strongest performer against gold, followed by the

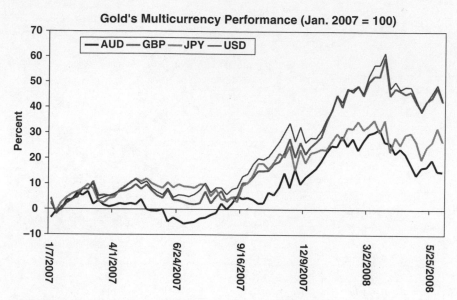

FIGURE 1.6 Gold's performance was weakest against AUD and JPY between January 2007 and May 2008, illustrating the strength in both of these currencies relative to GBP and USD.

yen, which fared significantly better than in Figure 1.5a. The yen's improvement owed primarily to the unwinding of carry trades as traders exited positions in high-yielding currencies and shifted their proceeds back to the lower-yielding yen for safety. Carry trades are discussed in more detail in Chapter 5.

GOLD'S SECULAR PERFORMANCE

The preceding exercise enabled investors to obtain a clearer picture of currencies' performances by valuing them against gold. Yet we could also aggregate each of the individual currencies' return performance against the price of gold to obtain gold's *total performance* for a specific period.

Figure 1.7 illustrates gold's aggregate annual returns against AUD, CAD, CHF, EUR, GBP, JPY, and NZD from 1999 to 2007 and the first five months of 2008. The chart shows a gradual increase in gold's aggregate annual growth from 1999 to 2001 before slowing the pace of growth in 2002 and 2003. Gold's aggregate growth rate was a negative 8 percent in 2004 before soaring by 239 percent in 2005. Growth was nearly halved in 2006 to 124 percent, then edged up to 145 percent in 2007. Since those returns are

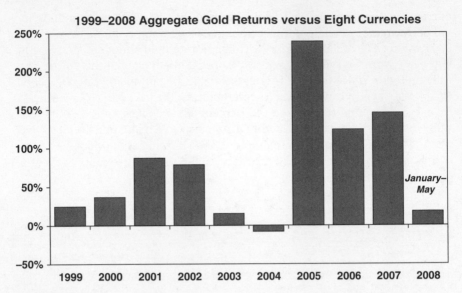

FIGURE 1.7 Gold's aggregate annual return versus AUD, CAD, CHF, EUR, GBP, JPY, and NZD illustrate the metal's broad performance between January 1999 and May 2008.

the aggregate of individual gold returns in distinct currencies, gold's performance is generally a function of the performance of individual currencies and paper currency in general.

By exploring the annual growth rates in detail, we note a sensible explanation to each of the moves. The 25 percent and 37 percent returns in 1999 and 2000 were clearly on the low side of the 82 percent annual average registered between 1999 and 2007. In those years, gold was under the dominance of a multiyear bull market in equities founded on low inflation and steady growth. Such were suitable ingredients for shutting investors' appetite in the precious metal. In fact, gold prices fell 6 percent in 2000 against the greenback, concluding a nine-year market. The following year, 2001, was the first in nearly a decade in which gold would rise against all of the major eight currencies. This increase was due to a combination of an ensuing bear market in U.S. and world equities as well as a general slowdown in the global economy. The September 11 attacks also had a role in lifting gold as investors sought refuge in its safe-haven status at a time when a major financial center was under assault.

Gold went on to rally in 2002, before showing a mere 15 percent increase in 2003 and an 8 percent decline in 2004. Since these returns are an aggregate of gold's individual performance against several individual currencies, the main driver to gold's retreat in 2003–2004 was the individual performance of each of the currencies. The common theme in 2003 and 2004 was broad dollar weakness. Thus, despite gold's modest showing in aggregate terms, it rallied 24 percent and 20 percent against the dollar. The rally halted in 2004 when global central banks began raising interest rates. But in the secular bull market in commodities, China's voracious appetite for metals and gold triggered an 18 percent advance against the dollar and a 239 percent rally against all eight currencies. Gold's bull market extended into 2006 and 2007 on a combination of deteriorating economic and financial conditions in the United States and a general shift of global investor capital into rising commodities such as gold and oil.

VALUING CURRENCIES VIA GOLD

While Figure 1.7 illustrated gold's aggregate returns over a 10-year period, we could also use gold to compare currencies' performances across different periods. Figure 1.8 shows how gold fared in 2000 against the eight different currencies. Note how gold's two highest rates of returns occurred against the so-called commodity currencies of Australia and New Zealand due to the 2000 price slump in wheat, copper, and dairy products, all of which are primary sources of export revenue for these two countries. Conversely, gold showed the highest negative performance against the USD, followed by the CAD, which helps traders conclude that the USD was the

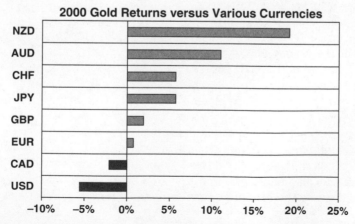

2000 Gold Returns versus Various Currencies

FIGURE 1.8 Gold's highest returns in 2000 fared against NZD and AUD, reflecting the slump in dairy products, copper, and wheat, primary exports in New Zealand and Australia.

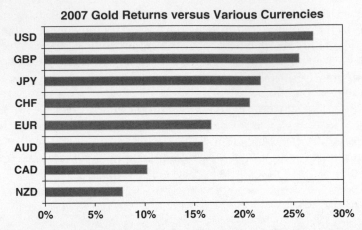

2007 Gold Returns versus Various Currencies

FIGURE 1.9 Gold's 2007 currency performances were almost a mirror image of 2000 as the commodities rebound lifted NZD, CAD, and AUD at the expense of USD.

highest-performing currency against all other currencies, with the CAD in second place.

It is important to note that currencies' ranking against gold does not always imply a similar ranking against one another. A few exceptions have occurred, such as in 2000 when the Swiss franc fared as the third-worst underperformer against gold due to the Swiss National Bank's sales of its bullion. In that year, however, the Swiss franc stood as the second-highest performer (after the U.S. dollar) when measured in aggregate terms against all seven other currencies.

Fast-forwarding seven years ahead, we find a largely different picture for gold in 2007. Gold had not only outperformed all currencies—reflecting the emerging bull market in the metal and commodities in general—but also showed the relative performance of currencies during the year. Put in another way, the 2007 relative performance of currencies was the near opposite of 2000, dominated by the commodity boom as well as commodity currencies. Similarly, with the U.S. dollar underperforming all major currencies during the commodity rally, gold showed the highest performance against the greenback. (See Figure 1.9.)

GOLDEN CORRELATIONS

The inverse relationship between gold and the U.S. dollar has implied a generally positive relationship between gold and currencies whose correlation with the dollar has the highest negative correlation. The euro has proven to be the most negatively correlated currency against the U.S. dollar due to the fact that EUR/USD is the largest traded currency pair in the foreign exchange market. And because the Eurozone is the world's second largest economy after the United States, its currency is most apt to act as the *anti-dollar*, rallying at the expense of the greenback and selling off to its benefit.

Figure 1.10 illustrates the six-month gold correlations with the dollar index, the aussie, the euro, the yen, and New Zealand dollar from January 2002 to May 2008. The USDX is the only currency with negative territory, illustrating an average rolling six-month correlation of −0.53. Both EUR and AUD show the highest average positive correlation at 0.53 each, with the former acting as the anti-dollar and the latter correlating with its vast mining industry. The JPY had the lowest positive average correlation at 0.39. Notably, NZD's six-month correlation with gold stood at 0.78 over the last four months of the measured period. Nonetheless, the *average* of the NZD's six-month rolling correlation from January 2002 to June 2008 stood at a mere 0.43. Any close correlation between the NZD and gold is attributed to the nation's dependence on dairy products as well as lamb and mutton, which have shown considerable proximity to the trend in gold. But the correlation between the agriculture-dependent currency and gold proves insufficient to last through most of the seven-year period.

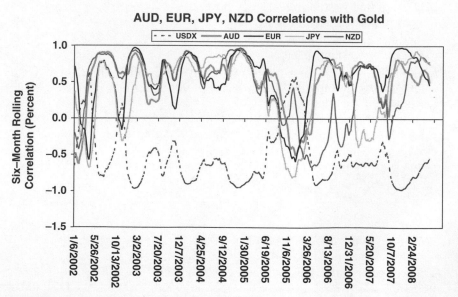

AUD, EUR, JPY, NZD Correlations with Gold

FIGURE 1.10 Gold's correlations are highest with Aussie and Euro.

DON'T FORGET FALLING GOLD PRODUCTION

So far, much has been discussed about the financial market underpinnings of the rally in gold: falling dollar, falling interest rates, rising inflation, and investors seeking the safety of the metal during equity market sell-offs. But, as is explored in more detail in Chapter 8, the gold rally has been founded considerably on major supply and demand conditions. These included plummeting world production, rising commercial demand by wealthier working class populations, and soaring demand for commodity-based funds.

Simply mentioning falling production as a reason is not enough for addressing factors behind the bull market in gold. Falling production has resulted from several factors, including chronic underinvestment in the mining sector; widespread power shortages in China and South Africa; prolonged strikes and mounting contract negotiations by mine workers demanding higher share of profits from surging metals prices; lack of skilled labor force as well as aging population of workers; and environmental restrictions adding to existing delays. World gold production fell more than 1 percent to 2,444 tons in 2007, reaching its lowest level since 2004. After producing as much as 1,000 tons of gold in 1970 and assuming the world's number one spot in gold production, South Africa has seen its mining production decline for five straight years into 2007. In 2007 alone, South African production fell 8 percent to 272 tons of gold, dropping to second place for the first time since 1905, according to GFMS.

Falling global oil production was somewhat stabilized by China's rising production, where output rose 12 percent to 276 tons of gold in 2007, accounting for 10 percent of total world production. China went from producing 71 tons in 1988 to 134 tons in 1998 and to 276 tons in 2007. (See Figure 1.11.)

GOLD AND EQUITIES: HARD VERSUS MONETARY ASSETS

Earlier in this chapter, several currencies were measured in terms of gold in order to gauge their true strength, rather than simply measuring them against the U.S. dollar or other currencies. Similarly, gold can fulfill the same purpose for major stock indexes. Instead of measuring the value of the S&P 500 or Dow Jones Industrial Average index against the U.S. dollar as is customarily done, we can price it in gold terms. As in the previous

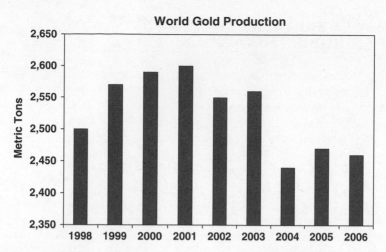

FIGURE 1.11 Falling gold production results from South Africa's supply problems, but China's recent number one position in world production fills the gap. *Source:* U.S. Geological Survey (http://www.goldsheetlinks.com/production.htm).

exercise with currencies, pricing the major stock averages in terms of gold enables a truer perspective for equities because they are compared against the currency of gold, whose value is solely influenced by natural forces of supply and demand and cannot be manipulated by any issuing authority as is done to national currencies by their central banks. And since gold cannot be easily produced as the way money is printed, its secular nature presents a fair benchmark for valuing other assets. By comparing gold with equities, we assess the two most popular measures of corporate market value seen in the major equity indexes (stock indexes) to a classic measure of real asset value (gold).

Before we look at the equity/gold ratios, let's examine the growth in gold prices versus that of major equity indexes. Figure 1.12 shows this growth comparison between January 2002 and May 2008. The beginning of the period occurred near the start of the bull market in gold while coinciding with the intensification of the bear market in equities. As of May 30, 2008, gold was 221 percent greater than where it was at the start of 2002, while the S&P 500 and the Dow Jones Industrial Average were 21 percent and 25 percent higher. But note that since their peak in October 2007, both the S&P 500 and the Dow have dropped nearly 20 percent, while gold rose by 50 percent over the same seven-month period.

For a longer-term perspective on equities and gold, Figure 1.13 compares their performances between January 1997 and May 2008. Note how gold carved out a bottom in early 2000, about the same time that equities topped out. What followed was a four-year inverse relationship

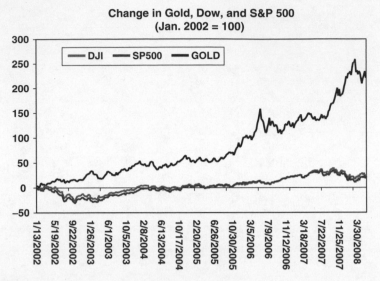

FIGURE 1.12 Gold rose 10 times faster than the S&P 500 and Dow Jones Industrial Average between January 2002 and May 2008.

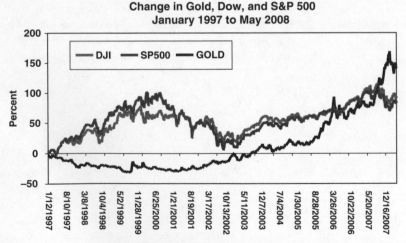

FIGURE 1.13 Although equities recovered from the 2000–2002 bear market, their gains paled compared to gold's recovery.

between equities and gold, with the latter prolonging its bull run and the former shedding losses during the post dot-com bust. When the U.S. and global economies recovered by the end of 2003, both equities and gold advanced higher, with the metal rising at a growth rate 10 times faster than equities.

EQUITY-TO-GOLD RATIOS

The rapid rise of gold relative to equities since the start of the decade may elicit some skepticism about the durability of the rally and whether the metal is in the midst of an expanding bubble. Having compared the growth of gold relative to equities, we now look at the two in relative terms by examining the equity/gold ratio. The ratio compares a commonly used measure of market value versus a decades-long measure of real asset value. Gold is known to measure real asset value because of its ability to preserve value during inflationary times. Since prior charts (Figures 1.12 and 1.13) have demonstrated a significantly faster growth rate in gold than in equities, it logically follows that the equity/gold ratio has fallen off its 1999 peak. Figure 1.14 charts the Dow/gold ratio and S&P 500/gold ratio since 1920. Both ratios have fallen more than 200 percent off their 1999 peak, which occurred when gold hit its 20-year lows and equities reached their highs at the top of the dot-com bubble.

Notably, since the 1920s, the equity/gold ratio has peaked approximately every 35 to 40 years: first in the late 1920s, then again in the mid-1960s, and once more in the late 1990s. Following each of these three peaks, stocks fell in a multiyear sell-off, accompanied by a rally in gold.

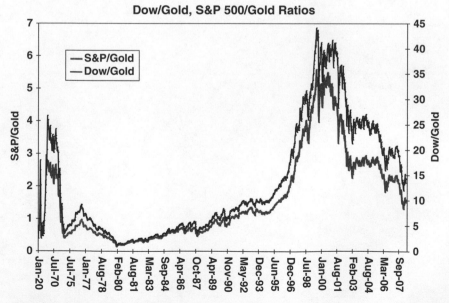

FIGURE 1.14 The plunge in the equity/gold ratio reflects the overall recovery in tangible versus monetary assets.

Once having peaked in 2000, stocks headed into a three-year bear market before recovering in 2003 and hitting new highs in late 2007. But as we saw earlier, stocks' 2003–2007 recovery did not prevent the equity/gold rally from extending its decline due to the accelerating advances in gold. (See Figure 1.15.)

The principal conclusion to be drawn from the near 90 years of equity/gold analysis is that each peak was followed by a full retracement to the lows preceding each advance. If this pattern holds into the future, then the equity/gold ratio has further declines ahead of it until recapturing the lows of the early 1980s. Whether this occurs via a faster decline in equities or persistent acceleration in gold's advances remains to be seen. Chapter 8 makes the case for a prolonged increase in the current commodities boom, in which gold will likely play a considerable role. The confluence of supply and demand factors boosting the broad commodity story suggests the bullish trend is unlikely to be reversed soon. Accordingly, prolonged declines in the equity/gold ratio will also imply that the real-asset values of tangibles such as metals, energy, and agriculture/food products will maintain their upward trajectory. A return in the equity/gold ratio to its low levels of the late 1970s through early 1980s is more than plausible.

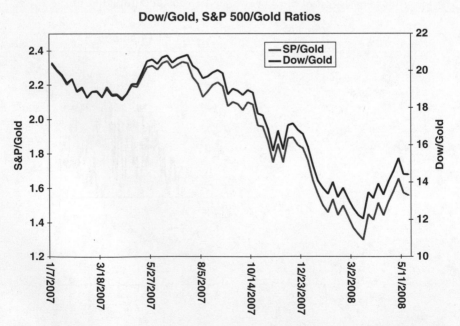

FIGURE 1.15 The equity/gold ratio recovered from its lows of March 2008, but the fundamentals underpinning commodities relative to equities suggest a limited rebound.

And while we are on the subject of the interaction between gold and monetary assets, it is worth weighing in on the current gold rally by comparing the amount of gold available versus the creation of monetary assets. Just as we have seen the ratio of major equity indexes to the price of gold falling to 13-year lows in late 2007, the ratio of total financial assets to physical gold is near the low end of its historical range. As a share of the valuation of all global stock markets and global bond markets, the world's available gold stands at a mere 3 to 4 percent, which is about four times lower than the ratio of the 1980s. Note how this difference in magnitude is similar to the aforementioned difference between the gold/equity ratio as of May 2008 and that of 1980, which was also four to five times greater.

THE ROLE OF THE SPECULATORS

As the commodity boom got under way, much talk circulated regarding the role of speculators in accelerating the rally in commodities. Chapter 8 is devoted strictly to the fundamentals underpinning the rise in gold and metals as well as energy and agricultural commodities. But let us take a glance at the role of speculators in gold over the past 17 years.

Figure 1.16 indicates a fairly positive correlation between the price of gold and the amount of net long/short positions accumulated in the metal

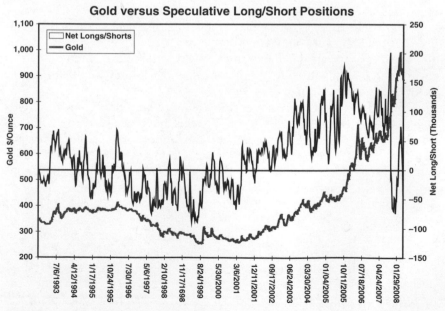

FIGURE 1.16 Speculators in gold futures contracts have helped boost gold prices but are not the main driver to the rally.

by futures speculators on the Chicago Mercantile Exchange in Chicago. Note, however, toward the end of the chart how the amount of interest plummeted from a record high of 201,859 net long contracts (more buyers than sellers) in October 2007 to an eight-year high of 74,343 net short contracts (more sellers than buyers) in January 2008. Despite the sharp reversal in net longs to net shorts during the three-month period, the price of gold remained on the rise, soaring from $750 per ounce to $895 per ounce over the same period. Thus, although the speculators have significantly curtailed their long positions, they could not reverse the price action in the metal, which was boosted by such events as the assassination of former Pakistani Prime Minister Benazir Bhutto, renewed erosion in U.S. and global financial markets over subprime loans in the United States, and aggressive interest rate cuts by the Federal Reserve.

GOLD IS PART OF A LARGER STORY

In further supporting the notion that speculators are not the principal drivers of gold's run-up, the breadth of the commodities story acts as a firm testament to the realities favoring metals and the rest of commodities. Figure 1.17 illustrates the evolution of the various commodity groups since January 2001. Note how the gold rally preceded all other commodities, starting as early as the third quarter of 2001 before accelerating its advances in the first quarter of 2002 once the dollar had peaked. Gold rallied more than 35 percent between January 2001 and February 2003, until oil caught up with the metal later that month as oil traders bid up the fuel ahead of the 2003 Gulf War. The relationship between oil and the dollar is discussed in more detail in Chapter 2.

For currency investors, not only is it important to determine the trend in gold versus the dollar and other currencies, but it is also essential to assess its performance relative to other commodities. Thus, if a rally in gold is accompanied by other commodity groups, as was the case in 2003, 2004, and 2007, then the U.S. dollar is more likely to be subject to broader secular pressure. If, however, a strengthening in gold occurs independently of the other commodity groups, then the dollar has more chances of holding its own.

The expansion of global foreign exchange markets, along with the emergence of a new array of several economies from the developed and developing world, has given rise to a multitude of new currencies to be traded by institutional as well as individual players. Making decisions about which currencies offer the most profitable opportunities can be as challenging as it is costly. Using gold as a common denominator measure of a group of

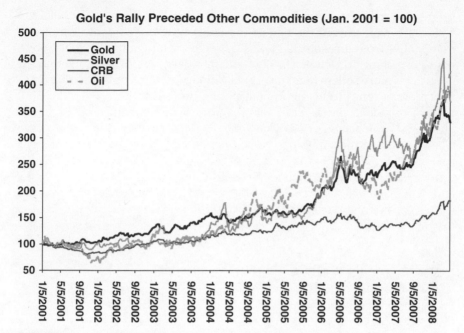

Gold's Rally Preceded Other Commodities (Jan. 2001 = 100)

FIGURE 1.17 Gold's bull market preceded other commodities by nearly a year, before the dollar decline triggered a more universal rally in commodities.

currencies enables one to rank these different currencies by order of performance, thereby facilitating the decision to buy the stronger currencies versus their weakest counterparts. For contrarian investors preferring to pick up trends before they occur, a similar exercise may be used to buy and sell currencies near the top and bottom of the ranking of returns. Besides currency valuation and ranking, traders may also compare gold's performance with that of other commodities to gauge whether the metal's behavior is part of an overall commodity trend or an exceptional phase pertaining to it exclusively.

Global financial markets have become more interconnected than they ever were in the past. Identifying the evolving forces shaping broader currency flows via gold is a prerequisite in grasping the currency-commodity relationship, which is explored in more detail in Chapter 8.

CHAPTER 2

Oil Fundamentals in the Currency Market

T he relationship between the most sought-after energy form and the world's reserve currency has invariably evolved via the intermediation of world economic growth and its response to energy prices. Each of the global recessions of the mid-1970s, early 1980s, and early 1990s was triggered by an oil shock stemming from soaring petroleum prices. As those recessions impacted the U.S. economy, the dollar came under pressure.

But oil prices did not always play the lead role in the dollar-oil causality. As this chapter will demonstrate, the tumbling dollar was a key factor in oil producers' decision to raise oil prices during the early 1970s in order to cushion the impact of a falling purchasing power as the weak currency eroded the value of their dollar-denominated oil receipts. In those cases, a falling dollar triggered rising oil prices, which in turn resulted in a global inflationary spiral and later a recession. As the Federal Reserve rushed to increase interest rates to counter the inflationary costs of high energy prices, U.S. yields gained in attractiveness, prompting the sharpest U.S. dollar rally in history.

But rising oil prices did not always boost the dollar. The arrival of alternative sources of energy, the rise of economic powers in the developing world, and the convergence of global economies via capital flows contributed to changes in the demand/supply equation for oil as well as its influence on different economies, whose currencies fluctuated significantly against the greenback. And no analysis of oil prices and the U.S. dollar can be undertaken without addressing the geopolitical events shaping the price of oil over the past half century, as well as the shifting dynamics in global

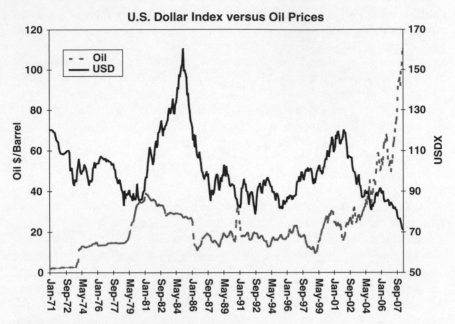

FIGURE 2.1 The inverse relationship between the U.S. dollar and oil was most striking during periods of protracted uptrends or downtrends in oil.

oil consumption and production. Finally, we will look at the relationship between the price of gold and oil over the past 30 years and how it helps investors assess the implications for the U.S. economy, interest rates, and the dollar (see Figure 2.1).

FROM A GOLD STANDARD TO AN OIL STANDARD (1970s–1980s)

The decline in the value of the dollar following the 1971 collapse of the gold-dollar exchange standard set up in Bretton Woods in 1944 played a vital role in fueling the upward spiral in oil prices of the first half of the 1970s.

Recall that during the Bretton Woods period, from 1944 until 1971, central banks converted their surplus dollars into gold in order to adjust for trade imbalances with their trade partners. The conversions were done at the fixed price of gold of US$35 per ounce. Oil prices, meanwhile, were mostly stable at about US$3.00 per barrel. But when Richard Nixon shut down the gold window, refusing to pay out nearly $300 million in ounces of gold to countries holding U.S. dollars, U.S. trading partners were left with mountains of surplus dollars that were no longer exchangeable into gold at $35 per ounce. Oil producers were forced to convert their excess U.S. dollars by purchasing gold in the marketplace, driving both the fuel and the metal higher and sending the value of the dollar lower.

The resulting devaluation of the surplus dollars around the world was a rude awakening to oil producers who had been receiving gold for their oil since 1933. From January 1971 to July 1973, the dollar index (measured against a basket of six currencies) lost 25 percent of its value, prompting the Organization of the Petroleum Exporting Countries (OPEC) to initiate its first price-boosting campaign. In October 1973, oil became a weapon when Arab oil producers set up an oil embargo against supporters of Israel in the Arab-Israeli war, cutting exports and reducing output by over 25 percent, thus producing the first oil shock in history. By the time the embargo was lifted against the United States in March 1974, oil prices had quadrupled to nearly $12 per barrel, triggering a global economic slowdown and inflation over the next three years.

In 1975, OPEC agreed to sell its oil exclusively for U.S. dollars, giving the depreciating U.S. currency the new role of world reserve currency and establishing oil as the preeminent energy resource of the world. While the Bretton Woods era of the 1950s to 1960s was known as the gold-backed standard, the 1970s and 1980s ushered in a de facto oil-dollar standard. It is no coincidence that the dollar value of the world's petroleum imports as a percentage of total fossil fuel imports fell from an average of 61 percent in the 1950s to 52 percent during the 1960s, before soaring to 70 percent in the 1970s. Unlike in the 1950s to 1960s when oil prices remained steady below $2.00 per barrel, partly due to the stable dollar/gold relationship of $35 per ounce, oil prices shot up in the 1970s as a result of the dollar's break from its fixed price against gold.

Oil Price Shocks Fueled by Mounting Inflation, Falling Dollar

Up to this day, many still attribute the quadrupling of oil prices in 1974 to OPEC's oil embargo and its increased political dominance. But in fact, it was the surging inflation of the late 1960s into the early 1970s and the falling value of the U.S. dollar that drove OPEC's decision to raise prices so as to make up for changes in real purchasing power. Recall that the pressure on the dollar escalated as early as the late 1960s when the cost of financing the Vietnam War and the Cold War drove up the balance of payments deficit. As dollars poured out of the United States and liabilities to foreign central banks soared, the world was flush with dollars while the U.S. gold stock was being depleted. Nixon's decision to shut the gold window in August

1971 ended the dollar's convertibility onto gold, prompting a collapse in the international financial system that was based on confidence in the U.S. dollar.

In December 1971, the dollar was devalued from the agreed-upon price of $35 per ounce of gold to $44.2 per ounce. A series of devaluations in 1972 culminated in the end of the Bretton Woods System in February 1973. The dollar became freely traded and freely sold. From January 1971 to February 1973, the dollar dropped 26.0 percent against the yen, 4.0 percent against the British pound, and 17 percent against the Deutsche mark.

First Oil Shock (1973–1974)

As the dollar tumbled in world markets, OPEC suffered from two fronts: being paid in a rapidly depreciating U.S. dollar, and facing higher costs of its imports as world inflation pushed up prices for commodities and industrialized goods. The Vietnam War played a key factor in lifting U.S. inflation to 4.2 percent in 1968 from 2.7 percent in 1967. In 1969 inflation hit 5.4 percent before reaching as high as 6.2 percent in 1970. The 47 percent increase in U.S. prices was exacerbated by the dollar decline at the turn of the decade.

No surprise that in early December 1970, the oil cartel began its first formal discussions about price increases, resulting from changes in foreign exchange rates. In the three years leading to the 1973 oil embargo, OPEC had made several price increases aimed at offsetting the declining value of oil receipts from the falling U.S. dollar. At its 1970 annual conference, OPEC passed a resolution expressing concern about "worldwide inflation and the ever widening gap existing between the prices of capital and manufactured goods and those of petroleum." Price increases were also accompanied by allowances for rising inflation. In 1971, 1972, and 1973, oil producers increased prices by 2.5 percent, 8.5 percent, and 5.7 percent, respectively.

One cannot assess the inflationary pressures triggering OPEC's price hikes in 1971 without addressing the expansive monetary policy pursued under the Fed Chairmanship of Arthur Burns. After Nixon became president in 1968, he appointed Burns as Fed Chairman in 1970—the same person who had advised him to cut interest rates prior to the 1960 election campaign. Burns had also served as a cabinet-rank counselor to the president on all economic issues for the year before becoming chairman of the independent Federal Reserve. Burns' pump-priming, aimed at ensuring Nixon a second term, catapulted money supply growth to 11 percent in the summer leading to the 1972 election, four times greater than the prior year. The inflationary consequences of those policies have played an unequivocally major role in the U.S. failure to maintain a fixed exchange rate regime against gold, eventually triggering the devaluation of the U.S. currency.

Figure 2.2 illustrates how Arthur Burns' easing monetary policy drove U.S. interest rates below those of the rest of the world, thus reducing the yield reward of the U.S. dollar and eroding 10 percent from its value between 1971 and 1972. Oil producers no longer content with being paid in depreciating dollars had to push up prices.

Against the backdrop of rising oil prices and a falling U.S. dollar in the first 2.5 years of the decade, the oil embargo of October 1973 precipitated the oil price hike on a global scale. Between 1973 and 1974, oil rose fourfold to nearly $12 per barrel, prompting sharp run-ups in U.S. gasoline prices and an abrupt decline in consumer demand. The plummeting dollar amplified the surge in prices and doubled inflation to an annual rate of 6.3 percent in major industrial economies, from 3.3 percent in 1972. In 1974, U.S. inflation soared to 11.0 percent while that of major industrial economies hit 13.7 percent, from 7.9 percent the prior year. In 1974–1975, the U.S. and major industrialized economies descended into recession.

Once U.S. inflation peaked at 12.3 percent in 1974, the dollar began a gradual rebound from March 1975 to May 1976, coinciding with a global recovery after nearly two years of recession. By the time the Fed halted its one-year easing campaign in summer 1975, gross domestic product (GDP)

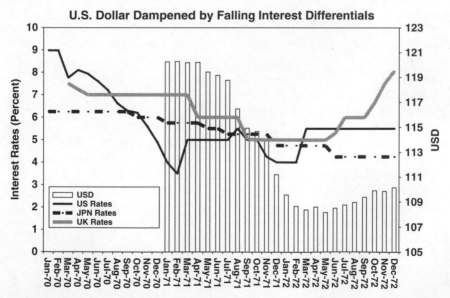

FIGURE 2.2 Easing U.S. monetary policy in 1970–1972 played a major role in the U.S. dollar's decline, stirring up inflation and encouraging OPEC to boost oil prices.

growth in the major industrialized economies rose 5 percent, thanks partly to a 5.3 percent increase in U.S. growth. The recovery lifted the dollar between summer 1975 and summer 1976, propelling the currency by 28 percent against the British pound, 10 percent against the deutsche mark, and 6 percent against the yen. The notable rise versus the pound was especially driven by soaring inflation in the United Kingdom, lifting the retail price index by as high as 27.0 percent in August 1975.

The First Dollar Crisis (1977–1979)

The U.S. dollar rebound of the mid-1970s came to a halt in summer 1976. What followed in the second half of the decade would be a five-year decline in the currency, unprecedented in the new post–gold standard era. Jimmy Carter's presidential campaign against Gerald Ford sought to lift the U.S. economy from its slowdown in the second half of 1976. Carter's currency policy was famously based on the talking down of the U.S. dollar, especially through his outspoken Treasury Secretary Michael Blumenthal, who pressured the Fed into monetary policy easing. The slide was accelerated in June 1977 when Blumenthal talked down the dollar after a meeting with his German and Japanese counterparts. The new policy sent the dollar tumbling more than 20 percent between January 1977 and October 1978, a dramatic plunge by postwar standards. Figure 2.3 shows how the

FIGURE 2.3   U.S. dollar drops nearly 40 percent against the Japanese yen as U.S. officials talk down the currency.

dollar tumbled 38 percent against the Japanese yen as Japan's trade surplus soared on its burgeoning exports industry. Figure 2.4 illustrates the 22 percent decline in the U.S. dollar index from its 1976 peak.

The dollar crisis was a vociferous manifestation of eroding market confidence in Carter's economic policies despite the fact that U.S. interest rates were yielding substantially more than those overseas. While the United States had embarked on a gradual tightening policy starting in early 1977, Germany and Japan were in the midst of an easing campaign that lasted well into 1978. From summer 1977 to autumn 1978, U.S. interest rates nearly doubled from 5.9 percent to 9.5 percent. In contrast, German and Japanese rates fell from 4.5 to 3.5 percent and from 5 to 3.5 percent, respectively, tripling the yield advantage in favor of the U.S. dollar.

So why did the dollar damage occur when the U.S. currency had yielded substantially higher rates than its German and Japanese counterparts? The answer lies in Carter's policy of targeting a 4.9 percent unemployment rate, following the stagflation days of the Ford administration where unemployment breached 9 percent and inflation crossed over 11 percent. As Carter pursued his unemployment target via major fiscal stimuli, inflation headed back up and so did the budget deficit—the two bogeymen of financial markets. Inevitably, confidence in the dollar continued to erode.

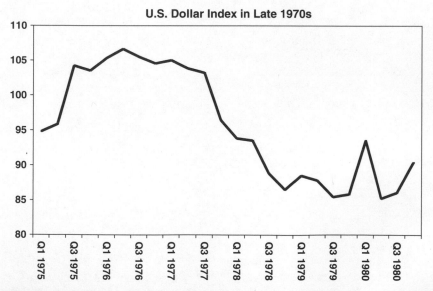

FIGURE 2.4 The 22 percent decline in the U.S. dollar index was less pronounced than the dollar's damage against the yen, as Japan's expanding trade surplus was a boon for the currency.

In November 1978, the United States mounted a massive joint intervention with Germany and Japan to buy dollars against foreign currencies. The move was supplemented with a 100-basis-point increase in the discount rate, the biggest in 45 years. The coordinated intervention proved limited in stabilizing the U.S. dollar. It wasn't until the Fed rewrote the rules of monetary policy management to combat soaring inflation in late 1978 that the currency began to turn around.

Second Oil Shock (1978–1980)

An unusual period of stability in oil prices during the period 1976–1978 proved short-lived. Oil prices had averaged about $12 per barrel partly due to a firm dollar in 1976 and early 1977, while major industrialized economies averaged annual growth rates at a brisk 5 percent accompanied by lower levels of inflation from the 1974–1975 period. But the 1977–1979 dollar crisis prompted more price hikes from OPEC, which were further accelerated by an increasingly unstable political environment in Iran. Surging social unrest in the second half of 1978 led to heated protests against the U.S.-backed Shah regime, culminating in the hostage crisis of the U.S. Embassy in Tehran and the Iranian Revolution of February 1979.

The combination of plummeting oil production in Iran and OPEC's price hikes resulting from a falling U.S. dollar pushed up oil prices by more than 200 percent between 1979 and 1980, giving rise to the second oil shock in less than 10 years. Just as in 1973–1974, the oil shock of 1979–1980 would trigger soaring inflation rates, which eventually eroded GDP growth, sending the world into recession. The relationship is cogently illustrated in Figure 2.5, where the three major oil shocks (1973–1974, 1978–1980, and the first Gulf War of 1989–1990) prompted the recurring pattern of mounting inflation followed by a contraction in economic growth.

OIL GLUT AND PRICE COLLAPSE (1981–1986)

Once prices peaked at a record high of $38 per barrel in February 1981, they descended on a six-year slide to reach below $10 in July 1986. Geopolitics again played a role, but this time the price impact was negative.

The outbreak of the Iran-Iraq war in autumn 1980 had the potential to produce further escalation in prices as the war involved two leading world producers of the fuel. But Saudi Arabia, the biggest producer, flooded the world market with inexpensive oil in 1981 and on into the mid-1980s, raising production to make up for the loss of Iranian and Iraqi production.

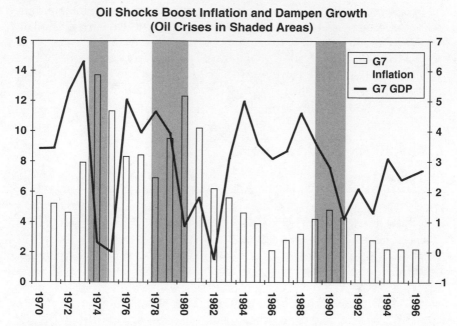

FIGURE 2.5 The pattern of soaring inflation rates followed by contractionary shocks in G7 economies (United States, Japan, Germany, Canada, United Kingdom, France, and Italy) was consistent throughout the three oil shocks, denoted in shaded areas.

Iran's annual oil production was cut by half, dropping from an average of 19 percent of OPEC's annual production in the first half of the decade to 10 percent of total production in the second half. Figure 2.6 illustrates the 1978–1981 oil price increase resulting from escalating uncertainty in the Middle East, which was followed by a 74 percent plunge in the ensuing six years.

The other main reason for OPEC's concerted price cuts was the gradual collapse of the world economy in 1980–1982. As the dollar began its five-year ascent in the first half of the 1980s, resulting from soaring U.S. interest rates (see next section), falling currencies outside the United States meant rocketing prices of imports from the United States and of higher-priced oil from OPEC. The double whammy of escalating import and oil prices triggered double-digit inflation in Europe and Japan, causing their central banks to embark on aggressive rate hikes at a time of already slowing growth and rising unemployment. The result was an economic slump in the industrialized world, giving rise to an unprecedented six consecutive annual declines in world imports for crude oil between 1981 and 1986. Global demand plummeted and so did consumption. The impact on oil

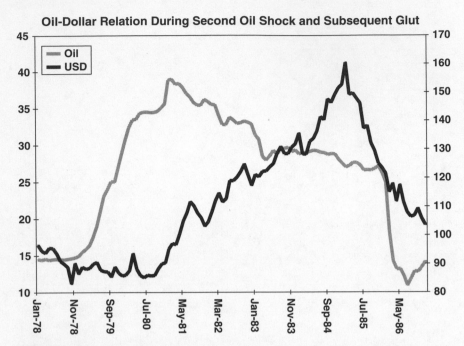

Oil-Dollar Relation During Second Oil Shock and Subsequent Glut

FIGURE 2.6 The 1978–1981 oil price shock triggered renewed inflation, causing the U.S. Federal Reserve to respond with soaring interest rates, eventually boosting the value of the U.S. dollar and raising the import burden on nations whose currencies are falling against the greenback. Oil prices began a six-year decline in 1981 due to falling world growth and rising supplies from OPEC.

prices was fast and deep. Figure 2.7 illustrates the prominent decline in global oil demand from 1980 to 1984, which played a significant role in exacerbating the price plunge.

Besides falling world demand and rising OPEC production as causes of the 1986 oil price plunge, improved conservation measures in the industrialized world also played a key factor in transforming the oil shortage into an oil glut. The emergence of cheaper alternatives to OPEC oil in the Alaskan and North Sea fields was also a factor in curtailing demand for the OPEC substance and its price.

THE SUPER DOLLAR OF 1980–1984: THE WORLD'S THIRD OIL SHOCK

The dollar decline of the late 1970s combined with the Iranian Revolution and the Iran-Iraq war weighed on the international economy in a way that

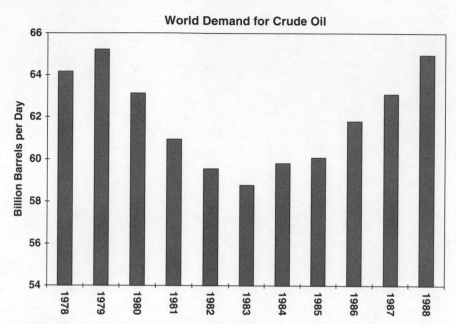

FIGURE 2.7 After peaking in 1979, oil demand headed for a four-year decline as central banks pushed interest rates to double digits to fight soaring inflation from the 1978–1980 oil price shock, driving the world economy into recession.

fueled a global inflationary spiral, soaring interest rates, and one of the longest and biggest rallies in the U.S. currency. Although oil prices fell 75 percent between 1981 and 1986, the decline followed a 200 percent price jump in 1979–1980, which was largely caused by the 20 percent slide in the dollar. Such a price surge in a relatively short period of time proved destabilizing for world trade and accelerated global inflation, which was already fed by the dollar declines of 1977–1979.

Aside from OPEC's oil spikes, inflation was also provoked by the Vietnam War, Lyndon Johnson's fiscal expansion to stimulate the Great Society, increased wage demands from labor unions that went beyond productivity growth, and finally the Federal Reserve's excessive pump-priming under the government-friendly Chairman Arthur Burns. Inflation hit 11.3 percent, 13.5 percent, and 10.4 percent in 1979, 1980, and 1981 respectively. Price growth also soared in major industrialized nations, reaching 9.5 percent, 12.3 percent, and 10.2 percent.

In August 1979, Paul Volcker took the helm at the Fed under the presidency of Jimmy Carter when inflation stood at 14 percent. It took two months before the Federal Reserve realized the urgency of adopting drastic measures to fight the destructive effects of an ever-growing price problem on incomes and purchasing power. The policy of targeting interest rates would no longer be effective in stabilizing monetary growth to its desired target of 1.5 to 4.5 percent. In autumn 1979, inflation hit 13 percent, surpassing the highs of 1974 and attaining levels not seen in 32 years. The Fed funds rate surged to a five-year high of 10.9 percent, and M-1 (the basic aggregate of monetary spending) hit 8.0 percent.

In October 1979, the Federal Reserve made a historical policy shift by adopting a new operating system of targeting money supply rather than interest rates. As it set targets for the *quantity* of money (money supply) and shifted away from targeting the *price* of money (interest rates), interest rates posted unforeseen sharp fluctuations in their postwar-era levels. Weeks after the Fed made its change, the Fed funds rate jumped to 17 percent in one day, dropped to 14 percent the next day, before rebounding again to 17 percent and back down to 10 percent. The new medicine of restrictive monetarism lasted for two years, driving up the Fed funds rate to as high as 20 percent in 1981.

As U.S. interest rates soared well above those in the industrialized world, so did demand for the greenback, resulting from global investors seeking higher-yielding returns to offset double-digit inflation rates. From January 1980 to February 1985, the U.S. dollar index soared 49 percent. One dollar bought 238.45 yen at the beginning of the period before reaching 259.45 yen five years later. Against the deutsche mark, the dollar climbed from 1.7245 marks to 3.2980 marks while more than doubling against the British pound, from 45 cents to 93 cents.

Figure 2.8 shows the U.S. dollar's performance against the Japanese yen, deutsche mark, and British pound. As the 1981 oil price peak culminated into broad interest rate cuts in Europe and Japan, their currencies were dragged down against the greenback. The appreciating dollar heightened the burden on non-U.S. purchasers of oil as they paid for the fuel, priced in higher-valued U.S. dollars, with their depreciating currencies.

The U.S. dollar's interest rate differential relative to the rest of the world played a major role in the dollar's ascent. In October 1979, the U.S. Fed funds rate stood at 15.5 percent compared to 7.0 percent in Germany and 6.20 percent in Japan. The U.S. yield advantage soared further as U.S. rates attained the 20 percent mark compared to 9.5 percent and 9.0 percent in Germany and Japan. After a temporary drop to 8.5 percent in June 1980, U.S. rates rebounded back toward the 20 percent mark over the following 10 months as double-digit inflation growth proved hard to abate. Renewed policy tightening once again lifted U.S. rates to twice the level in Germany and Japan as their central banks stopped raising their interest rates. The divergent interest rate picture between the United States and the rest of the world was a principal factor behind the dollar's haughty advances of the early 1980s.

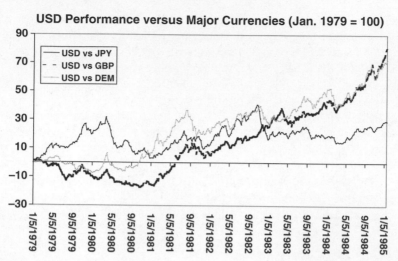

FIGURE 2.8 The U.S. dollar soared during the first half of the 1980s due to higher U.S. interest rates and struggling economies suffering from the high dollar cost of oil imports.

Figure 2.9 illustrates the role of the widening U.S. interest rate advantage in spurring the U.S. dollar's recovery. The currency, as in the case of most currencies, rallies not only when U.S. rates are on the rise but particularly when they are closing the margin below their foreign counterparts. The Federal Reserve's tightening policy shifted toward targeting money supply, while letting interest rates double to 20 percent. The rapid gains in U.S. yields increased appetite for holding dollars.

The 1979–1980 inflationary spiral forced major central banks into doubling their interest rates, and the world economy came to an abrupt halt in early 1981. The combination of soaring inflation and rising unemployment was a vicious pattern that pitted central banks against their governments, with the former focusing on combating inflation via higher interest rates and the latter aiming to fight unemployment through easing fiscal policies. The economic treatment of Paul Volcker's two-year dosage of hard monetary medicine succeeded in vanquishing inflation from its 30-year highs, but at the expense of a two-year recession that sent unemployment to a postwar high of 10.7 percent.

As the recession deepened in 1980–1981 and inflation peaked by the end of 1980, the Fed began a three-year easing campaign, slashing rates from 20 percent in May 1981 to 3 percent in February 1984. Despite the 87 percent decline in interest rates, the dollar was unrelenting during this three-year period, doubling against the deutsche mark and the British pound, while gaining 9 percent against the Japanese yen. The more

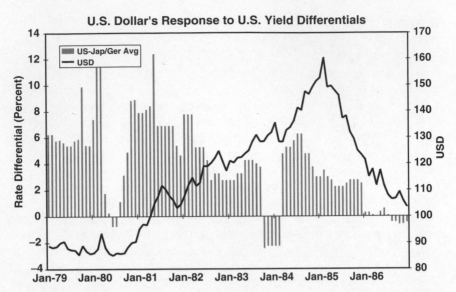

FIGURE 2.9 The U.S. dollar soared as rapid rate hikes increased appetite for holding dollars. The USD Index is plotted against a graph representing the Fed funds rate minus the average rate of Japanese and West German interest rates.

modest gains against the yen were attributed to the positive impact of Japan's surging exports on its currency and the fact that Japanese rates had ceased falling earlier in the period than had their German and British counterparts.

To the rest of the world, the soaring dollar meant falling currencies and rising inflation. The second oil shock of 1978–1979 was already driving up the oil import bill on world economies. As the dollar strengthened, nations had to spend more of their depreciating currencies to import high-dollar-priced goods. The externally driven inflation forced central banks to maintain interest rates higher than their domestic economies warranted, especially as nations such as West Germany and Japan were tightening their fiscal policies to trim down swelling budget deficits. Already in a campaign to fight the inflationary pressures of soaring oil, West Germany further raised rates from 3.5 percent in 1979 to 9.5 percent in 1980, causing a two-year contraction in economic growth, which included a doubling of unemployment to 2.3 million by 1982. Of the unemployed 32 million in OECD nations, half were from Europe. There was no growth contraction in Japan, largely due to the nation's burgeoning exports industry cushioning the overall economy. But GDP growth did enter the range of a *growth recession*, which is defined as a growth rate below 3 percent.

WORLD INTERVENES AGAINST STRONG DOLLAR (1985–1987)

The excessive strength of the U.S. dollar proved detrimental to the world economy. The U.S. trade gap moved sharply into a deficit and millions of manufacturing jobs were lost. Sharp depreciations in the currencies of the United States' trading partners triggered surging inflation that required central banks to tighten aggressively, sending their economies into recessions.

After 10 ineffective attempts of currency intervention aimed at stabilizing the dollar between 1981 and early 1985, the world's five biggest economies waged a global coordinated campaign to reverse the dollar's ascent. The dollar had already peaked in February 1985 before starting a gradual retreat over the next six months. The decline was especially helped by Fed rate cuts in the second half of 1984 while rates remained unchanged in West Germany and Japan, and rising in the United Kingdom.

Despite the dollar's 4 percent decline from its February peak to September, world leaders wanted more. In September 1985 at the Plaza Hotel in New York, representatives from the Group of Five (United States, Japan, Germany, United Kingdom, and France) agreed on coordinated operations to support non-U.S. dollar currencies. A series of joint interventions totaling nearly $13 billion in dollar-selling operations by the G5 over the following five weeks helped bring down the dollar. The interventions worked: The dollar lost 20 percent from September to December 1985, before shedding another 27 percent in 1986.

Falling Dollar and Oil: A Boon for Non-USD Importers

The oil factor once again played a prominent role in currency markets. As the oil price drop of the mid-1980s intensified—resulting from slumping world demand and OPEC's price declines—oil importing nations benefited significantly over time. The combination of a depreciating dollar and falling oil prices proved a boon for major oil importers, whose strengthening currencies increasingly absorbed cheaper oil, priced in a lower U.S. dollar. In the early 1980s, West Germany and Japan were the two countries with the highest dependence on imported oil as measured in terms of their overall economy.

Figure 2.10 shows Japan to have moved from being highly oil-import-dependent during the early 1980s—with an oil import/GNP ratio of 5.5 percent—to reducing its dependence fivefold over the following five years to become the most energy-efficient country in the industrialized world. An expanding Japanese economy and a strong yen were major

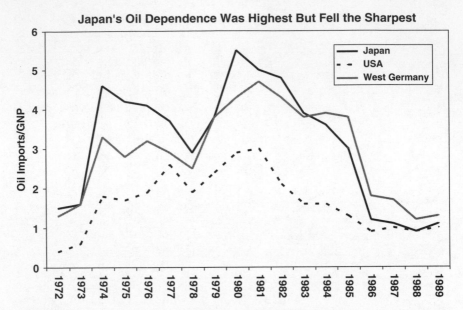

FIGURE 2.10 Japan's oil dependence, measured by oil imports as a percentage of gross national product, was reduced by five times into the end of the decade.

contributors in reducing the relative value of oil imports. The decline in West Germany's oil dependence during the latter half of the decade was far more modest, mainly due to slowing economic growth.

As concerted dollar-selling intervention took full force in autumn 1985, so did the decline in the currency. By January 1986, the dollar had dropped 9 percent from its February 1985 peak and its positive impact on the dollar cost of Japanese and West German oil imports became more evident. The windfall on these economies' external trade balance was especially ampli-fied by the 1986 decline in oil prices. Not only were they paying for cheaper oil but it required fewer Deutsche marks and yen to pay for it. Their imports fell relative to their exports, triggering a vital flip to their overall growth and further boosting their currencies.

To better illustrate the positive impact on the West German and Japanese currencies from falling oil prices and a falling dollar, one could compare the impact on the British pound during the 1986 oil price de-cline (see Figure 2.11). Unlike Japan and West Germany, the United King-dom had far lower dependence on imported oil, partly due to its status as an exporter of North Sea oil. Consequently, the windfalls of the oil price plunge were manifested more strikingly in Japan and West Germany than in the United Kingdom. The impact on its currency was evident. Against the backdrop of the 1986 plunge in oil prices, the British pound edged up

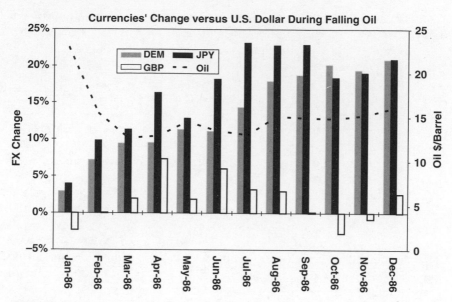

FIGURE 2.11 Superior percentage gains were made in the deutsche mark and Japanese yen against the U.S. dollar during the 1986 oil decline due to these nations' oil import capacity relative to the United Kingdom.

3 percent against the dollar, while the deutsche mark and the Japanese yen both soared 21 percent.

Less than five years after staging a remarkable 49 percent rally between 1980 and 1984, the U.S. dollar made an equally memorable 40 percent plunge in the ensuing two years. By the end of 1987, the currency lost all of the gains incurred at the first half of the decade. Once again, the world's top economies had to intervene, this time to support the falling dollar. The Louvre Accord of February 1987 was reached to stabilize the falling dollar and help other countries halt costly appreciations in their currencies. Both the dollar and oil eventually stabilized in 1988 and 1989, until Iraq's 1990 invasion of Kuwait drove prices to an eight-year high, creating a new oil price shock.

IRAQ'S INVASION OF KUWAIT AND THE GULF WAR (1990-1991)

On August 2, 1990, Iraq's invasion of Kuwait gave oil prices their sharpest percentage increase over any two-month period, lifting them by 48 percent to $41 per barrel in October 1990 from their $15 per barrel mark in June

1990. Over 1.59 million barrels of Kuwait oil was cut off from world production, or 0.5 percent of total world output. It took over five months for the Gulf crisis to turn into the outbreak of the Gulf War on January 17, 1991. The coordinated effort from the industrialized world and Arab countries to participate in the U.S.-led military operations in ousting Iraq from Kuwait resulted in a relatively quick end to the war, which lasted 42 days until the official cease-fire on February 28, 1991.

As in most geopolitical conflicts involving oil, prices make their biggest jumps during the period leading to war when the risk of the unknown triggers fears of uncertainty regarding the fate of oil supplies. Prices soared from $23.70 per barrel on the day of the August 2, 1990, invasion to over $40 per barrel in mid-October, before heading mostly lower the rest of the year and into the war outbreak of January 1991. The price decline resulted in assurances that Saudi Arabian oil would make up for the loss of Kuwaiti supply on expectations that the war would come to a relatively swift end. After having reduced production by an annual average of 40 percent during the 1980s, Saudi Arabia hiked production by 27 percent in both 1990 and 1991, attaining a 10-year high of 8 million barrels per day.

The currency impact was largely negative for the dollar in the eight weeks following the August 2 invasion, as escalating oil prices hampered a U.S. economy already troubled by the savings and loans (S&L) crisis of the late 1980s. Savings and loans had been struggling to balance the rising cost of their liabilities with the falling portfolios of their mortgage assets. By the late 1980s, hundreds of banks failed as the funds available to bail them were eroded. Real estate prices tumbled across the board and the economy slowed sharply.

In the second quarter of 1990, GDP growth slowed to 1.0 percent from 4.7 percent in the first quarter. Soaring oil prices of summer 1990 exacerbated the slowdown and sent the economy into recession from third quarter 1990 to second quarter 1991. The Fed began cutting rates in July 1990, while Europe and Japan were either raising rates or holding them steady into the end of 1990. Diverging global interest rates and a stalling U.S. economy dragged the dollar down by 15 percent from early 1990 to summer 1991. The role of falling U.S. differentials was indisputably punishing for the U.S. dollar.

Figure 2.12 shows how the U.S. dollar fell sharply against the yen and Swiss franc as oil prices nearly tripled after Iraq's invasion of Kuwait, which is marked by the first shaded column, 165 days prior to the official outbreak of the war. As oil prices broke the $30 per barrel mark, the dollar's declines accelerated amid protracted risks for the already slowing U.S. economy. The dollar's losses bottomed once oil began pulling back below the mid-$30s level. Note how oil prices declined sharply on the day the war broke (second shaded column) with the rationale being that the

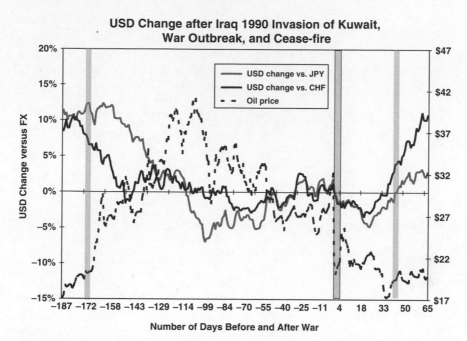

FIGURE 2.12 Oil prices and the percentage change of the U.S. dollar in the period spanning from Iraq's invasion of Kuwait to the outbreak of war, and from the war's outbreak to the cease-fire.

conflict would come to a quick end and oil supplies would be secure. The third shaded column marks the day of the official cease-fire, 41 days after the war began, coinciding with the dollar's percentage change crossing above the zero level.

Another main factor weighing on the U.S. dollar was foreign selling of U.S. equities. As the S&L crisis began to bite into the U.S. economy in late 1989, non-U.S. investors became net sellers of U.S. equities. The selling intensified in summer August 1990 when the invasion of Kuwait increased geopolitical uncertainty and drove oil prices sharply higher. U.S. Treasuries have often served as a safe haven during global uncertainty, but foreign net flows into U.S. bonds were outweighed by the increased selling of U.S. equities, hence weighing on the U.S. dollar. But once the cease-fire was announced on February 28, 1991, oil prices had dropped by more than 50 percent from their $41 high and the dollar pared all its postwar losses against major currencies.

Figure 2.13 shows the sharp decline in net purchases of U.S. equities in the months of the Iraqi invasion, dropping from a net buying balance of $1.4 billion in July to $3.8 billion in net selling in October. But the rebound

FIGURE 2.13 The decline in net foreign purchases of U.S. stocks upon the August 1990 Iraqi invasion of Kuwait was greater than that in U.S. Treasuries, but the rebound was more prolonged after the February 1991 cease-fire.

in stocks purchases grew more definite in January 1991, when the outbreak of war increased chances of a speedy resolution to the conflict. Although U.S. Treasuries involved greater dollar amounts in capital flows, their behavior was more volatile after the cease-fire due to the combination of the competing returns from stocks and global bond portfolio redistribution.

THE ASIAN CRISIS AND OPEC's MISCALCULATION (1997–1998)

The next major move in oil would take place in 1997–1998, when a mistimed decision by OPEC to raise production coincided with a two-year recession in Southeast Asia. Oil prices had doubled between 1994 and 1996, thanks to a combination of oil workers' strikes disrupting production in Nigeria, extremely cold weather in the United States and Europe, and the strike of U.S. cruise missiles into southern Iraq following an Iraqi invasion of Kurdish safe-haven areas in northern Iraq. In December 1996, oil peaked at $23.22 per barrel, its highest level since the 1991 Gulf War.

Prices began their steep decline in January 1997 when the United Nations authorized Iraq to double the amount of oil it could export as part of the oil-for-food sales agreement. But the oil price decline was interrupted in summer 1997 when Iraq refused United Nations weapons inspectors admission into key sites, raising fears of a renewed conflict in the Middle East. The run-up in oil prices extended into the fourth quarter of 1997, pushing OPEC to make the first output increase in four years, raising its production ceiling by 2.5 million barrels per day to 27.5 million barrels per day. OPEC's 10 percent production increase drove up total world output by 3.1 percent in 1997, the highest annual increase in 10 years.

Figure 2.14 shows the resulting price decline of OPEC's supply hikes to have been especially accelerated by the so-called Asian flu of 1997–1998. Economies in newly industrial Asian countries (Hong Kong, South Korea, Singapore, and Taiwan) saw their GDP growth drop from 4.5 percent in 1997 to −3.6 percent in 1997, while total domestic demand plummeted from 4 percent in 1997 to −9.2 percent in 1998. Unemployment growth went from 2.1 percent in 1996 to −2.7 percent in 1998, and import volumes tumbled 8.9 percent in 1998 after averaging 7.1 percent in 1993–2002. It was Pacific Asia's first drop in oil demand since 1982. Sharp currency depreciations, soaring interest rates, and political unrest damaged domestic demand. What began as an attack on local currencies in 1997 translated into massive debt defaults and the freezing of foreign capital in 1998. Oil prices continued to plummet as increased production from Iraq coincided with zero growth in Asian oil demand due to the Asian crisis and escalating oil inventories. Prices dropped to $9.40 per barrel in December 1998, losing 60 percent from their December 1996 high.

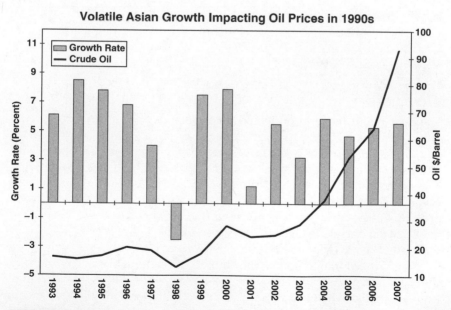

FIGURE 2.14 The sharp tumble in Asian economic growth exacerbated the 1997–1998 decline in oil prices, but the recovery in subsequent years was swift in both growth and prices.

OIL THRIVES ON WORLD GROWTH, DOT-COM BOOM (1999–2000)

The U.S. economy remained largely insulated from the Asian crisis, and the dollar held firm all through 1997–1999. Beginning in 1996, U.S. interest rates were higher than those in Germany (and later the Eurozone after 1999) and Japan. Low interest rates and a shrinking budget deficit helped the economy grow by more than 4 percent in 1997, 1998, and 1999, the highest three-year growth period since the mid-1980s. The global tech rally powered by the Internet bubble was a boon for U.S equities as it was for the dollar. After averaging a monthly drop of 99 percent and 134 percent in 1996 and 1997 respectively, growth of net foreign purchases of U.S. equities rose 1,448 percent, 59 percent, and 34 percent in 1998, 1999, and 2000 respectively. The dollar increased in value by 13 percent in 1997, fell 6 percent in 1998 due to three Fed rate cuts in the third and fourth quarters, and then rose 8 percent and 9 percent in 1999 and 2000.

The period 1999–2000 proved a rare example of a broadening global expansion feeding into higher demand for the fuel. Even the Eurozone area, which averaged an annual growth of 2.2 percent between 1980 and 1998, broke the 3 percent growth mark in 1999 and 2000, registering the first 3 percent handle in nine years. Oil rallied from a low of $9.40 per barrel in December 1998 to a high of $30.50 per barrel in September 2000.

The burst of the technology bubble in 2000 culminated in a prolonged worldwide stock market decline, which was further exacerbated by the September 11 attacks the following year. The U.S. economy entered a recession in 2001, dragging world GDP growth down to 2.5 percent in 2001 from 4.8 percent in 2000. Growth in advanced economies cooled down to 1.2 percent in 2001 from 4 percent in 2000. U.S. oil demand slowed to 0.9 percent in 2000 before contracting 0.3 percent in 2001. Oil prices fell 50 percent from their September 2000 high to under $16 per barrel in December 2001.

IRAQ WAR FUELS OIL RALLY, DOLLAR FLOUNDERS, CHINA TAKES OVER (2002 TO PRESENT)

The 2001–2002 economic slowdown proved only temporary. The 2003 Iraq war was more of a burden on U.S. fiscal affairs than on the rest of the global economy. By the outbreak of war in March 2003, oil prices had doubled to $35 per barrel from their December 2001 lows. Concerted interest rate cuts in major industrialized economies, along with broad tax cuts in the United States, reenergized aggregate demand and spurred corporate spending. Global unemployment started heading lower, while rallying stock markets and improved balance sheets spurred household confidence and spending.

In January 2002, the U.S. dollar index peaked at 120.51, just short of its 15-year highs attained six months earlier. The peak marked the end of a seven-year bull cycle from 1995 to 2001 and ushered in the beginning of a new bear market, currently in its seventh year. It was no coincidence that the dollar's peak of spring 2002 coincided with President Bush's trade war action of slapping foreign steel producers with tariffs in order to secure the Republican Party victory in key states ahead of the Congressional elections later that year. Escalating protests by U.S. manufacturers calling the administration to weaken the strong dollar were heeded by Washington. The message was also loud enough for currency traders to begin selling the dollar against all major currencies, including the euro, which had become an obligatory legal tender in the Eurozone that year.

Neither the swelling budget deficit resulting from soaring war costs in Iraq nor escalating geopolitical risks helped the U.S. currency. More is discussed on the geopolitical dynamics of the currency market in Chapter 9. The Federal Reserve's slashing of interest rates by 550 basis points (bps) in the Fed funds between 2001 and 2003 weighed heavily on the U.S. currency as investors sought higher yields in other currencies. With the Fed funds rate reaching a 45-year low of 1 percent in June 2003, U.S. short-term rates were the lowest in the industrialized world with the exception of Japan and Switzerland. From 2002 to the end of 2004, the U.S. dollar dropped 53 percent against the euro and the Australian dollar, 32 percent against the British pound, 22 percent against the yen, and 25 percent against the Canadian dollar. The Fed's rate hikes of 2004–2005 gave the U.S. dollar a prolonged reprieve in 2005, before renewed selling eroded the currency's value in 2006 and 2007.

Figure 2.15 shows the clear inverse relationship between the U.S. dollar (bottom graph) and oil and gold prices (top graph) between 2002 and 2007. The U.S. dollar index lost nearly 40 percent of its value from its 2002 high to a new all-time low in November 2007, while oil prices surged fivefold from their 2002 lows to an all-time high in late 2007. Gold surged 290 percent from its 2002 low to breach the $800 per ounce mark in later 2007.

As the dollar tumbled in world markets, commodities soared across the board. Metals, fuels, and agricultural commodities woke up from their 1990s slump as their currency of exchange, the dollar, began its secular bear market. From 2002 to 2004, crude oil soared 200 percent to $55 per barrel, reaching its highest level since 1981, while gold gained 65 percent to break above $450 per ounce for the first time in 14 years.

China's energy appetite was also a major factor in escalating commodity demand. Its weak currency and ultralow labor and costs helped lift the trade surplus by more than 300 percent from 2000 to 2005. The resulting

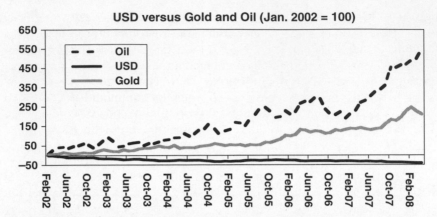

FIGURE 2.15 The 40 percent decline in the U.S. dollar index during 2002–2007 was closely correlated with the surging prices of oil and gold.

increase of more than $120 billion in China's current account surplus gave China the newly acquired status of world's leading consumer of coal, copper, and iron ore.

China's growth rate has become synonymous with global demand for commodities. Figure 2.16 shows that China's oil demand stood at

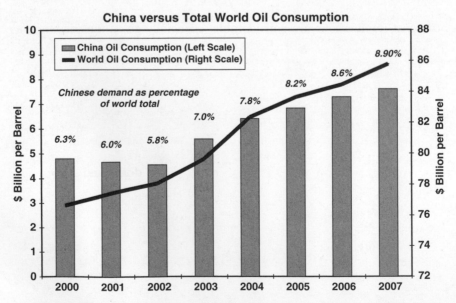

FIGURE 2.16 China's oil consumption grew from less than 6 percent of the world's total in 2002 to 9 percent in 2006.

4.80 billion barrels per day in 2002, or 5.8 percent of the world's total. Two years later, China's share of global demand rose to 7.8 percent in 2004, beating Japan to second place behind the United States. The correlation between China's strengthening oil demand and oil prices remained robust throughout. With GDP growth topping 11 percent in 2007, elusive signs of an economic slowdown have yet to weigh on commodities. Until then, China's accumulation of the biggest armory in currency reserves at $1.5 trillion should maintain the country's support for commodities prices.

SUMMARY

We have seen in this chapter how strong global growth can be instrumental in boosting oil prices. The years 1976–1979, 1994–1997, 1999–2000, and 2003–2006 were all periods of steady import demand sustained by robust growth in both the developed and developing world. While Saudi Arabia's status as the world's largest oil producer has enabled it to act as the swing producer during supply uncertainty, China has assumed an increasingly similar role on the demand side.

The United States remains the world's biggest economy as well as the world's biggest oil consumer. But this also means that 5 percent of the global population is consuming 25 percent of the world's energy supplies. Given that the United States imports 58 percent of the oil it consumes, the cost implications are considerable, especially given that dependence on foreign oil has risen from about 36 percent in the first and second oil crises, and is expected to reach 68 percent in 2025. At what cost? The dollar amount of total U.S. petroleum products pyramided from $103 billion in 2002 to $302 billion in 2006, doubling its share of total imports to 14 percent over the same period. As a share of the trade deficit, petroleum imports surged from 25 percent to 40 percent of the U.S. trade imbalance. With world oil supply struggling to catch up with soaring demand, and the world's biggest consumer continuing to grow at subpar rates, conditions remain ripe for a prolonged bear market in the U.S. dollar and an extended bull market in oil.

CHAPTER 3

When the Dollar Was King (1999–2001)

D etermining *why* foreign exchange rates move the way they do may seem a far too ambitious and challenging task, as it requires making sense of an unlimited array of factors ranging from fundamentals (macroeconomic changes, central bank actions, capital markets changes, corporate/dealer transactions, political and geopolitical factors, and news reports) to technicals (price charts, momentum, oscillators, moving averages) to pure flow-driven developments. Other books tackle the theories of international economics and finance that explain the principle drivers of foreign exchange rates. Since this book aims at focusing on the real-world developments impacting currencies, textbook theories take a secondary role in shedding light on the major developments in currencies. These theories are only briefly mentioned. Chapter 3 and 4 tackle the trends in major foreign exchange rates between 1999 and 2007, identifying the highest- and lowest-performing currencies, and citing the fundamental reasons for these developments.

This analysis calculates the annual changes in the values of currencies against one another to determine a ranking of currency returns. Performances are examined against a host of fundamental variables such as national GDP growth, world and regional GDP growth, interest rates and central bank action, capital flows, current account balances, and export dynamics such as commodities markets. The real-world developments that dictate the major trends in global currencies demonstrate the theories and paradigms that worked, and the reasons for their prevalence during those years.

THE MAJOR THEORIES

As mentioned earlier, we will give a brief account of the major theories of international economics seeking to explain foreign exchange market values, before tackling the practical underpinnings behind the performance of each of the nine major currencies. This way, those not familiar with the theories will be able to reconcile and relate the real-life dynamics of foreign exchange movements to the theoretical properties, wherever possible.

Purchasing Power Parity

The theory of purchasing power parity (PPP) states that exchange rates are determined by deriving relative prices of similar baskets of goods across different currencies. Changes in inflation rates are expected to be offset by equal but opposite changes in the exchange rate.

The major advantage of PPP is that it provides for convenient and easy comparisons when using similar products. However, the theory is valid *only for goods that are easily tradable, with no transaction costs taken into consideration*, such as tariffs, quotas, and taxes. In fact, PPP is only valid for goods, not for services or in cases of significant differences in values. One clear disadvantage of PPP is its disregard for market dynamics such as economic releases, asset markets, sentiment, and the role of political and geopolitical factors. There was little empirical evidence of the effectiveness of PPP prior to the 1990s. Thereafter, PPP was seen to have worked only in the long term (three to five years) when prices eventually correct toward parity.

Interest Rate Parity

The theory of interest rate parity (IRP) holds that a currency's appreciation (depreciation) versus another currency in the future must be neutralized by the interest rate differential. If Eurozone interest rates exceed their U.S. counterpart, then the euro should depreciate against the U.S. dollar by the percentage that prevents riskless arbitrage. That depreciation (appreciation) is reflected into the forward exchange rate stated today.

Interest rate parity theory is the underlining foundation of pricing currency forward and futures contracts. Its main weakness is the lack of proof after the 1990s. Contrary to the theory, currencies with higher interest rates characteristically appreciated rather than depreciated on the reward of future containment of inflation and a higher-yielding currency.

Balance of Payments Model

The balance of payments model (BOP) maintains that a nation's currency must be at the rate that produces a stable current account balance. This rate is known as the rate of equilibrium. A nation with a trade deficit experiences erosion in its foreign exchange reserves, and a subsequent decline in its value. As the currency becomes cheaper, it renders exports more affordable and imports more expensive, thus reducing the trade imbalance.

As in the case of purchasing power parity, the balance of payments model addresses mainly tradable goods and services, while ignoring the increasing role of global capital flows. As investors purchase other nations' stocks and bonds, their flows are added to the *capital account* (also known as the *financial account*) item in the balance of payments, thus balancing the deficit in the current account. The increase in capital flows has given rise to the asset market model.

Asset Market Model

The asset market model (AMM) addresses cross-border portfolio flows (purchases/sales of stocks and bonds) in evaluating currency values. The emergence of cross-border capital flows and trading of financial assets has reshaped the way markets approach currencies. Only 1 percent of all foreign exchange (FX) transactions are trade-related.

Economic variables such as growth, inflation, and productivity are no longer the only drivers of currency movements. The proportion of FX transactions stemming from cross-border trading of financial assets has dwarfed transactions in goods and services by several hundred times.

ANNUAL PERFORMANCE ANALYSIS OF INDIVIDUAL CURRENCIES

The following sections show the highest- and lowest-performing currencies from 1999 to 2001, a period marked by general strength in the value of the U.S. dollar. In Chapter 4, we tackle currency performances from 2002 to 2007, a period involving the protracted decline in the dollar and the broad strengthening of the euro. The following currencies are examined in this analysis:

- U.S. dollar (USD)
- Euro (EUR)
- Japanese yen (JPY)

- British pound (GBP)
- Swiss franc (CHF)
- Canadian dollar (CAD), also known as the loonie
- Australian dollar (AUD)
- New Zealand dollar (NZD), also known as the kiwi

Currency returns are based on a yearly percentage return aggregating each currency's bilateral returns against all other seven currencies. These performances are then measured against the backdrop of variables like world, regional, and national GDP growth, interest rates and central bank action, capital flows, current account balances, and commodities markets.

1999: Risk Aversion, Bottom Fishing Boosts Japanese Stocks and the Yen

The year 1999 witnessed the simultaneous recoveries of East Asian and Russian economies following the market crisis of 1997–1998, and the continued boom into the equity markets of industrialized economies. Global fund managers exhibited a high degree of risk aversion from the emerging markets of Asia, Eastern Europe, and Latin America, opting to capitalize on higher growth in more developed economies. The Japanese yen was the highest-performing currency of 1999 as Japan offered the combination of *industrialized economy* status and cheap valuation, as the country was widely expected to finally recover from its decade-long economic slump. The "buy-the-Japanese-dip" strategy mobilized massive flows of funds into Japanese equities, propping up the yen across the board. While the introduction of the euro to currency trading replaced the national currencies of 11 European nations, U.S. equity markets were busy absorbing foreign flows chasing an increasingly solid bull market in high-growth technology stocks. (See Figure 3.1.)

The commodity currencies of Canada and Australia ranked second and third respectively in their rankings as the aussie benefited from high crop and copper prices and the loonie gained from a 134 percent increase in oil prices. Meanwhile, the euro found no other way but down after the currency was inaugurated at an uncompetitive exchange rate against the dollar, yen, and pound, while devaluations of Asian currencies of 1997–1998 exacerbated Europe's already lackluster exports foundation to the Far East. In its first year of trading, the euro registered what would become its worst performance out of the eight years that followed. But the euro was not the worst performer in 1999. The New Zealand dollar held that title due to a swelling trade deficit, falling dairy prices, and a slowing economy. Figure 3.2 provides a summary of how the currencies fared against each other in trading pairs.

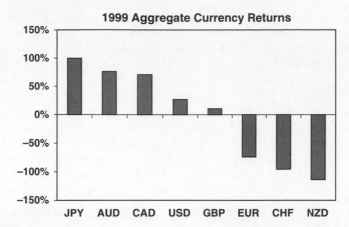

FIGURE 3.1 The Japanese yen was the biggest gainer amid major currencies in 1999, as world growth and equities recovered from the Asian crisis.

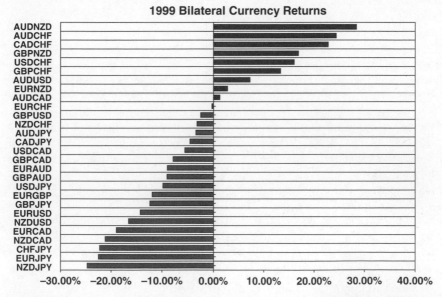

FIGURE 3.2 The 1999 returns of individual foreign exchange rates indicate the yen crosses were at the bottom of the rank, reflecting the yen's broad strength.

Japanese Yen: +99 percent The Japanese yen's 1999 performance was a resounding attack on conventional theories indicating that rising or high interest rates boosted currencies, while low or falling interest rates were negative for currencies. In 1999, Japanese short-term rates started the year at a postwar low of 0.25 percent—already the lowest among

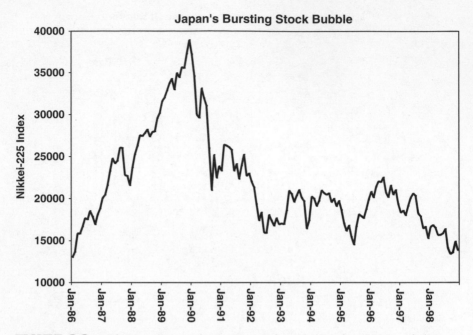

FIGURE 3.3 With Japanese stocks at 12-year lows in October 1998 and down 66 percent from their peak of 1989, global fund managers rushed into cheap Japanese valuations, giving the yen its best performance in decades.

G7 economies—before being cut to 0.15 percent. Instead, the yen was boosted by a surge of global funds into Japanese stocks with the notion that Japanese markets were set to gain the most from the global recovery story, especially that Japan's main equity index Nikkei-225 was drifting at 12-year lows in October 1998. The notion of cheap bargain stocks in the world's second-largest economy during a global boom was the underlying theme to the yen recovery. Figure 3.3 shows how tumbling Japanese equities reached 12-year lows in September 1998, prompting investors to seek bottom-fishing opportunities in Japanese stocks.

Figure 3.4 shows how net foreign purchases of Japanese stocks soared throughout 1999, producing a record total of 11.9 trillion yen for the year in net foreign purchases. These flows boosted the currency against the USD, EUR, and GBP by 10 percent, 23 percent, and 12 percent respectively for the year.

Australian Dollar: +76 percent   The Australian dollar was the second-highest-performing currency in 1999, boosted by a 30 percent increase in copper prices as the world economy headed into recovery mode

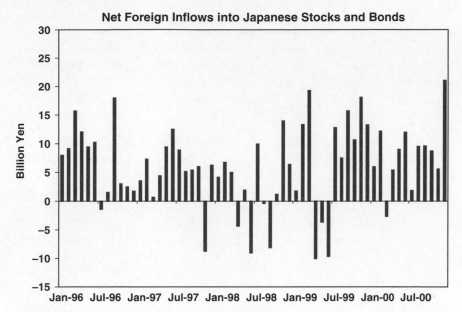

FIGURE 3.4 Net foreign purchases of Japanese stocks soared to a record high in 1999, giving the yen its biggest rally in six years.

after the financial turmoil of 1997–1998. With minerals making up 50 percent of Australia's total exports and copper accounting for 6 percent of mineral exports, the Australian dollar's performance is closely correlated with the price of copper. As GDP growth in major industrialized economies rose to 3.5 percent in 1999 from 2.6 percent in 1998, the demand for copper was robust and so was demand for Australian exports.

Australia's 4.4 percent GDP growth in 1999 was slower than the 5.3 percent rate of 1998, but higher than the average of the G7 economies. Surging demand from newly industrialized economies (Hong Kong, Korea, Singapore, and Taiwan) was also a boon for the aussie as these economies posted an impressive 7.5 percent recovery in GDP growth following the 2.5 percent contraction in 1998.

Canadian Dollar: +70 percent As was the case with the aussie benefiting from rising copper prices due to the global recovery of 1999, the Canadian dollar was boosted by higher oil prices resulting from growing world demand. In 1999, energy products made up 11 percent of Canada's total exports, with crude oil accounting for 5 percent of exports. The 132 percent increase in the price of crude oil was an undisputable boon for CAD, lifting it by an aggregate 71 percent against the major seven currencies. The loonie also gained more than 5 percent against the USD, its best performance versus the greenback since 1988.

Soaring oil exports lifted GDP growth to 5.5 percent from 4.1 percent in 1998, exceeding the 2.1 percent average growth of 1989–1998. Soaring global demand for Canada's hottest commodity more than offset any negative impact the currency would have otherwise sustained from the two interest rate cuts at the first half of the year.

U.S. Dollar: +27 percent　The combination of strong growth in the industrialized world and fund managers' risk aversion to nonindustrialized economies rendered the quality and safety of U.S. stocks a fundamental factor in going for U.S. markets, as was the case with Japan. Consequently, net foreign purchases of U.S. stocks soared to a record $107.5 billion in 1999, a 53 percent increase from the 1998 total.

From an interest rate perspective, surpassing the 4 percent handle for the third consecutive year, U.S. real GDP growth allowed the Federal Reserve to raise interest rates by a total of 75 basis points (bps), taking back the rate cuts made during the 1998 market turmoil/liquidity crisis. U.S. interest rates were raised back to 5.5 percent, making them the highest in the G7 along with UK rates. In fact, it was the first time since 1984 that U.S. rates had matched their UK counterpart after 15 years of underperformance. These factors helped the dollar gain an aggregate 27 percent return against the major seven currencies.

British Pound: +11 percent　The British pound ended up gaining only against EUR (12 percent), CHF (13 percent), and NZD (17 percent) thanks to improved economic growth and a favorable interest rate environment as GDP growth remained at the 3 percent handle and the Bank of England raised rates by 50 bps. Continued erosion in EUR, lackluster growth in Switzerland, and a swelling trade deficit in New Zealand dragged these currencies down against GBP. But GBP lost ground against the JPY (−12 percent), AUD (−9 percent), CAD (−8 percent), and USD (−2 percent) due to equity flows, and commodity market developments prevailing in Japan, Australia, and the United States.

Euro: −74 percent　The first year of the euro was its worst performance to date as the single currency began trading at $1.1740 in 1999, a rate that turned out to be unsustainably high for the fundamentals of the 11-nation Eurozone. Notably, the Asian flu of 1997–1998 did leave some damage on German exports, 11 percent of which went to the continent. German and French exports had continued to struggle, especially with 11 percent of German exports sold to Asia. Consequently, net exports' contribution to German growth fell from 1.7 percent in 1997 to −0.4 percent and −0.6 percent in 1998 and 1999. And although Eurozone GDP growth stood at 2.7 percent in 1999, growth rates in Germany and Italy were subpar at 1.9 percent and 1.7 percent. Against the backdrop of sluggish growth, interest rates were at 3 percent, already deemed too high, especially as the late European Central Bank (ECB) president Duisenberg persisted in emphasizing the upside risks to inflation at the expense of ignoring the ongoing downside risks to growth.

The euro was also saddled by heightened uncertainty related to the war in the former Yugoslavia, verbal clashes between Eurozone politicians, and the ECB regarding the need for the central bank to cut interest rates. Intense pressure on the ECB even caused speculation about the breakup of the Eurozone due to falling central bank credibility regarding monetary policy and inflated prices following the conversion from national currencies to the euro.

Swiss Franc: −95 percent The Swiss franc was the second-worst performer in 1999 amid the eight major currencies due to a combination of sluggish growth and cooling demand from the Eurozone. Swiss GDP growth more than halved in 1999 to 1.3 percent from 2.8 percent in 1998, falling below the 1.4 percent average of 1989–1998. Although Swiss rates were increased, they remained well below 2 percent, surpassing only their counterpart in Japan. Yet Switzerland lacked the size of Japan's stock market capitalization, and thus was unable to absorb the magnitude of global capital flows that lifted Japanese stocks and the yen.

New Zealand Dollar: −114 percent With triple-digit losses, the kiwi was the worst performer in 1999 as slumping dairy prices dragged exports lower, exacerbating the swelling trade deficit. Over 50 percent of New Zealand's exports came from agriculture, with dairy products accounting for 20 percent of total exports. Declining dairy prices led to a negative price growth and pushed up the trade deficit to 6.2 percent of GDP from 3.9 percent in 1998. Food prices fell 12.6 percent in 1999 following an 11 percent decline. The currency was also hit by falling poultry prices due to falling Russian demand following the Russian currency crisis of 1998.

2000: Tight Fed, Soaring Foreign Flows Boost the Greenback

As the world economy gathered further strength in the aftermath of the 1997–1999 market crises, investors grew bolder in their appetite for stocks, bolstering their already solid interest in U.S. assets and the U.S. currency. (See Figure 3.5.) But despite strengthening global growth, metals failed to sustain the solid performance of 1999 as paper currencies proved

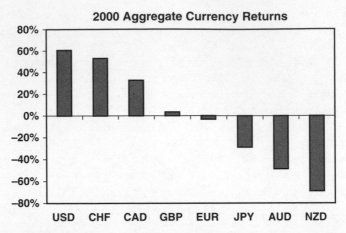

FIGURE 3.5 Massive foreign purchases of U.S. stocks in 2000 powered the dollar to the top-ranking position of aggregate currency returns.

triumphant due to interest rate hikes throughout the industrialized world. Oil prices, meanwhile, were up as much as 48 percent on the year in the third quarter before cancelling nearly all of the gains in the fourth quarter.

To tackle rising inflation, the Federal Reserve raised rates by 100 bps to a nine-year high of 6.5 percent, while the Bank of England and European Central Bank raised rates by 50 bps and 175 bps to 6 percent and 4.75 percent respectively. There were also rate hikes from Australia, Canada, Japan, New Zealand, and Switzerland.

The technology stocks bubble combined with accelerating growth gave the USD its strongest showing among the eight currencies, while exacerbating the lackluster performance in metals. Consequently, the oil-dependent Canadian dollar showed the third-best performance, tracking oil's rise. The New Zealand dollar remained the worst performer for the second consecutive year due to the nation's high trade deficit, while the aussie was dragged down by a 3 percent decline in copper prices. The yen made a sharp U-turn, losing 29 percent as global investors mostly sold off the stocks they had purchased the prior year. (See Figure 3.6.)

U.S. Dollar: +61 percent   Interest rate hikes, surging capital flows, strong growth, and rising inflation were all reasons for the dollar's stellar performance in 2000. After rising 59 percent to a record $107.9 billion in 1999, net foreign purchases of U.S. stocks rose 39 percent to a new record of $174.9 billion in 2000, chasing the bull market in technology stocks.

But U.S. stocks weren't the only destination of record foreign flows. Figure 3.7 shows the breakdown of foreign flows into U.S. assets between

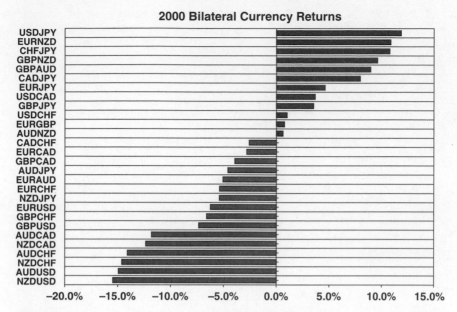

FIGURE 3.6 U.S. dollar pairs dominated the best-performing foreign exchange rates of 2000.

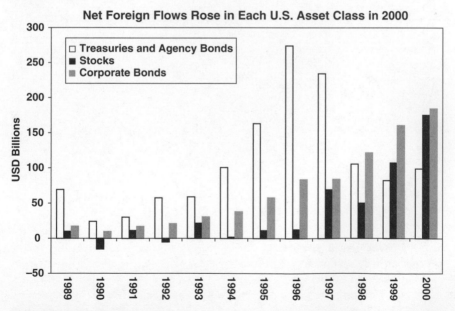

FIGURE 3.7 The year 2000 was the only year when foreign purchases of U.S. assets rose in each asset class (stocks, Treasuries, corporate bonds, and Agency bonds over the prior year).

1989 and 2007, illustrating that 2000 was the only year with an increase in net purchases of U.S. stocks, corporate bonds, Treasury securities (bills and bonds), and agency bonds (bonds of local agencies and municipalities). Every other year in the chart shows a decrease in at least one of these U.S. asset classes. Such a remarkable trend in 2000 proved to be the backbone of the dollar's resulting 61 percent increase against AUD, CAD, CHF, EUR, GBP, JPY, and NZD.

The U.S. presidential elections of November 2000 also had considerable impact on currency markets, as the victory of Republican candidate George W. Bush over Democrat candidate Al Gore was cheered by U.S. markets due to market-friendly economic policies of the Republican Party. The positive impact on the dollar was especially highlighted during the several reports that erroneously announced victory for Gore, whose planned tax hikes were seen as negative for stocks and the currency. The dollar then rallied strongly during the recount period in mid-November with each subsequent news story rectifying the claim of a Gore victory.

Swiss Franc: +53 percent The Swiss franc proved an unlikely second-highest performer in 2000, despite low interest rates and relatively small capital markets. But the highest GDP growth rate in over a decade and a doubling of interest rates to 3.5 percent stood in the way of carry trades betting on a weakening and low-yielding franc. Swiss GDP growth nearly tripled to 3.6 percent, enabling the Swiss National Bank to raise rates without worrying about restraining growth. The growth story was also bolstered by robust neighboring economies, such as the Eurozone and the United Kingdom both growing by 3.8 percent, rates not seen in over a decade.

But the franc's gains were also related to risk appetite. Once global equities peaked in the second quarter of 2000 and the tech rally began to falter, stocks grew more volatile. What followed was a decline of 42 percent and 18 percent in the NASDAQ and S&P 500, respectively, from September to December 2000, which prompted currency traders to seek the safety of the franc, as the Swiss economy remained sheltered from the slowing U.S. economy and bolstered by a growing European recovery. The franc particularly rose across the board in November and December when market volatility was heightened by the uncertainty surrounding the U.S. presidential election and the intensifying sell-off in Wall Street amid the slowing U.S. economy.

Canadian Dollar: +33 percent The Canadian dollar ranked third-highest returning currency for the second straight year, benefiting from a combination of accelerating growth, rising interest rates, and a temporary jump in oil prices. The 45 percent summer price increase to a 10-year high of $37 per barrel sufficed in spurring the CAD higher for the rest of the year despite a retreat in oil later in December. The oil pullback in late fourth quarter gave oil a modest 4 percent increase for the year, but the $20 price spike between May and September 2000 was a boon for the oil-dependent loonie.

On the growth side, Canada's GDP maintained a growth rate of 5.2 percent, following 5.5 percent in 1999, well above the 2.1 percent average of 1989–1998. In addition to the oil and growth windfall, the loonie was boosted by a 100 bps increase in overnight interest rates to 6 percent, the highest in five years.

British Pound: +3.5 percent Sterling's lackluster 3.5 percent cumulative return against the other seven major currencies shows that despite the United Kingdom's stellar GDP growth of 3.8 percent and the Bank of England's (BoE) rate hikes to 6 percent, it was not enough to prevent the currency from losing 7 percent against the USD, 4 percent against CAD and CHF, and 0.8 percent against EUR. Speculators also began exiting long GBP positions after midyear when the BoE's first-quarter tightening was perceived to have begun threatening a protracted slowdown. Indeed, the Bank of England joined the Fed in January 2001 to begin an extended easing campaign.

Euro: −3.2 percent The 175-point rate hikes from the ECB proved too little too late in stemming the euro's losing tide, whose intensification began amid eroding credibility with ECB policy. Recall that a large reason for the euro's aggregate 74 percent tumble against the major seven currencies in 1999 was the excessively hawkish ECB policy. While the ECB was mandated to keep inflation below the 2 percent ceiling, inflation remained below that ceiling throughout the year—despite rising from under 1.0 percent to 1.8 percent.

Foreign exchange markets suspected that the ECB was behind the curve in shoring up growth, especially when it raised rates by 225 bps from fall 1999 to fall 2000. Rather than boosting the currency, the rate hikes were punishing the already struggling German and Italian economies. In 2000, inflation exceeded the 2.0 percent ceiling while money supply growth remained well above the ECB's policy pillar of maintaining monetary growth at an annual three-month average of 4.5 percent.

The bulk of the euro's losses stemmed from an excessively restrictive monetary policy and a central bank largely deemed to be inexperienced, especially as differing points of view and statements from within the policy makers started to be more prominent. That contrasted with the central banks of the United States, Japan, and the United Kingdom, whose

FIGURE 3.8 The euro's intensifying sell-off of 2000 prompted the ECB to intervene with other major central banks on at least four occasions.

governors at the time (Greenspan, Hayami, and George) were associated with respect and proven experience.

In the last week of January 2000, the euro broke below parity with the U.S. dollar, culminating a decline from its $1.1740 opening level a year earlier. EUR went on to lose 6 percent versus USD to reach an all-time low of 82.25 U.S. cents, prompting a series of concerted interventions by the European Central Bank, Federal Reserve, Bank of Japan, Bank of England, and Bank of Canada. There were four officially reported interventions between September and November 2000, the last two of which took place one day before and after the closely contested U.S. presidential election so as to contain excessive dollar rally versus the euro. (See Figure 3.8.)

Japanese Yen: −29 percent   The same factors prompting the yen's outperformance of 1999 were also behind the currency's 29 percent sell-off of 2000. Just as Japanese stocks were among the first to be snapped up by global fund managers during the global economic recovery of 1999, these were unloaded aggressively throughout 2000 as the global tech wreck turned into an all-around global market corrosion. Foreign investors *sold* a net 234.0 billion yen of Japanese stocks in 2000, following the record total net purchases of 11.9 trillion yen in 1999.

Australian Dollar: −49 percent   The aussie's underperformance of 2000 underlines the currency's high correlation with copper prices, which overrides the impact of growth and interest rates. Although GDP growth slowed from 4.4 percent in 1999 to 3.4 percent in 2000, it remained well above the 1989–1998 average of 3.3 percent. Yet it was the 3 percent decline in copper prices that weighed on the currency, following a 31 percent increase in 1999. The aussie's losses especially intensified when a robust rally in the second quarter peaked in September at 16-year highs, before starting a 12 percent decline into the rest of the year. Consequently, the aussie tumbled to an all-time low against the USD, reaching the 50-cent figure in November 2000, down from the February high of 67 cents. Copper's decline in the fourth quarter emerged as slowing world growth was on the cusp of recession.

New Zealand Dollar: −69 percent   The kiwi finished at the bottom of the return ranking for the second consecutive year as it remained hit by a mediocre environment for dairy prices and investors clustered the aussie and peripheral currencies across the board. Although New Zealand's current account deficit stabilized from 6.2 percent of GDP in 1999 to 5.1 percent in 2000, it remained the highest among developed nations, especially as the global price environment for agriculture and dairy products turned lackluster in the second half of the year. GDP growth slowed to 3.9 percent from 4.3 percent.

2001: Recession Favors Dollar Due to Aggressive Fed Cuts

The U.S. slowdown of the second half of 2000 intensified in 2001, causing the economy to slip into recession, and dragging the rest of the world into a standstill. This was especially intensified by a sell-off in world stock markets triggered by the burst of the U.S. tech bubble. As the U.S. imported nearly a fifth of the world's exports, the proverbial U.S. sneeze left the rest of the world with a cold. Neither the U.S. economic contraction nor the aggressive easing by the Federal Reserve could destabilize the dollar from its top-performing position. (See Figure 3.9.)

Since the downside risks to growth were markets' top priority, traders rewarded currencies whose central banks were boldest in cutting interest. GDP growth in the seven most advanced economies slowed from 4.0 percent in 2000 to 1.2 percent, well below the 2.7 percent annual average of the prior decade. We see in this section how the EUR/USD bipolarity seen in 1999–2000 took further hold in 2001 and beyond, whereby the performances between the two currencies were consistently in opposite directions. Figure 3.10 shows that the USD pairs occupied most of the top-performing pairs, while the JPY crosses reflected broadening weakness in the Japanese currency.

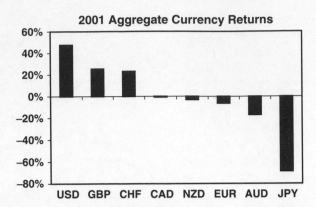

FIGURE 3.9 U.S. dollar retains top position in 2001 as Fed rate cuts are seen as most pro-growth policy among major central banks.

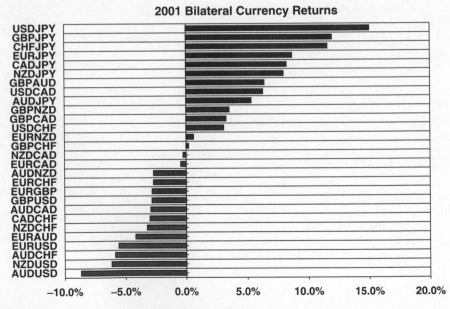

FIGURE 3.10 U.S. dollar and Japanese yen were on opposite sides of the 2001 return spectrum.

U.S. Dollar: +48 percent   Contrary to conventional theory stating that currencies are favored by higher yields and vice versa, the U.S. dollar's outperformance of 2001 resulted from aggressive rate cuts, signaling to markets that the U.S. economy may be the first to recover from the global slowdown. Two business days into the beginning of January 2001, the

Fed delivered an unscheduled 50 bps interest rate cut to start a 475-point rate reduction campaign that took the Fed funds rate to a 45-year low of 1.75 percent by year-end.

Although the Fed funds rate dropped below the overnight rates of all G7 nations with the exception of Japan, the U.S. dollar outperformed all currencies in 2001. The rate cuts were insufficient to prevent 21 percent and 13 percent declines in the Dow and the S&P 500 for the year, but they proved instrumental in the dollar's broad gains, especially as the central bank was perceived to be in the forefront of battling the ensuing recession, rather than being behind the curve. Such perception was also a result of the fact that the easing campaign included two rate cuts during unscheduled central bank meetings, highlighting the sense of urgency to stimulate the economy back into growth.

Finally, the September 11 attacks proved a minor blip in the currency radar screen, as the Fed coordinated with other central banks to inject the financial system with added liquidity. The dollar went on to rally by 3 percent in the fourth quarter in trade-weighted terms as fears inside the United States were perceived to have been largely fended off when the country took the offensive abroad to start the war against the Taliban in Afghanistan. (See Figure 3.11.)

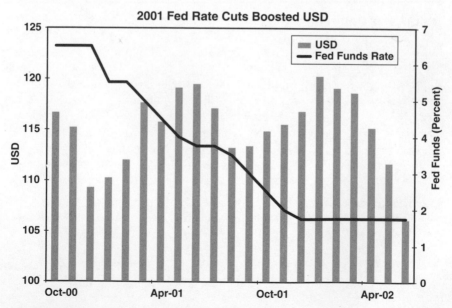

FIGURE 3.11 The Federal Reserve's aggressive easing of 2001 boosted the dollar because markets' primary concern lay primarily with slowing economic growth.

British Pound: +25 percent The sterling was the second-best-performing currency in 2001 because the Bank of England was nearly as aggressive as the Fed in cutting interest rates, slashing the overnight rate by 200 bps to 4.0 percent. Most remarkably, the United Kingdom's GDP growth slowed from 3.8 percent in 2000 to 2.4 percent in 2001, which was still above the growth rates of the United States and Eurozone of 0.8 percent and 1.9 percent respectively. In fact, UK growth was highest among G7 nations in 2001. The GBP's broad strength was also highlighted by its 5 percent decline against gold, which was the smallest decline of any currency behind the USD against the metal during the year.

Swiss Franc: +23 percent At a time of escalating stock market volatility, subpar global economic growth, and weak commodity prices—gold up only 2 percent and oil down 25 percent—the Swiss franc was partially boosted by its role as a so-called safe currency. The Swiss National Bank cut rates from 3.5 percent to 2.75 percent, making them the lowest behind Japan and the United States in 2001, a year when currencies thrived on the deepest of interest rate cuts. The currency also manifested its ability to strengthen in times of geopolitical uncertainty, as was the case during the September 11 attacks. Consequently, CHF lost a mere 3.1 percent against the dollar on the year.

Canadian Dollar: −1 percent The Bank of Canada (BoC) delivered the biggest magnitude of rate cuts behind the Fed out of the eight major central banks in 2001, reducing overnight rates by 350 bps to a 41-year low of 2.5 percent. The BoC was mindful of the repercussions of a U.S. recession, especially as the United States imports over 80 percent of Canada's oil exports. Indeed, 90 percent of the $6 dollar decline in the price of oil for the year took place after the September 11 attacks, on fears that the deteriorating recession would further weigh on oil demand. Although Canada's GDP growth tumbled to 1.8 percent from the 5 percent handle of 1999–2000, the currency fared well as FX traders rewarded the BoC's proactive response.

New Zealand Dollar: −3 percent The kiwi finally rebounded from the bottom of the ranks, but barely generated cumulative negative returns. The Reserve Bank of New Zealand cut rates from 6.5 percent to 4.75 percent while GDP growth slowed to 2.7 percent from 3.9 percent. The slowdown in Japan (to 0.2 percent from 2.9 percent in 2000) and newly industrialized Asian economies (to 1.2 percent from 7.9 percent in 2001) created a drag on New Zealand's economy, as they account for a quarter of the nation's total exports. The year 2001 was a year of consolidation for the kiwi after a 22 percent decline in the currency's trade-weighted index during

1999–2000. This consolidation preceded what would later become a multi-year secular rally.

Euro: −6 percent The ECB took back all but one of the 2000 rate hikes, slashing rates by 175 bps to 3.25 percent. Despite ending the year in negative territory, EUR had a strong run between July and September, taking advantage of a broad summer decline in the U.S. dollar as U.S. economic data began to deteriorate. But the dollar staged a broad fourth-quarter rebound in the aftermath of the September 11 attacks as the United States fended off the geopolitical threat and waged war in Afghanistan.

One noticeable pattern between EUR and USD developing in the first three years in the life of the young currency is the bipolarity between the two pairs. In 2001, the EUR/USD pair accounted for 30 percent of total currency market turnover, before rising to 28 percent of the total in 2004 and 27 percent in 2007. This compared to a 13 percent share of trading volumes for USD/JPY and 12 percent for GBP/USD. The growth in the EUR pair trading volumes accelerated consistently, rising 42 percent to $501 billion in 2004 from 2001 and up 67 percent to $840 billion in 2007 from 2004. We note later in the book the intensification in the bipolarity of returns between USD and EUR and touch upon its reasons and implications.

Australian Dollar: −17 percent The high-yielding aussie ended the year as the worst-performing currency in 2001 as copper prices fell 21 percent, prolonging their sell-off after hitting 16-year highs in 2000. The global slowdown dragged G7 GDP growth to 1.2 percent from 4 percent in 2000, prompting a retreat in construction and infrastructure spending, all of which are major sources for copper. The Reserve Bank of Australia's (RBA) 175 bps of rate cuts were the smallest among the eight currencies, with the exception of the JPY, whose central bank cut rates by merely 10 bps. Australia's GDP slowed to 2.1 percent from 3.4 percent as newly industrial Asian economies (Hong Kong, Korea, South Singapore, and Taiwan) struggled during Japan's renewed dip into recession territory.

Japanese Yen: −69 percent While 2001 rewarded currencies whose central banks delivered the most aggressive easing campaigns to tackle the deteriorating growth climate, the already ultralow rate environment in Japan meant the central bank was unable to deliver any further meaningful easing to stimulate the ailing economy. In March 2001, the Bank of Japan (BoJ) cut its overnight rate target to 0.15 percent from 0.25 percent, sending the actual market rate to zero percent. But the BoJ's policy bind was underlined in the *real* interest rate (nominal interest rates minus inflation), which was higher than the nominal rate because inflation stood below zero. This meant that interest rates were too high for the deflationary environment, suggesting that the BoJ was powerless in shoring up the economy with interest rate policy alone. Investors found no choice but to sell the zero-yielding JPY, especially as Japanese stocks hit 15-year lows to lose 24 percent for the year.

SUMMARY

The years 1999 to 2001 were dominated by a 24 percent rally in the USD Index, emerging on a combination of solid economic growth, soaring equity markets, and relatively weaker performance abroad. As the world economy emerged from the Asian crisis of the late 1990s, U.S. markets provided global investors with a winning combination of safety and growth. In June 2001, the dollar index surged to a 15-year high, which was partly a result of the euro's struggle during its early years. But 1999–2001 culminated in the end of the dollar's seven-year bull market. As the world slipped into the 2001–2002 recession and equity markets descended in a four-year bear market, China sought to fill the void via its voracious appetite for commodities.

What followed next was the beginning of a protracted decline in the U.S. currency along with a historic recovery in the euro and commodity currencies, all of which are the subject of Chapter 4.

The Dollar Bear Awakens (2002–2007)

T he 2002–2007 period was a major turning point in global currency markets, which triggered the start of a new bear market in the U.S. currency and the reemergence of a broad strengthening in the euro. The falling value of the dollar brought about a super rally in commodity prices, culminating in new record highs in precious metals, energy fuels, and agricultural products. This chapter tackles the annual performance of the world's eight major currencies (U.S. dollar, euro, yen, British pound, Swiss franc, Canadian dollar, Australian dollar, and New Zealand dollar) between 2002 and 2007. As in Chapter 3, the annual performance of each currency is measured by aggregating a currency's percentage changes against each of the other seven currencies.

2002: THE BEGINNING OF THE DOLLAR BEAR MARKET

The year 2002 marked the end of the U.S. dollar's seven-year cyclical appreciation from 1995 to 2001 and ushered in the beginning of a bear cycle, entering its seventh year as of this writing in 2008. U.S. manufacturers stepped up their complaints about an overvalued U.S. dollar eroding their competitiveness, demanding that President Bush impose tariffs on U.S. trading partners and declaring that the currency needed to depreciate by about 40 percent.

The president heeded those complaints, and U.S. Treasury officials began adopting a policy of benign neglect, whereby they implicitly wanted the dollar to depreciate, despite mechanically reiterating declarations that a strong dollar is in the interests of the United States, a mantra widely adopted—and fully intended—under the second Clinton administration. The dollar ceiling was firmly reached in spring 2002 when President Bush launched a trade war, slapping foreign steel producers with tariffs in order to secure the Republican Party victory in key steel and manufacturing states ahead of the Congressional elections later that year. Trade actions, such as tariffs, always beget currency depreciations as countries aim at increasing the competitiveness of their products in the global marketplace.

As a result, selling the dollar across the board became the trade of choice, especially amid the successful conversion of the euro into an obligatory currency of exchange in the Eurozone in 2002. The swelling U.S. budget deficit was exacerbated by soaring war costs in Iraq, while the trade deficit soared due to rising oil imports and the relatively lackluster growth of exports. (See Figure 4.1.)

Meanwhile, commodity prices rebounded due to the falling value of the currency in which they were denominated, and partly due to a modest pickup in demand for energy and agriculture products. Metals, however, did not share in the wealth as the world economic growth remained below its potential trend and financial markets extended their erosion from the heights of 1999–2000. Interestingly, of the eight currencies under examination, only the central banks of commodity-based economies—Australia, Canada, and New Zealand—raised their interest rates in 2002. (See Figure 4.2.)

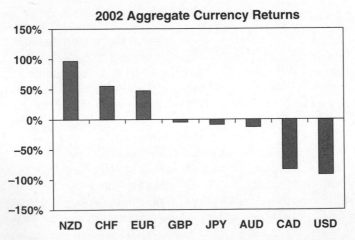

FIGURE 4.1 U.S. dollar drops to bottom of currency returns in 2002.

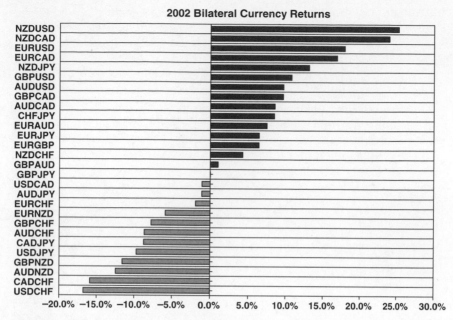

FIGURE 4.2 Kiwi-related currency pairs dominated foreign exchange in 2002 as the greenback was sold across the board.

New Zealand Dollar: +97 percent

New Zealand's dependence on agriculture exports was instrumental in the kiwi's recovery, which was made possible by a 3.4 percent increase in general food prices following a rise of 2.5 percent and 0.2 percent in 2000 and 2001, respectively. Prices of agricultural raw materials moved from a 4.9 percent decline in 2001 to a 1.8 percent increase in 2002, surpassing the 1989–1998 average of −0.3 percent. These price developments helped stabilize the country's swelling trade deficit, especially as neighboring Asian economies' growth rate rebounded to 5.5 percent from 1.2 percent in 2002. New Zealand's GDP growth soared from 2.7 percent in 2001 to 5.2 percent, exceeding the 1989–1998 average of 2.1 percent.

All of these developments pushed the Reserve Bank of New Zealand to make its first rate hike in two years, pushing up the overnight rate by 75 bps to 5.75 percent. Most notably, the kiwi's 25 percent gain versus USD was a combination of the aforementioned NZD fundamentals and deteriorating USD dynamics that would trigger another 25 percent rally in 2003 and a 10 percent rally in 2004, totaling an impressive 60 percent gain in three years against the greenback. (See Figure 4.3.)

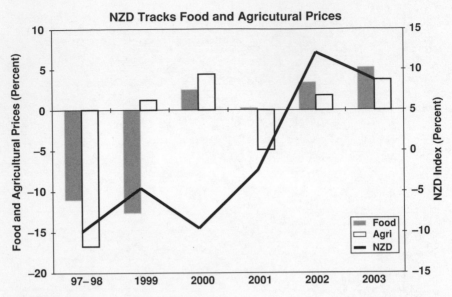

FIGURE 4.3   New Zealand dollar recovers from 1990s slump along with food and agricultural prices.

Swiss Franc: +55 percent

The strong performance of the Swiss franc was largely a reflection of a resurgence in European currencies exploiting the broad decline in the U.S. dollar, which set them off on a positive footing against other currencies such as AUD and CAD, whereby the former was dragged down by weak copper prices and the latter weighed down by the U.S. recession. Global portfolio managers also boosted European currencies as they increased their allocation in Western European markets at the expense of their U.S. counterpart. The CHF gained only 1.8 percent against EUR, while rising 15.8 percent and 8.7 percent against CAD and AUD. The CHF gained versus all of the currencies under examination with the exception of the kiwi. Although Swiss GDP growth more than halved to 0.4 percent in 2002, the CHF rally reflected a broad vote of confidence in European currencies (EUR, GBP, CHF), as these benefited from the solid Asian recovery.

Euro: +47 percent

Once it was evident that the Bush administration of 2002 wanted a weaker U.S. dollar—without necessarily having been explicit about it—currency traders sold the U.S. currency, with the euro acting as the primary beneficiary to the trend. The steel tariffs announced in March 2002 were also a green light to sell the dollar, as international trade actions are associated with nations increasing the competitiveness of their products abroad. Also by spring 2002, the European Central Bank had successfully accomplished its mission of ensuring that each of the 13 nations in the Eurozone made a smooth transition into making the euro the legal tender in all commercial and retail transactions in 2002. The ECB allayed public concerns of notes and coins shortages and worries about the spread of counterfeit currency.

In its third year of life, the euro had already cemented its role as the so-called anti-dollar, reacting to each and every dollar-specific development and benefiting from the downtrend in the greenback. Just as the euro suffered from the dollar's solid performances in 2000–2001, it exploited the dollar's woes quite thoroughly. The EUR-USD polarity was already seen in 1999–2000, but was magnified in 2001 and beyond, as the two currencies consistently moved in opposite directions. Figure 4.4 illustrates the persistently opposing directions between the two currencies, with the dollar's outperformance in 1999, 2000, 2001, and 2005 being accompanied by negative euro returns, while the euro's outperformance in 2002, 2003, 2004, 2006, and 2007 was accompanied by negative dollar returns.

The main reason for the EUR-USD polarity is related to the growth of trading volumes in the EUR/USD pair. The creation of the euro meant that the EUR/USD pair eliminated trading in 11 individual currency pairs against the dollar, one of which was U.S. dollar/deutsche mark (USD/DEM), which accounted for 22 percent of global foreign exchange

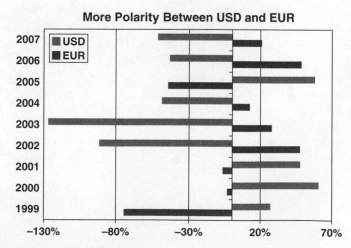

FIGURE 4.4 The diverging paths of the dollar and the euro reflect the increased duality between the two currencies.

turnover in 1995. In 2004, trading in the EUR/USD pair accounted for 28 percent of all transactions, compared to 17 percent and 14 percent for USD/JPY and GBP/USD. In 2007, the share slipped to 27 percent, but it remained clearly the top traded pair versus 13 percent and 12 percent for USD/JPY and GBP/USD.

The euro's dominance in the U.S. Dollar Index, a futures instrument traded at the New York Board of Trade, also explains the polarity between the two currencies. The euro's weight in the six-currency index is 57.6 percent, followed by the JPY, GBP, CAD, the Swedish krona (SEK), and CHF at 13.6 percent, 11.9 percent, 9.1 percent, 4.2 percent, and 3.6 percent respectively.

The other reason for the EUR/USD polarity is the euro's potential to threaten the dollar's role as the world's reserve currency. In 1999, the euro's share of global foreign exchange reserves stood at 25 percent versus over 70 percent for the U.S. dollar. In 2002, the euro's share edged up to over 26 percent. Meanwhile, more central banks have already started diversifying their currency holdings, including more euros as a percentage of reserves at the expense of the U.S. dollar. Later in this chapter we consider how this relationship is maintained during both positive and negative phases for the two currencies.

British Pound: −4 percent

Sterling's cumulative return against the seven major currencies was negative due to losses against NZD, EUR, and CHF, but gains elsewhere were partially a result of those currencies' losses against European currencies. The year 2002 was the only year when the Bank of England made no change in interest rates since the central bank gained independence in May 1997. It was also the only central bank besides the constrained Bank of Japan to hold rates unchanged in 2002. GDP growth rate slowed further, reaching 2.1 percent from 2.4 percent in 2001.

One noteworthy development weighing on GBP in late 2002 was that of geopolitics. As then British Prime Minister Tony Blair stepped up his support for a U.S.-led attack in Iraq, the UK position began to weigh on sterling as the market punished currencies whose nations were pursuing an increasingly isolated pro-war position. Aside from the economic costs of a prolonged involvement in the war, participating countries were at risk of reprisal and terrorist attacks on their own soil. In November 2002, the United Kingdom was the only G7 nation and permanent member of the UN Security council supporting the United States in drafting a UN resolution supporting war. Sterling's tenuous position was exacerbated when Prime Minister Tony Blair faced heightened opposition by his own party and the majority of the British public.

Consequently, sterling's trade-weighted index (basked against selected currencies) fell for seven consecutive months, between November 2002 and May 2003, the longest monthly losing streak since 1995.

Japanese Yen: −9 percent

The yen's negative cumulative gains versus the seven other major currencies were largely a result of losses against the strengthening European currencies (−6 percent and −8 percent versus EUR and CHF) as well as −13 percent versus the NZD. But the currency was unchanged against GBP as the latter staged broad declines in the fourth quarter due to geopolitical factors impacting the British pound. The yen's 10 percent rally against the USD was largely a reflection of the dollar's deterioration, considering intensifying deflationary pressures in Japan as consumer price growth dropped from −0.7 percent in 2001 to −0.9 percent in 2002.

Australian Dollar: −13 percent

The aussie gained only against the USD (10 percent) and CAD (9 percent) in 2002, the two currencies whose economies were interconnected via the sluggishness in the United States. Despite the rise in agricultural prices, which boosted the kiwi, copper prices returned a lackluster 2 percent gain, which was particularly negative for the aussie as the metal reversed most of the 16 percent gains sustained in first half of the year. The aussie's negative reaction to the late developments in copper was similar to that in 2000 when copper prices fell 12 percent in the third quarter, following an earlier rally to 16-year highs. Rather than focusing solely on what copper did on the year, one must take note of the price developments during the latter part of the year (three to six months) for the impact on the currency aussie.

Canadian Dollar: −83 percent

Despite the 56 percent rise in oil prices and the Bank of Canada's rate hikes to 3 percent, the Canadian dollar fell against each of the said currencies with the exception of the USD, against which it eked out a 1 percent gain. The Canadian dollar's losses were primarily a result of eroding confidence based on the conclusion that Canada would be hardest hit from the U.S. recession. Indeed, exports fell 1.6 percent in 2002, dragging the trade surplus down 19 percent as exports to the United States accounted for 84 percent of the total. And although Canada voted against the Iraq war, once again its proximity to the potential war-related economic downdrafts from the United States was highly considered as a negative for the currency. Falling exports and a falling trade surplus dragged GDP growth from 2.5 percent in 2001 to 2.3 percent in 2002.

U.S. Dollar: −91 percent

The aforementioned shift of currency policy by the Bush administration toward that of a benign neglect (indirectly encouraging a dollar decline) as well as the imposition of trade tariffs on foreign steel producers was a green-light signal to sell the U.S. dollar regardless of fundamentals in other economies. The Fed cut rates by 50 bps to 1.25 percent, while the broad equity indexes tumbled to five-year lows on a combination of continued fallout from overvalued valuations in technology and escalating news of corporate malfeasances such as Enron, WorldCom, and Arthur Andersen.

2003: DOLLAR EXTENDS DAMAGE, COMMODITY CURRENCIES SOAR

The major differences distinguishing the global economic/market environment surrounding the 2003 dollar sell-off from that of 2002 were (1) the breadth of the commodity rally; (2) increased geopolitical uncertainty weighing on the U.S. dollar and U.S. assets after the outbreak of the Iraq war; and (3) deteriorating budget deficit and current account deficit balances. Prolonged interest rate cuts by the Federal Reserve to a 45-year low of 1 percent also accelerated the dollar decline and boosted commodities as the Fed vowed to inject the liquidity to allay the risk of deflation. This readiness to debase the currency via aggressive rate cuts and injection of liquidity was likened to dropping money from helicopters, a metaphor that would earn its author, former Fed Board governor Ben Bernanke, the moniker "Helicopter Ben." The Fed's so-called *reflationary* monetary policy—boosting liquidity to lift inflation above zero—was a significant negative for the U.S. dollar and a windfall for commodities as investors fled the low-yielding currency for the high-growth commodities as these appreciated against their principal invoicing currency.

The September 2003 G7 meeting in Dubai proved a highly eventful development for currency markets, when the seven most powerful economies urged China and Japan to refrain from intervening by maintaining their competitive currencies. The reaction to the unusual request was a rapid decline in USD/JPY, which is explored later in this section under JPY.

The three major commodity currencies—AUD, CAD, and NZD—were the top three performers on a cumulative return basis in 2003, returning their biggest gains versus the dollar at 34 percent, 18 percent, and

25 percent, respectively, hitting their highest levels against the greenback in a decade. (See Figure 4.5; their positioning in pairs trading is shown in Figure 4.6.) The rally in metals, foodstuffs, and agricultural raw materials was a boon for the three currencies, with the trend especially enforced by the deepening bear cycle in the dollar.

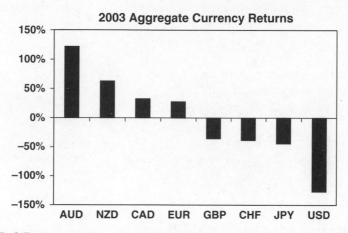

FIGURE 4.5 Commodity currencies dominate the foreign exchange market in 2003 with the aussie at the top.

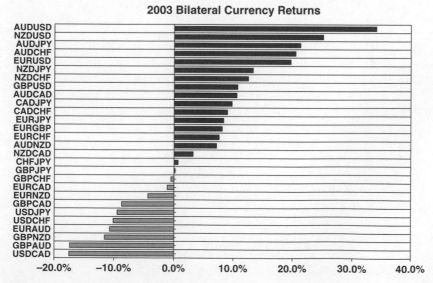

FIGURE 4.6 AUD, NZD, and CAD occupy highest-performing FX pairs in 2003 due to broad rally in commodities.

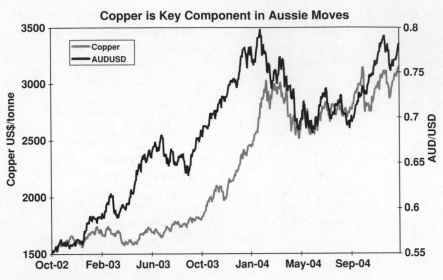

FIGURE 4.7 Copper prices are instrumental in aussie price action.

Australian Dollar: +122 percent

Although Australia's GDP growth slowed to 3.1 percent in 2003 from 4.1 percent in 2002, the aussie rallied aggressively as China, the world's largest importer of copper, stepped up its demand, benefiting Australia, the world's largest copper exporter. The resulting 45 percent increase in copper prices prompted currency traders to automatically bid up the aussie, lifting it against all seven other currencies, while taking advantage of the USD's woes and dragging it down by 34 percent. (See Figure 4.7.) Ultimately, 2003 was a year with a rare triple boost for the Aussie:

- Reserve Bank of Australia (RBA) hikes rates to two-year high.
- Fed cuts rates to 45-year lows.
- Copper rallying to multiyear highs.

In trade-weighted terms, the aussie reached its highest since January 1989.

New Zealand Dollar: +63 percent

The price acceleration in agricultural raw materials and food items of 3.7 percent and 5.2 percent following 1.8 percent and 3.4 percent gains in

2002 provided considerable boost for the kiwi. The currency was hardly fazed by 50 bps of rate cuts in the spring, as they were followed by a quarter point hike, taking the overnight rate to 5.25 percent.

Canadian Dollar: +32 percent

Tracking the rise in oil and decline in the U.S. dollar, CAD posted its biggest percentage gain versus the U.S. currency, rallying 18 percent to 10-year highs. Oil rose 16 percent in the first nine weeks of 2003 and peaked out at a 13-year high of $38 per barrel just two weeks before the official start of the Iraq war on March 19. Once U.S. and British troops took Baghdad in April and President Bush announced "Mission accomplished" in early May, oil prices fell back to as low as $25 per barrel amid fading risk premium in the region. But the war was further complicated by sectarian violence and the murders of pro-U.S. Iraqi clerics, which catapulted oil back above the mid-$30s into the end of the year. Although prices closed 2003 barely $1 above where they had opened the year, all signals pointed to further price escalation, which boosted the oil-dependent Canadian dollar.

Euro: +28 percent

In its fifth year of life, the euro had its second consecutive rising as it increasingly assumed the role of the anti-dollar, exploiting the downtrend of the greenback. Just as the euro had suffered from the dollar's solid performances in 2000–2001, it now exploited the dollar's woes quite thoroughly. In December 2003, EUR/USD ended the year at $1.2590, closing well above the $1.1740 rate at which it had opened in 1999. The EUR-USD polarity had already been seen in 1999–2000, but was magnified in 2001 and beyond as traders adopted an increasingly negative stance toward the U.S. dollar. The converse also worked in 2005 when the dollar made a broad recovery, dragging the euro sharply lower.

In 2002, although Eurozone GDP growth slowed for the third consecutive year reaching 0.8 percent, growth rates made little difference as traders focused on selling the dollar on a combination of rising twin-budget and trade deficits, as well as 45-year low interest rates. Specifically, the euro appreciated 20 percent against the U.S. dollar, the highest annual increase it attained against the major seven currencies over the 1999–2007 period.

British Pound: −35 percent

The sterling's woes in 2002–2003 were especially notable as the currency decoupled from the euro, reflecting the extent of bearishness toward the currency. Looking at the performances of 1999, 2000, 2001, 2005, and 2006, EUR and GBP showed similar magnitudes in their returns as these currencies were deemed economically interconnected. This was especially seen via their similar behavior against the U.S. dollar. But the relationship began to fade in the third quarter of 2002 when the United Kingdom increasingly supported the tenuous U.S. cause to invade Iraq. (See Figure 4.8.) Prime Minister Tony Blair drew heightened opposition from his own party and the majority of electorate. Aside from the issues of popularity and isolation, Britain subjected itself to the risk of terrorist attacks by groups staunchly opposed to the war. These risks were later substantiated during the London bombings of July 2005.

Aside from geopolitics, the economic reasons for the sterling's 2003 downfall included an unexpected interest rate cut in February, followed by a subsequent cut in June to 3.75 percent. The renewed easing from the Bank of England punished GBP against major currencies, triggering a decline even against the ultralow-yielding CHF. Sterling's trade-weighted index (basked against selected currencies) fell for seven consecutive months between November 2002 and May 2003, its longest monthly losing streak since 1995.

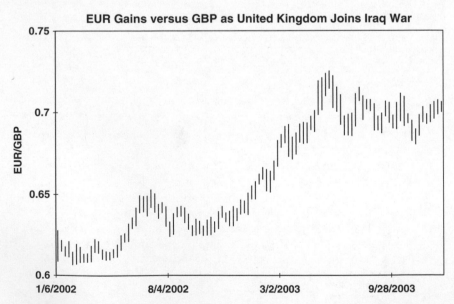

FIGURE 4.8 EUR breaks out of flat trend versus GBP in 2002–2003 as United Kingdom supports case for Iraq war.

Swiss Franc: −38 percent

A combination of ultralow interest rates, falling domestic growth, and weak external demand weighed on the Swiss currency against most major currencies with the exception of the struggling GBP and low-yielding JPY. Swiss GDP growth dipped to −0.2 percent in 2003 after slowing in the prior two years due to stalling demand from the sluggish Eurozone whose GDP growth hit 0.8 percent, down from 0.9 percent and 1.9 percent in 2002 and 2001 respectively.

Seeking to prevent geopolitically driven safe-haven flows from boosting CHF excessively at a time when the world economy was already dragged by higher oil prices, the Swiss National Bank eased monetary policy substantially. Interest rates fell to the low end of its 0.00–0.75 percent target range at a historically low 0.25 percent, driving away investors from the ultralow-yielding currency.

Japanese Yen: −44 percent

As Japan entered its sixth straight year of deflation, interest rates remained at virtually zero percent and currency traders found no interest in snapping up the low-yielding yen against the soaring commodity currencies and rallying European currencies. But the yen rallied as much as 10 percent against the U.S. dollar for the year in reaction to one of the key developments dominating currency markets in 2003. At the September G7 meeting in Dubai, the top seven economies agreed on encouraging Asian economies to refrain from capping their currencies to gain competitive edge in the global market place. The message was directed at China and Japan, which were notorious for keeping their currencies artificially weak against the U.S. dollar. Once the communiqué was issued by the G7, USD/JPY tumbled from 117.70 to 113.50 within a week, losing 6 percent on the month to reach two-year lows.

U.S. Dollar: −127 percent

The year 2003 was the U.S. dollar's worst year in terms of total returns against the seven other major currencies, losing a cumulative 127 percent against AUD, CAD, CHF, GBP, EUR, JPY, and NZD by 34 percent, 18 percent, 10 percent, 11 percent, 20 percent, 10 percent, and 25 percent, respectively. Increased geopolitical uncertainty, record high budget and trade deficits, and prolonged Fed rate cuts were all drivers of the greenback damage. Markets clearly understood that Washington's currency policy of benign neglect stemmed from its desire to see further decline in the dollar as long as it was orderly and did not erode general confidence in U.S. assets.

2004: GLOBAL RECOVERY BOOSTS CURRENCIES AGAINST U.S. DOLLAR

For the second year in three years, the New Zealand dollar was the highest-performing currency of the eight major currencies in terms of cumulative returns, due to a favorable environment in monetary policy, global growth, and commodities (see Figure 4.9). In contrast, the U.S. dollar was the worst performer for the third consecutive year as the broadening global recovery maintained bullishness in non-USD currencies. Swelling U.S. trade and budget deficits combined with a currency policy of benign neglect accelerated the declines. GDP growth in G7 nations rose to 3.1 percent in 2004, the highest growth rate since 1999. The emerging theme of central banks slowing their accumulation of U.S. dollar reserves in favor of euros, sterling, and gold was taking hold and acted as a negative for the greenback.

Currencies in general delivered their strongest performance against gold since 1999 as central banks reached the end of their easing campaigns and shifted to tighter monetary policies. The end of the global interest rate–cutting cycle meant that projected increases in interest rates would challenge the returns on gold as an asset class. Both the Federal Reserve and the Bank of England began raising interest rates for the first time in

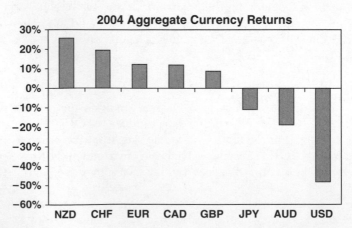

FIGURE 4.9　NZD regains top position in 2004 FX performance while USD remains at bottom of league.

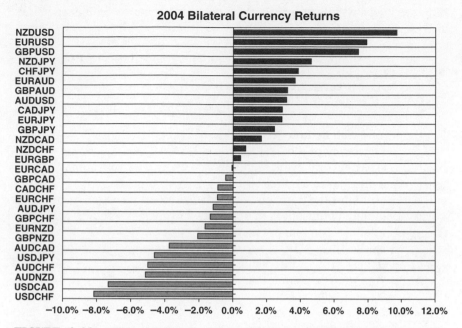

FIGURE 4.10 USD and AUD pairs dominated the bottom of the rank as U.S. interest rates underperformed and Australia's real estate slowdown hampered the aussie.

three years, while the European Central Bank held rates unchanged after cutting them in each of the previous three years. The Reserve Bank of Australia held interest rates unchanged for the first time since 1995, opting not to join the global tightening due to the broad decline in house prices following a decade-long housing bubble. Figure 4.10 shows the currency pairs trading results for 2004.

New Zealand Dollar: +26 percent

For the second year during this nine-year analysis period (1999–2007), the NZD was the highest-ranking currency in terms of cumulative returns. A combination of aggressive tightening from the Reserve Bank of New Zealand (RBNZ) and a favorable price environment in New Zealand's top exporting commodities provided an attractive recipe to currency traders.

The RBNZ raised rates on five occasions, boosting the cash rate to 6.50 percent at a time when inflation rose to 2.3 percent from 1.7 percent and GDP growth recovered to 4.4 percent from 3.5 percent. As long as the growth and inflation arguments were in place for aggressive rate hikes, investors were willing to chase the higher-yielding kiwi as a carry-trade investment. Carry trades involve borrowing funds in low-yielding currencies such as JPY and CHF and investing the proceeds in higher-yielding currencies. Consequently, investors reap the benefit of the interest rate differential as well as the appreciation of the target currency. As we shall see in subsequent chapters, carry trades can involve investing not only in high-yielding currencies but also in high-growth assets such as appreciating stock indexes, gold, and oil.

Rising commodities was another factor behind the soaring kiwi. Prices of nonfuel commodities rose 18.5 percent in 2004 after 6.9 percent and 1.7 percent in 2003 and 2002, respectively. Food prices rose 14.3 percent after 5.2 percent and 3.4 percent, while prices for agricultural raw materials increased 5.5 percent from 3.7 percent and 1.8 percent. With over 50 percent of New Zealand's exports coming out of the agriculture sector, and with dairy products accounting for 20 percent of total exports, the continued price growth was a clear windfall for the nation's GDP growth and currency. The currency was also boosted by the growth rebound in the newly industrialized Asian economies (NIAEs), attaining 2.4 percent GDP growth rate after 3.5 percent in 2003.

Swiss Franc: +19 percent

Though not spectacular, the cumulative returns of the Swiss franc were sufficient to place it in second position in the 2004 ranking due to a robust export-led recovery following the 2003 recession. GDP growth rose to 2.5 percent from −0.2 percent, while growth in its major trading partners, the Eurozone and the United Kingdom, rose to 2.0 percent from 0.8 percent and to 3.3 percent from 2.8 percent. Battling the risk of deflation, the Swiss National Bank held rates unchanged, which increased demand for currency deemed to have been undervalued, relative to the nation's GDP growth rate.

Euro: +12 percent

Although its returns were well below those of the strong cumulative gains of 47 percent and 28 percent in 2002 and 2003, the euro managed to rank third-best performer in 2004 with a 12 percent cumulative gain versus the other seven major currencies. Gaining from a jump in GDP growth to 2.0 percent from 0.8 percent in 2003, and from the absence of ECB policy tightening, the euro accumulated a strong boost of confidence in its sixth year of operation. Bank of France president Jean-Claude Trichet's assumption of the ECB presidency in November 2003 added a vital vote of confidence to the young central bank due to his proven record as a credible and highly respected central banker in the Eurozone's second-largest economy. Trichet also became the single dominant voice of the euro, unlike in the early years when several policy makers tended to give misleading and inconsistent signals.

Most notably, the euro's robust performance was a reflection of the dollar's woes as the U.S. currency was saddled with further swelling in the twin deficits (budget and trade) resulting from lower taxes, surging war spending, and rising energy imports. EUR maintained its role of the anti-dollar in global currency markets as the EUR/USD pair accounted for 28 percent of all transactions, compared to 17 percent and 14 percent for the USD/JPY and GBP/USD pairs. The euro breached above the $1.30 mark for the first time in history, delivering a resounding signal of confidence to currency traders and global asset managers.

Canadian Dollar: +12 percent

The loonie fully exploited the 34 percent rise in oil prices, which at one time during the year were up 72 percent, the highest since Iraq's 1990 invasion of Kuwait. Exports rose 7.5 percent in 2004 after declining 1.4 percent and 1.6 percent in 2002 and 2003 respectively. The role of rising oil prices was highlighted in the fact that energy exports accounted for 16 percent of total exports in 2004, following 15 percent and 12 percent in the prior two years. Crude oil exports rose 24 percent, more than doubling the growth of 2003. Benefiting from the impact of higher oil and a sharp recovery in GDP growth to four-year highs at 3.7 percent, the loonie surged 7 percent against the U.S. dollar to 12-year highs, following an 18 percent increase in 2003. Those returns placed the CAD on the radar screen of asset managers seeking returns from a nation with budget and trade surpluses—the antithesis of the U.S. economy.

British Pound: +9 percent

The sterling's 2004 performance came under pressure mainly in the second half of the year when house price growth slowed sharply, risking a standstill in the highly leveraged household spending sector. The Bank of England's five rate hikes between November 2003 and August 2004 had started to take effect in summer 2004. In August, the Halifax measure of house prices fell by 0.6 percent, posting its 10th monthly decline in the preceding five years, a period when home prices had more than doubled. Nationwide's housing price data showed growth of only 0.2 percent and 0.1 percent in September and August respectively, rates not seen since summer 2000. (See Figure 4.11.)

FIGURE 4.11   Slowing growth in UK home prices weighed on the British pound's trade-weighted index.

In addition to the housing slowdown, central bank policy makers had begun signaling the peak in interest rates, thus accelerating the declines in the currency.

Japanese Yen: −11 percent

The losses in the Japanese yen against individual currencies were mostly moderate, ranging from 1 to 4 percent, with the exception of the NZD and USD against which it fell 5 percent. The decline against the NZD was based on surging carry trade, whereby investors funded investments in low-yielding JPY (0.15 percent interest rate) to deposit the proceeds in higher-yielding NZD (over 6 percent interest rate).

So why did the JPY fall by the same amount against the USD when U.S. interest rates stood at the relatively low levels of 1.0 percent? The main reason was persistent currency interventions by the Bank of Japan, whereby it sold its own currency in the open market to buy U.S. dollars in order to prevent the yen from appreciating markedly and weighing on Japanese exports. A lower yen also helped Japan fight its deflation problem as negative price growth entered its sixth consecutive year. Oftentimes, Japanese officials succeeded in steering the yen lower simply by jawboning the market—in other words, threatening to intervene or expressing concern with rapid currency appreciation. Unlike the 2003 interventions, which were carried out almost every month, the yen-selling interventions of 2004 lasted only the first four months of the year, albeit on a greater scale.

Australian Dollar: −19 percent

The main reason for the aussie's 2004 underperformance was the accelerating decline in home prices, threatening to halt the nation's longest economic expansion. Despite a 46 percent increase in copper prices and an increase in GDP growth from 3.7 percent in 2003 to 3.1 percent, many home buyers were forced to let their properties go into foreclosure, thereby impacting consumer expenditure.

Australia's house price boom began in the mid-1990s, and gathered speed after the 2000 Olympics with a 20 percent annual increase in some cities. The peak was reached in mid-2003. As house price growth slowed markedly, inflation fell from 2.8 percent to 2.3 percent, the lowest since 1999. The interest rate hikes of November and December 2003 helped accelerate the slowdown into the first half of 2004, and caused the central bank to refrain from raising rates for the first time since 1999, when the economy struggled following the 1997–1998 Asian crisis.

Although rates were held at 5.25 percent throughout the year, speculation of an RBA rate cut was behind the aussie's declines. But the economy was spared the threat of recession thanks to the price surge in Australia's minerals, powered by China's growing demand for commodities.

U.S. Dollar: −48 percent

Despite 10 rate hikes of 25 bps each by the Federal Reserve, the U.S. dollar ended at the bottom of the performance rank for the third straight year in 2004. The widening budget deficit hit a record $412.55 billion in fiscal 2004 following a record $377.14 billion in fiscal 2003. The fiscal profligacy of the Bush administration and its negative impact on market sentiment was largely the cause of the renewed attack on the currency after his reelection in the 2004 elections. The decision to extend the first term's income tax and dividend tax cuts has also eroded any hopes of stabilizing the fiscal imbalance. The U.S. trade gap hit a record 5.7 percent of GDP as soaring oil exacerbated the rise in oil imports. Despite the 30 percent drop in the dollar's trade-weighted value since January 2002, the U.S. trade gap had risen by over 80 percent.

The falling dollar also reduced foreign investors' interest in U.S. assets to the extent of curtailing the inflows required to finance the swelling deficit. The currency policy of benign neglect also hurt the greenback. Treasury Secretary John Snow's insistence that the dollar's value must be "decided by the markets," at a time when traders had shaved 30 percent off the currency's value in trade-weighted terms since January 2002, left markets no choice but to conclude that the U.S. administration was encouraging a weaker dollar. It wasn't until 2005 that prolonged Fed tightening would begin helping the U.S. currency.

2005: COMMODITIES SOAR ALONGSIDE DOLLAR, CARRY TRADES EMERGE

The widely held notion stating that commodity prices are inversely related to the U.S. dollar was largely debunked in 2005 as the greenback rallied along with oil, gold, and most other primary commodity prices. There were several reasons for these developments:

- Continued Fed rate hikes into 2005 lifted U.S. rates back above their Canadian, Eurozone, and UK counterparts, offering USD holders a more favorable interest rate differential.
- Repatriation of foreign-based earnings by U.S. multinationals to take advantage of a provisional tax had increased USD-bound flows.
- Soaring demand for commodities was amplified by China's advance as the world's top consumer of most agricultural and metal products.
- Robust growth rates in G10 nations complemented China's demand.

Figure 4.12 shows the U.S. dollar was the second-highest-performing currency in aggregate terms, standing among the three major commodity currencies (CAD, NZD, and AUD).

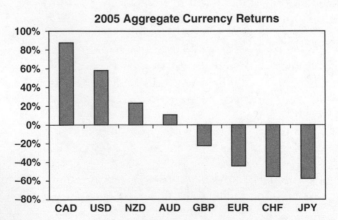

FIGURE 4.12 The U.S. dollar joined commodity currencies among top-performing currencies of 2005 as the Fed tightened and world commodities rallied.

This was also the year of carry trades as global investors benefited from diverging monetary policies between the low interest rate currencies of Japan and Switzerland, and higher interest rate currencies of the United States, Canada, Australia, and New Zealand. Investors particularly sought currencies with the greatest potential for appreciation and rising interest rates. As these flows were mobilized, the higher-yielding currencies outperformed, while lower-yielding currencies headed down across the board (see Figure 4.13).

Canadian Dollar: +88 percent

The Canadian dollar attained a cumulative 88 percent increase against the seven major currencies in 2005, its highest return during 1999. A 41 percent increase in oil prices boosted Canada's oil exports to a 19 percent share of total exports in 2005, from a 16 percent and 15 percent share in the prior two years, providing the overall economy and the currency with significant windfall. The combination of an external-led expansion and strong domestic demand fed into rising inflation, which reached 2.2 percent from 1.8 percent, driving the Bank of Canada to raise rates by 75 bps to a two-year high of 3.25 percent.

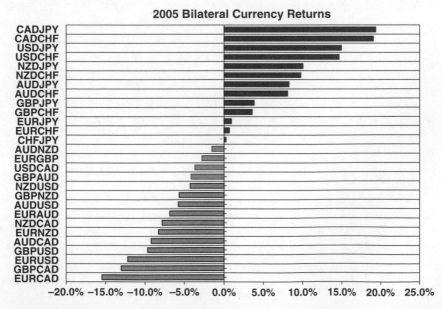

FIGURE 4.13 The Canadian dollar prevailed throughout the top-performing currency pairs of 2005.

Although Canadian interest rates were lower than in the United States, United Kingdom, Australia, and New Zealand, the CAD delivered the better performance against those currencies due to its benefiting from rising oil. The currency rose from 12-year highs against the U.S. dollar in 2004 to 15-year highs in 2005. It also delivered solid gains versus CHF, JPY, EUR, and GBP at 19 percent, 19 percent, 15 percent, and 13 percent respectively.

U.S. Dollar: +58 percent

After a three-year slump at the bottom ranking of cumulative returns, the U.S. dollar staged a broad comeback in 2005 due to a steady dose of interest rate hikes, USD-bound capital flows, and political uncertainty in the Eurozone. After slashing rates to a 45-year low at 1 percent in 2003, the Federal Reserve began a gradual policy of normalizing monetary policy in 2004 and 2005, with five and eight 25 bps rate hikes respectively, taking the Fed funds rate to 4.25 percent by the end of 2005. The incremental tightening served to contain inflationary pressures without hampering the economic recovery from the 2000–2001 recession as the Bush $212 billion tax stimulus worked its way through the economy. U.S. interest rates rose back above their Eurozone counterparts, extending the yield differential to 225 bps, while cutting their yield disadvantage relative to rates in the United Kingdom.

The dollar also benefited from the Homeland Investment Act, which was part of the American Jobs Creation Act of 2004, signed into law by President Bush, allowing U.S. companies to repatriate earnings permanently reinvested abroad. Funds were taxed at 5.25 percent, rather than the normal tax rate of 35 percent, prompting companies to bring back an estimated total of $180 to $210 billion.

Political uncertainty in the Eurozone emerging from France's rejection of a European Union referendum spelled trouble for political union ambitions and dragged an already retreating euro farther down.

New Zealand Dollar: +23 percent

The kiwi maintained its strong positive correlation with rising food and agricultural raw materials, while gaining from a rising interest rate environment as the central bank tightened rates by 75 bps to 7.25 percent. As central banks raised rates in concert, investors sought added returns in growth and yield, which was on offer by the kiwi. Although GDP growth in NIAEs slowed from 5.9 percent to 4.7 percent, demand for kiwi was largely driven by carry-trade investors, especially as Japanese and Swiss interest rates offered attractive funding means for such trades. Offering the highest interest rates among the eight currencies, the kiwi was a popular destination for carry trades, appreciating 10 percent against JPY and CHF. At some point in January, the kiwi soared to a 14-year high against the U.S. dollar before the Fed rate hikes triggered a broad run-up in the greenback.

Australian Dollar: +11 percent

The aussie managed to stand out as a net gainer in 2005 as the Australian economy struggled to recover from the housing correction. Although GDP growth had slowed from 3.7 percent in 2004 to 2.8 percent in 2005, the aussie benefited from a 76 percent increase in copper prices as China stepped up its consumption of minerals and commodities with the help of its appreciating currency. And despite slowing GDP growth in Australia and the NIAEs, the bulk of the aussie's gains were a result of broadening carry trades as the RBA raised rates to 5.50 percent. The central bank kept the door open for further tightening as inflation rose to 2.7 percent from 2.3 percent.

British Pound: −22 percent

The sterling's declines were largely a result of fears that the 10-year-old housing bubble was finally about to burst. The slowdown of 2004 grew more pronounced in 2005, and annual home price growth hit its lowest in nine years, while month-to-month rates were showing declines. The sterling's losses were magnified by the fact that the Bank of England was the only central bank among those analyzed to have cut interest rates, which proved to be a punishing outcome in a year when FX speculative flows thrived on carry trades. Sterling's worst performances were against the CAD and USD and −13 percent and −10 percent respectively.

Euro: −44 percent

The euro sustained its first decline in three years as a result of weak Eurozone growth, political uncertainty, and the euro-dollar duality obtaining the best of the single currency. Eurozone France's rejection of a proposed European Union Constitution dealt a blow to confidence in the European Union and the future of its currency, especially with France being the second-largest economy of the Eurozone. The rejection raised questions about the political unity of the Eurozone, adding to speculation that some member-nations would exit the currency area and trigger a crisis of confidence in the seven-year-old currency. The slowdown in Eurozone GDP growth to 1.5 percent from 2.0 percent as well as that in the United Kingdom and Switzerland also weighed on the region's net external trade.

The euro-dollar polarity was once again in play, as gains in one currency shed losses in the other. The euro's dominance in the U.S. Dollar Index caused the polarity between the two currencies. The euro's weight in the six-currency index is 57.6 percent, followed by the JPY, GBP, CAD, SEK, and CHF at 13.6 percent, 11.9 percent, 9.1 percent, 4.2 percent, and 3.6 percent respectively. As the dollar rallied strongly against most currencies, the euro took the short end of the stick.

Swiss Franc: −55 percent

The low-yielding CHF was hit across the board as 2005 marked an escalation of carry trades, with investors showing risk appetite in leveraging their trades in high-yielding assets by borrowing in lower interest rate CHF and JPY. The Swiss franc's woes were magnified by the fact that the Swiss National Bank had kept rates unchanged around their 0.75 percent target since July 2002 while the rest of major central banks—other than the Bank of Japan—had pushed rates higher. As global growth picked up and equity indexes recovered to five-year highs, investors developed higher risk appetites, using low-yielding currencies as funding vehicles.

Japanese Yen: −58 percent

The Japanese yen fell 14 percent in trade-weighted terms, the biggest decline on record. The 57 percent cumulative decline against the group of seven currencies was the second biggest in this 1999–2007 period as investors borrowed in ultralow Japanese interest rates to finance higher-yielding investments. Such investments included currencies with higher interest rates and those with the greater potential for appreciation without necessarily any substantially high interest rates, such as CAD, whose rates were lower than those for USD, GBP, NZD, and AUD (see Figure 4.14).

2006: DOLLAR VULNERABLE AS FED ENDS TWO-YEAR TIGHTENING

The conclusion of the Federal Reserve's two-year tightening campaign in summer 2006 was one of the most important developments in financial markets, as investors braced for the policy implications of the deteriorating U.S. housing market. No longer obtaining a boost from Fed rate hikes and repatriation flows, the U.S. dollar gave back most of its 2005 gains to end among the big losers in 2006. (See Figure 4.15.)

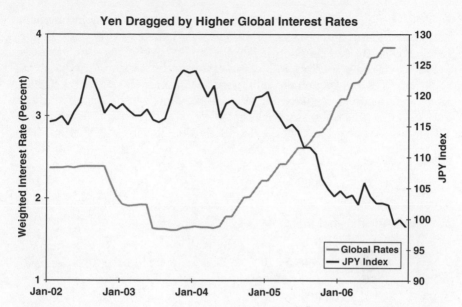

FIGURE 4.14 Higher global interest rate* drove down JPY as investors sold the low-yielding currency and placed proceeds in higher-yielding currencies and investments.

*Global interest rates are the growth-adjusted weighted average of the top eight currencies.

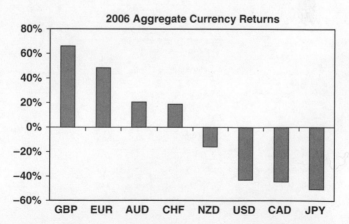

FIGURE 4.15 Both GBP and EUR rallied significantly due to higher GDP growth rates and rising interest rates in contrast to USD, whose growth rate moved below par and interest rates peaked out.

The British pound made an aggressive comeback from its sluggish 2003–2005 performances as the Bank of England delivered two surprising rate hikes in the second half of the year aimed at containing rapid credit growth and house price appreciation. Gold prices soared to a 26-year high of $735 in May before retreating by year-end, yet still gaining 23 percent. Gold's retreat was a result of midyear nervousness with emerging markets and fears that high interest rates in Japan would reduce global liquidity and weigh on risk appetite. A series of gradual rate hikes by the ECB boosted the euro to the second-highest return ranking position, while the Japanese yen was the biggest loser for two consecutive years as continued rate hikes elsewhere further reduced the attractiveness of the yen. (See Figure 4.16.)

British Pound: +66 percent

The sterling delivered its strongest annual cumulative performance against the seven major currencies in 2006, its best showing during the 1999–2007 period. In trade-weighted terms, GBP rose 5.16 percent, its highest level since 1999. The main reason for those gains was the timing of the Bank of England's monetary policy cycle. While the Federal Reserve, European Central Bank, Bank of Canada, Reserve Bank of Australia, and Reserve

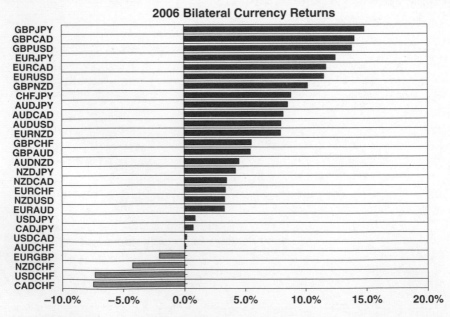

2006 Bilateral Currency Returns

FIGURE 4.16 The British pound was the highest-performing currency of 2006 while the euro followed closely behind.

Bank of New Zealand each began raising rates in 2005, the Bank of England was forced to cut rates due to slowing home prices. It wasn't until August 2006 that the BoE began raising rates as inflation exceeded the 2.0 percent target and house prices continued accelerating earlier in the year. With UK interest rates already at a relatively high 4.5 percent, the new tightening cycle promised to take those rates to the upper range of G7 rates, while most other central banks were mulling the end of their tightening campaigns and holding rates steady. A surprise BoE rate hike on August 3 extended sterling's gains across the board, and hawkish inflation reports from the BoE in August and November confirmed that further increases were in store for 2007. GBP went on to gain versus all currencies: JPY (15 percent), USD (14 percent), CAD (14 percent), NZD (10 percent), EUR (2 percent), CHF (6 percent), and AUD (5 percent).

In December 2006, sterling broke above $1.955 against the U.S. dollar, reaching its highest level since September 1992, when it had broken off the Exchange Rate Mechanism (ERM) due to its inability to sustain high levels during the recessionary early 1990s. The new landmark provided a particularly tremendous boost of confidence for the currency, as the landmark signaled the shifting of billions of U.S. dollars among asset managers in asset allocation plays, and among central banks considering rebalancing their reserves into higher-yielding currencies.

Euro: +48 percent

Steady rate hikes from the ECB, improving growth differentials, weak U.S. fundamentals, and a prolonged sell-off in the U.S. dollar were the main drivers of the 2006 euro rally. On the monetary policy front, the ECB delivered well-telegraphed rate increases with the aim of normalizing policy— after slashing rates aggressively in 2001–2003 and containing inflation without endangering growth. ECB president Jean-Claude Trichet was credited with continuously improving the central bank's communications to the financial markets to the extent that the outcome of each interest rate announcement was never a surprise to market participants. Such is the trademark of central bank credibility. On the growth front, Eurozone GDP growth rose above that of the United States for the first time since 2001, thereby accelerating the currency's winning run against the greenback.

On the U.S. front, persistent declines in housing prices and falling construction spending were showing nascent signs of extending to the rest of the economy, forcing the Federal Reserve to end its two-year tightening campaign after 17 rate hikes. While U.S. interest rates peaked at 5.25 percent in June 2006, Eurozone interest rates rose to 3.5 percent, narrowing the U.S. yield premium to 2.25 percent in January from 3.5 percent by year-end. With Eurozone GDP growth continuing to grow faster than its U.S.

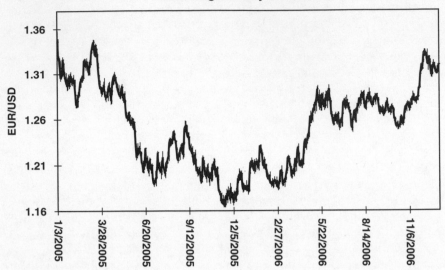

FIGURE 4.17 The euro regained the psychologically important $1.30 level in October 2006 on reports that German growth would surpass that of the United States.

counterpart and the ECB maintaining its preoccupation with rising inflation, markets anticipated more ECB rate hikes and prolonged narrowing in the U.S. yield advantage.

The euro also benefited from increased speculation that global central banks would reduce their buildup of USD-denominated currency reserves in favor of the euro. (See Figure 4.17.) China's central bank had already reduced the proportion of its USD reserves from over 90 percent in 2000 to less than 70 percent in 2005. Central banks from Arab Gulf nations made several statements signaling their willingness to diversify reserves into non-USD currencies and gold. Chinese officials also made comments about the need for reserve diversification. Although such pronouncements meant that central banks would slow their future accumulation of U.S. dollars, rather than dump their U.S. reserves, they triggered various bouts of selling in the greenback.

Australian Dollar: +21 percent

The aussie's strong 2006 performance emerged on the heels of a continued favorable environment for commodities prices, robust GDP growth, falling unemployment, higher interest rates, and rising inflation. An emerging drought pushed up prices of wheat by over 50 percent, boosting revenues of Australia's biggest-selling crop. Australian wheat exports make up approximately 15 percent of the world's wheat trade. Copper prices rose as much as 75 percent in the first half of the year but lost a third of their gains into the second half. Continued strength in East Asian GDP growth was also a valuable source of demand for Australian minerals and agricultural exports. The resulting increase in inflation from 2.7 percent in 2005 to 3.5 percent was above the preferred range of the central bank, forcing interest rates to rise by 75 bps to a 10-year high of 6.25 percent.

Swiss Franc: +19 percent

A sharp increase in Swiss GDP growth and the largest interest rate increase in decades gave the Swiss franc the best cumulative return among the eight major currencies under review. Although all major central banks had begun raising interest rates by 2004, the Swiss National Bank hadn't raised its rates since summer 2000, after which it reduced them to 0.75 percent over the next two years. In 2006, the central bank raised rates five times, taking them to 2.0 percent, as GDP growth jumped to a six-year high of 3.2 percent from 2.4 percent.

CHF was particularly boosted during the global stock market correction occurring between May and June, as investors cut back from their carry trades, which financed speculation in high-growth currencies, equities, and metals. The unwinding of carry trades shifted capital back to the lower-yielding franc. Between May and June, the currency rallied by as much as 6 percent against the higher-yielding aussie and kiwi, while gold tumbled 25 percent from its 26-year highs and the S&P 500 shed more than 8.0 percent. As we will see later in this section, the Japanese yen failed to prolong the gains shown by the Swiss franc during the temporary correction because of currency jawboning by Japanese authorities.

New Zealand Dollar: −16 percent

It was a tale of two halves for the kiwi as the currency tumbled 11 percent in trade-weighted terms in the first six months, before regaining 90 percent of those losses in the second half of the year. The currency failed to share its Australian counterpart despite agricultural raw materials soaring 10 percent above their 20-year average. There were three main reasons for the kiwi's 2006 performance:

1. Treasury officials persistently talked down the currency in an attempt to prevent further run-ups after the kiwi hit 14-year highs in early 2005 and was set to revisit those levels in the midst of the global commodity boom. Finance Minister Cullen went as far as taking the unorthodox

step of warning speculators of a currency loss of as high as 40 cents amid dimming prospects of further rate hikes.

2. The unwinding of carry trades away from high-yielding currency was accelerated late in the second quarter as global equity markets tumbled by 7 to 8 percent from their first-quarter highs.

3. The Reserve Bank of New Zealand held rates unchanged at 7.25 percent throughout the year so as to prevent further advances in the currency. It was the first time in five years that rates were not hiked by the central bank. GDP slowed to 1.6 percent from 2.7 percent.

U.S. Dollar: −43 percent

The much-anticipated end of the Federal Reserve's two-year campaign took place in summer 2006, prompting currency markets to begin paring their dollar longs. Once it concluded its 17 consecutive rate hikes, the Fed took a wait-and-see approach to gauge the upside risks of inflation and the downside risks from the slowing housing market. One year after peaking out, the U.S. housing market was signaling increasingly consistent signs of weakness, from falling home prices to sluggish construction spending and falling housing starts and permits. By the second quarter of 2006, the monthly price growth of U.S. existing and new home sales had reached double-digit levels on year-to-year basis. Although the Federal Reserve persisted in signaling its preoccupation with rising inflation, markets were beginning to perceive the Fed's concerns as largely tactical rhetoric aimed at supporting the U.S. dollar and bond yields without following through with an actual rate hike.

Meanwhile, GDP growth rates in the Eurozone, the United Kingdom, and Asia were exceeding those in the U.S., sending a vocal message to the market that the U.S. dollar was losing its growth and interest rate differential relative to other currencies. This was confirmed across the board as the Bank of England, Bank of Japan, European Central Bank, Swiss National Bank, and Reserve Bank of Australia continued raising rates in the second half of the year, a situation of contrasting monetary policies not seen in over a decade. Strong economic reports from the Eurozone showed that the general economy was unfazed by the euro's 8 percent appreciation against the U.S. dollar, encouraging traders to boost EUR/USD past $1.30 and extending it by 11 percent for the year.

Canadian Dollar: −44 percent

The Canadian dollar was rallying for the fourth consecutive year until it sustained a drag by a sharp retreat in oil prices and a change in Canada's tax laws. Oil reached a record $77 per barrel in August 2006, posting a 26 percent increase on the year before losing all of those gains in the fourth quarter. Profit-taking among oil speculators sent prices back to where they had begun the year, causing a drag on the oil-dependent loonie. The currency had climbed 7 percent against the U.S. dollar to hit 28-year highs at $1.0960 during the oil price rise.

The subsequent sell-off in CAD was exacerbated in October when Canada's government announced a new tax on income trusts, whose exemption had enabled domestic and foreign companies to avoid paying hundred of millions of dollars in taxes each year. The announcement wiped out more than $30 billion off the market value of unit trusts over a few days. The consequences were equally negative for the CAD, which lost more than 5 percent in the fourth quarter alone. The Bank of Canada's conclusion of its two-year tightening campaign in June also helped weigh on the Canadian dollar.

Japanese Yen: −51 percent

The Japanese yen lost a cumulative 51 percent against the other seven major currencies in 2006, to fall into the bottom rank of returns for the second consecutive year. Unlike its low-yielding counterpart, the Swiss franc, which was the beneficiary of risk aversion and unwinding of carry trades during the year, the yen made limited gains.

One reason for that is the highly defensive rhetoric communicated by Japanese policy makers in signaling the much-anticipated rate hike. Prolonged deflation was the reason Japanese rates weren't raised since 2000. As the Bank of Japan prepared to raise rates from their ultralow levels of 0.15 percent, the Japanese yen was already rallying across the board during the first five months of the year, benefiting from the correction in global stock markets. A rate hike would have accelerated the yen's appreciation, thereby possibly throwing the economy back into deflation mode. At the same time, policy makers were obliged to begin normalizing interest rates as the Japanese economy and rest of the world continued their expansion, and inflation remained on the rise. Failure to raise rates would have prolonged carry trades' negative impact on the yen and discouraged global capital flows away from yen-denominated assets.

Policy makers did all they could to signal that the rate hike would be a minor step to normalize monetary policy, rather than the beginning of a series of rate increases. By the time the rate hike took place in July 2006, equity markets had stabilized and global investors gradually shifted to low-yielding currencies to fund a renewed run-up in high-yielding currencies, equities, gold, and oil.

2007: RECORD OIL BOOSTS LOONIE, HELPLESS FED HITS GREENBACK

The year 2007 was a year of records broken in currencies and commodities as the corroding dollar drove the former and demand/supply forces propelled gold and oil to or near record highs. The currency developments of 2007 were largely dominated by two main themes:

1. Risk appetite trades benefiting AUD, CAD, NZD, and GBP at the expense of USD, CHF, and JPY.

2. USD-specific selling against all major currencies as the Federal Reserve was forced to slash interest rates by 100 bps to stabilize the crisis in credit markets and contain the economic impact of deteriorating housing. (See Figure 4.18.)

The Japanese yen amassed broad gains during periodic episodes of risk appetite reduction as global stocks sold off aggressively in the midst of subprime-related losses in the U.S. financial sector.

The USD was the broadest loser in 2007, with its trade-weighted index hitting all record lows, while the top four performing currencies against the USD were CAD, AUD, EUR, and NZD. The commodity currencies of CAD, AUD, and NZD were boosted by new record highs in prices of energy, metals, and agriculture as well as high interest rate policies. EUR was propped by its role as the anti-U.S. dollar and by the European Central Bank's persistently hawkish rhetoric. While the three commodity currencies

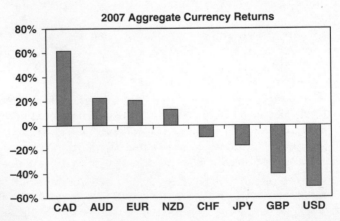

FIGURE 4.18 Soaring oil prices fueled the Canadian dollar to the top of the currency performance league of 2007.

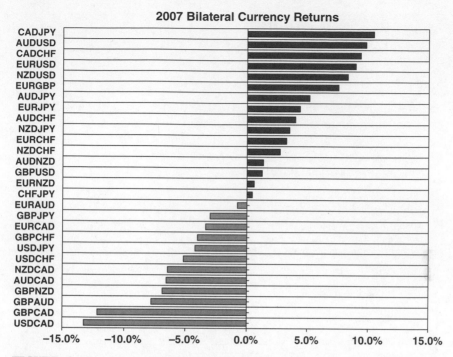

FIGURE 4.19 The euro's presence among the commodity currencies in the top performers of 2007 reflects its broadening strength.

(CAD, AUD, and NZD) were clearly in command in the ranking of currencies' performance against gold, no currency registered any gains versus the metal, illustrating the secular rally in gold and other commodities. (See Figure 4.19.)

Canadian Dollar: +62 percent

Record levels in oil prices gave the Canadian dollar a cumulative 61 percent return against the seven major currencies, as energy exports made up over 20 percent of total exports and 10 percent of GDP. Crude oil soared 60 percent to a new all-time high of $96 per barrel, propelling the CAD to 50-year highs against the USD, 14-year highs against GBP, and 6-year highs against EUR. Especially favorable for the CAD were continued signs of expansion in Canada's economy despite the sharp slowdown south of the border. Canada's unemployment rate dipped to a 33-year low of 5.8 percent, while GDP growth rate cooled to 2.5 percent from 2.8 percent. The Bank of Canada raised rates on one occasion to a six-year high of 4.5 percent. The

Canadian dollar had become an asset class of its own, representative of the secular rally in oil prices.

Australian Dollar: +22 percent

The aussie surged against the USD, GBP, and EUR to the highest levels in 23 years, 10 years, and 7 years, respectively, as interest rates hit 11-year highs at 6.75 percent and GDP growth matched 8-year highs at 4.4 percent. The combination of high growth and relatively low inflation of 2.3 percent offered high real interest rates (nominal rates less inflation), an attractive combination to investors. Much of the growing GDP rate emerged from soaring prices of Australia's best-selling commodities. Prices of wheat doubled for the year to hit a record high of $10 per bushel, while copper prices rose 30 percent due to surging demand from China. With the unemployment rate falling to 33-year lows at 4.2 percent and GDP growth at decade highs, traders found proof of a surging economy in the face of protracted currency strength, thereby further bidding up the currency to multidecade highs.

But as high Australian interest rates helped the aussie benefit from rising carry trades, they also proved to be the source of its declines during the unwinding of these carry trades. (See Figure 4.20.) Between November and December 2007, the aussie's trade-weighted index lost 7 percent as global equities fell across the board on write-downs from struggling U.S. banks. Risk appetite and volatility will be covered in more detail in Chapter 5.

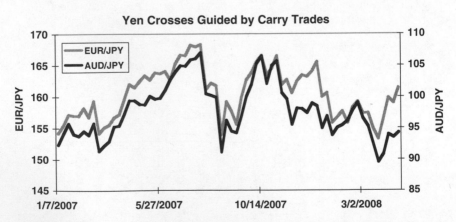

FIGURE 4.20 Increased market volatility triggered sharp fluctuations in carry trade currency pairs such as AUD/JPY and EUR/JPY.

Euro: +21 percent

The strength of the euro's 2007 performance was particularly highlighted by the contrasting growth and interest rate climates between the Eurozone and the United States, as the former grew at a rate of 2.5 percent compared to 1.9 percent for the latter. Meanwhile, the ECB raised interest rates by a total of 50 bps to 4 percent, while the Fed cut rates by a 100 bps to 4.25 percent, taking down the U.S. rate advantage to a three-year low. As a result, the premium of German 10-year yields over their U.S. counterpart widened further, which bolstered the euro's ascent against the greenback. (See Figure 4.21.)

Unlike in previous years of EUR strength and USD weakness when the euro largely benefited from USD weakness, the 2007 dynamics were a result of eroding USD fundamentals as well as cyclical Eurozone strength. Improved domestic demand in the Eurozone also proved that the economy was better equipped to contain the pressures of a rising euro than was the case in 2003 and 2004. Having said that, the single currency continued to play the role of the antidollar, helping to bolster its upward run to record highs versus the USD, GBP, JPY, and CHF.

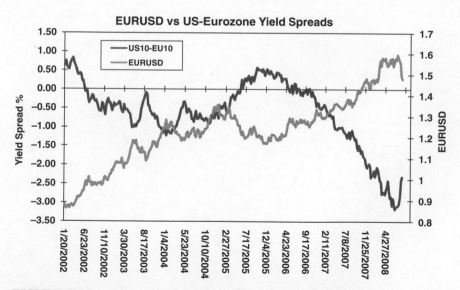

FIGURE 4.21 Widening interest rate differentials between German and United States 10-year bond yields left little choice for currency traders but to send EUR/USD higher.

New Zealand Dollar: +13 percent

The kiwi's performance resulted from aggressive rate hikes and soaring dairy prices, which provided a robust growth foundation for the rising currency. Speculative interest also played a vital role in sustaining the kiwi's gains, especially from traders who funded their investments with low-yielding currencies such as the yen. The Reserve Bank of New Zealand (RBNZ) raised the official cash rate four times, driving it to 8.25 percent, the highest level since its introduction in 1999. Persistent demand strength from Asia was supported by strong growth GDP rates in China and NIAEs at 11.3 percent and 3.9 percent respectively. Currency strength lifted the kiwi to 25-year highs against the U.S. dollar, prompting the central bank to intervene by selling kiwis in the open market to stabilize the trend.

But the interventions proved too little against the speculative interest propping the currency. The RBNZ gave up intervening after three failed attempts and the kiwi pursued its run-up to multidecade highs. The threat of rising inflationary pressures emerging from record-breaking dairy prices was stabilized by the strong currency, thus providing an impetus to real interest rates. GDP growth hit a three-year high of 2.8 percent, while inflation stabilized at 2.4 percent. Similar to the aussie, the kiwi sustained sharp declines during the stock market corrections of February–March, August, and November 2007.

Swiss Franc: −10 percent

The low-yielding Swiss franc served its role of a funding currency to carry trades targeting higher-yielding currencies and growth alternatives such as stock indexes, individual stocks, oil, and gold. Consequently, the franc came under sharp pressure during periods of rising risk appetite and low market volatility during which investors leveraged their investments in the rallying markets by borrowing in cheap francs. Conversely, the franc rallied significantly as those trades were unwound during periods of rising volatility. During the weeks of surging volatility, on March 2, August 17, and November 9, the S&P 500 dropped 5.2 percent, 6.5 percent, and 4.7 percent respectively, while the Swiss franc rallied against the USD and AUD by 0.2 percent and 2.9 percent, 1.7 percent and 9.0 percent, 3.3 percent and 4.4 percent respectively.

Japanese Yen: −17 percent

Similar to the Swiss franc, the Japanese yen had its share of carry trade sales, shedding 7 percent in trade-weighted terms to reach a 22-year low in July 2007. Once the summer market turmoil deteriorated into the rest of the year, JPY rebounded 4 percent, ending down 0.5 percent on the year. The currency was characterized by several episodes of extremely rapid gains, gaining more than 4 percent or 500 points in a single day (August 16). But unlike its Swiss counterpart, the Bank of Japan held rates unchanged at 0.5 percent, worrying that slowing U.S. growth would drag down Japan's economy and a rate hike would risk jeopardizing the fragile recovery.

British Pound: −40 percent

The British pound was the worst-performing currency in 2007 behind the beleaguered U.S. dollar. Despite having breached the $2.00 level, hitting 26-year highs, sterling gave up most of its earlier 9 percent gains versus the greenback to end the year barely 1 percent higher. The currency closed at all-time lows against the euro to lose 8.0 percent.

After a strong seven months, sterling's fundamentals began to deteriorate due to prolonged declines in housing prices, a struggling banking sector suffering from dried-up liquidity, and a near collapse of the nation's biggest mortgage lender, as well as eroding confidence among households and businesses. Personal debt had been stretched to the extent that the savings ratio headed below zero, a level not seen since the late 1980s, while household debt service soared to 14 percent of incomes, the highest since 1991. House price indexes began showing three consecutive monthly declines, a pattern not seen in over 12 years. With over a million fixed-rate mortgages due for reset in 2008, the risks to UK personal debt were considerable and also for consumer demand. Estimates placed the number of homes to be repossessed in 2007 at 30,000 to 45,000 in 2008, the highest since the property crisis of the 1990s. In other sectors of the economy, the services sector dropped to its lowest level in four and a half years.

UK interest rates were raised three times, reaching a six-year high of 5.75 percent. But as the cracks began to show, the Bank of England was obliged to cut rates by 25 bps in December, earlier than it anticipated in the November inflation report. Considering the aforementioned downside risks, traders perceived UK rates as the highest in the G7, but also with the greatest potential for rate cuts by the central bank. The Bank of England had already been forced into a unanimous decision to cut rates in December, one month earlier than it predicted at the November inflation report. We expect the BoE to cut rates by 100 bps in 2008, taking down rates to 4.50 percent, which would deal sharp erosion to real interest rates, currently at 3.4 percent as of this writing.

U.S. Dollar: −51 percent

The dollar's trade-weighted index dropped 9 percent to 74.79, its lowest level ever since it was created in 1967. The speed of the 2007 dollar decline was particularly intensified by two factors: (1) the speed at which the

Federal Reserve shifted its policy emphasis from worrying about inflation—in August—to making an about-turn and slashing interest rates within less than four weeks; (2) the continued divergence in growth and interest rates between the United States and the rest of the G7, to the extent of driving the Federal Reserve to cut interest rates, while the ECB, United Kingdom, Canada, and Australia were raising interest rates. Less than five months after the U.S. central bank told the markets that inflationary pressures were the greater risk to policy and that U.S. growth would revert to its trend growth within a year, the interest rates were cut by 100 bps, a magnitude that reflected the Fed's considerable underestimation of the downside risks to the economy and the deterioration in housing.

One other factor behind the falling value of the dollar is that of reserve diversification away from U.S. dollars among global central banks and private asset managers. China's central bank had already reduced the proportion of its $1.7 trillion in currency reserves from over 90 percent USD-denominated in 2000 to less than 70 percent in 2005. Chinese officials also made comments about the need for reserve diversification. Although such pronouncements meant that central banks would slow their future accumulation of U.S. dollars, rather than dump their U.S. reserves, they triggered various bouts of dollar selling and worsening sentiment for the currency.

Speculation also emerged that some Arab Gulf nations (United Arab Emirates and Saudi Arabia) would end their policy of pegging their currencies to the U.S. dollar and move toward a basket of currencies due to the falling value of the dollar fueling these nations' inflation rates. With the dollar having lost over 30 percent of its value in trade-weighted terms over the previous five years, the currency's decline sent inflation soaring in the Gulf countries, prompting Kuwait to break from its dollar peg in early 2007 and to revalue its currency twice after inflation hit an all-time high of 14.8 percent in March. Speculation abounded that the UAE, another country maintaining its dollar peg, may either revalue its currency to a new peg or break off the currency system altogether after inflation reached a 19-year high of 9.3 percent. In early January, officials from Saudi Arabia and the UAE said they would continue pegging their currencies to the U.S. dollar and no revaluation will take place. We suspect the issue will be revisited when the greenback sustains its next bout of declines, prompting the Gulf nations to rethink their currency regimes.

LESSONS LEARNED

Several lessons can be learned from the currency developments of 1999–2007.

The most striking pattern prevailing through the eight-year period is the growing polarity between EUR and USD. As the two currencies dominated trading in global foreign exchange markets, one currency would persistently act as an opposite for the other. Daily trading averages in EUR/USD accounted for 30 percent of total market turnover in 2001, before retreating toward 28 percent in 2004. However, trading in the currency pair increased 42 percent to $501 billion between 2001 and 2004, before leaping 67 percent to $840 billion from 2004 to 2007.

On the commodities front, the demonstrable link between global growth and commodity currencies (AUD, NZD, and CAD) was brought to the fore at the turn of the new millennium, especially on the heels of China's tremendous appetite for commodities. Consequently, foreign exchange markets became segmented into a new set of currencies, against which low-yielding currencies were the first to drop during any signs of improved global growth such as strong economic data from the United States or China, or any signs of reduced risk appetite.

Since the late 1990s, risk appetite and carry trades have grown to form the single most influencing dynamic in foreign exchange markets since 2005. The combination of the widening gulf between low- and high-yielding currencies, and the reduction of fear—as gauged via falling volatility and rising global equities—had triggered a nearly systematic shift into higher-yielding currencies at the expense of the low-yielding CHF, JPY, and the USD. Among these three currencies, JPY fares as the most consistent loser during risk appetite trades—in other words, the accumulation of carry trades. Conversely, JPY is the main winner out of these three currencies during rising volatility and falling equities.

The multicurrency performances of 1999–2007 have also proven that interest rate differentials do not always succeed in solely influencing currency values. Other important factors such as global growth, risk aversion, carry trade unwinding, and the direct relationship between commodities and their currencies have had significant weight. The year 2001 proved to be one of those situations, when the deepening slowdown in the United States and an impending cooling abroad led investors to reward the dollar during the Fed's aggressive easing.

Capital flows are another reason why interest rate differentials may not work in driving currencies. In 1999, the lowest-yielding currency, the yen, was the highest performer among the major eight currencies, while NZD was the highest-yielding and lowest-performing currency. Escalating anticipation of an eventual Japanese recovery following the slump of the 1990s drove asset managers to snap up Japanese stocks, which were largely deemed to be undervalued. Conversely, a soaring trade deficit in New Zealand, partly as a result of declining food and agricultural prices, sent the kiwi to the bottom of the league. In such cases where the interest rate landscape is largely unchanged, other dynamics succeed in taking over the influence over foreign exchange values.

Increasingly regionalized economic activity within Asia Pacific and East Asia has acted as a quasi hedge for the AUD and NZD from economic headwinds in Western Europe and North America. The reverse relation took place in 1998–1999 when regional trade was hampered by the 1997–1999 Asian crises. The relationship is particularly robust between the annual aggregate returns of the aussie and annual GDP growth of newly industrialized Asian economies. The powerful advance in China's GDP growth between 2004 and 2005 proved a vital source of demand for Australia's iron ore industry, thus alleviating the fallout from the burst of Australia's real estate bubble.

The strong positive correlation between copper prices and the Australian dollar was instrumental in identifying turnarounds in the aussie that may have not been anticipated via interest rates. The extent of the relationship is also underlined by not only whether copper has ended higher or lower at year-end but also by the metal's most recent performance shift during the year. Thus, even if copper has ended the year on a high note, it may have a negative impact on the aussie in the event of a decline in the latter part of the year, such as was the case in 2000 and 2002.

CHAPTER 5

Risk Appetite in the Markets

M anaging risk has become an increasingly integral part of the risk/return trade-off in financial markets over the years as participants seek to improve the profitability of their investments while attempting to reduce their downside. Increasing risk can adopt one of the following forms: (1) concentrating assets in securities with similar risk/return attributes; (2) holding securities with the probability of high rates of return and correspondingly high probability of losing the initial investment; (3) selecting securities with relatively high volatility or variability of returns; and finally, (4) borrowing funds with the intention of enhancing the rate of return at the risk of magnifying the potential of a loss.

The latter type of investment risk is most relevant to this chapter as it involves risk appetite in the way funds are raised and where they are invested. *Speculation* may be more apt to describe this type of endeavor due to the high potential of losing all of one's initial capital in a relatively short period of time as well as the use of borrowed funds. Yet, regardless of the likelihood of recouping one's initial investment, the principal idea is underlined by the notion of minimizing the use of one's own funds with the hope of maximizing the rate of return.

The following example can be used to illustrate risk appetite relevant to this chapter. Let's say Jane purchases 200 shares of a pharmaceutical company priced at $50 each with the intention of selling them in two weeks based on her expectation of a favorable ruling by the Federal Drug Administration. Jane evaluates two options to go about her $10,000 investment: (1) Use her own funds to pay $10,000 for the shares, or (2) borrow $10,000 from a bank at a 7 percent interest rate repayable in one year. Assuming the

FDA rejects the introduction of a new drug by the company and the stock price plummets to $15 per share after one year, Jane's holdings would drop to $3,000. Had Jane used her own funds in the first option, her total loss would be $7,000. Had she borrowed the funds at 7 percent, Jane would be obligated to return the initial $10,000 loan plus the interest rate cost of $722.90 resulting from 7 percent charged monthly, bringing her total cost to $10,722.90. Spending $10,722.90 on an investment that fell to $3,000 entails a loss of 357 percent, versus a loss of 40 percent in the case of the no-loan option.

If, however, the price of the stock rises by 40 percent to $70 after one year, following a favorable ruling by the FDA, Jane's holdings would grow to $14,000, netting her a 40 percent gain on her investment. Under the same price increase scenario, Jane's 7 percent loan would have an interest cost of $722.90, netting her a profit of $13,277.10 or a 1,837 percent rate of return. By leveraging her investment through borrowing, Jane has magnified her rate of return to 1,837 percent compared to only 40 percent when she uses her own money. Conversely, the loan would have magnified her loss to a 357 percent loss compared to 40 percent using her own money.

There are several factors driving Jane to embrace risk and borrow money to fund her investment. But for the sake of relevance to this chapter, I focus on the *environmental* factors impacting her tolerance for risk. These may include a generally favorable stance by the FDA toward new drugs, a bull market in pharmaceutical stocks prompted by rising health care costs, expanding economic growth, or broader media attention on the disorder that the pharmaceutical company aims to treat. None of these dynamics are related to the company per se, but they do shape the general climate impacting the share price. As these factors bolster Jane's confidence in the stock, her risk appetite is improved, prompting her to magnify her bet by leveraging the purchase of the stock. Thus, even if there is no improvement in the company's specific fundamentals, Jane's risk appetite may be driven by a generally positive environment, conducive to raising risk appetite and confidence, sometimes at the expense of overlooking some vital elements pertinent to the individual stock.

Similarly, we will see next how emerging shifts in economic growth, market volatility, liquidity, and confidence can lead to fluctuations in risk appetite over relatively short periods of time, triggering tremendous fluctuations in the foreign exchange market.

CARRY TRADES IN FOREIGN EXCHANGE

Borrowing money at low interest rates to fund higher-yielding loans has been the conventional source of revenue for banks for as long as credit providers have been around. The same principal is also the basis of currency carry trades, whereby hedge funds, asset managers, or individuals borrow funds in low-yielding currencies (funding currencies) to convert and deposit the proceeds in bonds or certificates of deposit in higher-yielding currencies, aiming to reap the return from the interest rate differential. An extra return can be obtained during the appreciation of the high-yielding currency, while in other cases the currency depreciation is greater than the interest rate differential, making the carry trade a losing investment. The two components on which carry trades rest are therefore currency- and yield-related.

Carry trades are also used in bond investing within the same currency by borrowing (selling) bonds at short-term interest rates to finance the purchase of long-term bonds at higher rates. The difference between the coupon received from the higher-yielding bond and the interest cost paid on the shorter-term bond is called the *carry return*. The downside risk entails an unexpected decline in the price of long-term bonds (and rising long-term interest rates), and a rise in the price of short-term bonds (falling short-term rates). As investors unwind these positions (i.e., sell their holdings of long-term bonds and repay their short-term borrowing), they accelerate the decline in the price of long-term bonds, exacerbating the rise in their yield and triggering the opposite reaction in the price and rates of short-term bonds.

Let's return to carry trades in currencies. Suppose an investor borrows 100,000 yen from a Japanese bank at 0.70 percent interest and deposits the proceeds in a U.S. dollar–denominated 10-year government bond worth $1,000, paying 5 percent interest. The investor stands to make 4.3 percent from the interest differential plus or minus the exchange rate risk. If the U.S. dollar appreciates by 5 percent over the duration of the investment, the investor makes 9.3 percent (4.3 percent yield differential plus 5 percent currency gain). If the dollar loses 5 percent against the yen, the investment nets a loss of 1.3 percent (4.3 percent yield differential minus 5 percent currency loss).

This example illustrates that currency carry trades have interest rate and currency elements. While higher interest rate differentials play a major role in spurring interest in carry trades, the potential for currency appreciation or depreciation is also essential in sustaining the viability of the trade.

Such a straightforward investment endeavor is the basis of hundreds of billions of dollars worth of daily carry trades by foreign exchange dealers, proprietary traders, and hedge fund managers. As these players aim at reaping the gains from the interest rate differential, they tend to leverage their positions to magnify their returns from what appears to be an assured investment. Accumulating over $2.3 trillion in daily turnover, currency markets thrive on trading volumes among bank dealers, corporate treasuries, and speculators. As participants increasingly exploit emerging opportunities of widening interest rate differentials, volumes expand and momentum intensifies, resulting in self-reinforcing trends, whereby high-yielding currencies rally against their lower-yielding counterparts. The result could entail prolonged trends lasting for several weeks and months.

Every Trend Has Its End

But every trend reaches an end, at least a temporary one. Carry trades are notably visible once they start to unwind. As funds exit high-yielding currencies back into the low-yielding currencies, the latter tend to appreciate in value relative to the former. Such unwinding takes place upon the following:

- Anticipation of a decline in the high-yielding currency or an actual decline in its value.
- Anticipation of a rise in the low-yielding currency or an actual rise in its value.
- Anticipation of a decrease in interest rates of the high-yielding currency, or the end of its tightening cycle.
- Anticipation of an increase in interest rates of the low-yielding currency, or the end of its easing cycle.
- A sudden decrease in risk appetite, which normally leads to a decrease in the high-yielding currency and an increase in the lower-yielding currencies. This type of development is the primary focus of this chapter.

The above scenarios may result from new economic data, speeches or reports from central banks, or, in the case of the fourth scenario, a reduction in market confidence, eroding risk appetite due to market declines or geopolitical events. Recall that the profitability of carry trades is reinforced by the buildup of positions, which accelerates the strengthening of higher-yielding currencies and deepens the declines in the lower-yielding ones (funding currencies). Conversely, the unwinding of carry trades can be accelerated by the execution of multiple margin calls and the subsequent opening of new positions, triggering further selling in high-yielding currencies. What may be a 3 percent or 5 percent differential in interest rates between two currencies can be completely eroded during a 6 percent slide (rally) in the high- (low-) yielding currency.

Japanese Yen and Swiss Franc: Thriving During Uncertainty

Due to structurally low interest rates in Japan and Switzerland, the yen and the franc often served as *funding* currencies, used by speculators to borrow in lower rates and invest the proceeds in higher-yielding currencies and other assets such as gold, oil, and equities. Both the yen and franc have commanded interest rates lower than those in other G10 nations mainly due to their expanding current account surplus. A surplus in the current account signifies that both countries' exports of goods and services are greater than their imports. It also tells us that both nations are net savers—in other words, creditors of capital—rather than net investors or debtors, thereby not requiring their interest rates to be as high as the rest of the G10 economies experiencing current account deficits.

By contrast, countries with high current account deficits such as the United States or the United Kingdom command higher interest rates because they require capital from abroad to finance these deficits. The capital consists of foreign purchases of U.S. and UK financial assets such as stocks and bonds. Generally, the wider the current account deficit, the higher the required financing from abroad and the higher the cost of financing—hence the interest rate. These interest rates are of 5- to 10-year durations rather than the overnight benchmark rates controlled by the central banks.

Just as a person with $20,000 in credit card debt is more likely to be charged a higher interest rate than someone with a $2,000 credit debt, current account deficit nations incur higher interest rates and their currencies are said to be *riskier* than those of current account surplus nations. Foreign investors require a higher rate of return to compensate for the risk of buying assets from debtor nations.

Figure 5.1 illustrates this point via the clearly inverse relationship between current account balances and interest rates. New Zealand, the United States, Australia, and the United Kingdom each have current account deficits and boast higher interest rates than in Japan and Switzerland, whose lower interest rates are explained by current account surplus balances. Canada is the exception to the rule in that its interest rates were as high as those in current account deficit nations despite boasting current account surplus. When Canada's current account balance became positive in early 2000, interest rates fell from 5.75 percent in 2000 to 2.0 percent in 2002. But the subsequent rebound in oil prices boosted the nation's economy by bolstering its current account balance, ultimately fueling inflation and forcing the central bank to raise interest rates.

Yet the relationship between current account balances and interest rates remains clear. Since carry trades involve the purchase of higher interest rate currencies against lower interest rate currencies, they are

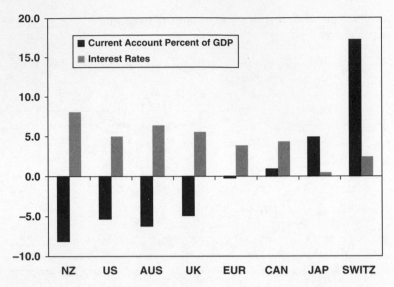

FIGURE 5.1 Currencies of nations with positive current account balances are typically characterized by low interest rates.

considered risk-seeking trades, or reflective of rising risk appetite. Such risky trades are therefore vulnerable to any negative developments that create fear in the market, causing investors to scale down their risky bets by shifting funds back to yen and francs to repay their low interest rate loans, ultimately boosting the two currencies against their higher-yielding counterparts. An illustration of the development in global interest rates such as in Figure 5.2 helps investors determine the ensuing opportunities obtained from interest rate differentials.

High Interest in Yen's Low Yield

While both the Japanese yen and Swiss franc are characterized by their low-yielding status, the Japanese yen is more notorious for its sharp declines during the accumulation of carry trades as well as for its rapid gains during the unwinding of carry trades. This is largely owing to the size of the Japanese economy, whose GDP of $4.3 trillion is the world's second largest, more than 10 times the size of the Swiss economy. More significantly, only 1 to 2 percent of Japan's 1,500 trillion yen (US$14 trillion) in household financial assets is invested overseas, while the rest is desperately searching for higher yields in an economy with predominantly low interest rates.

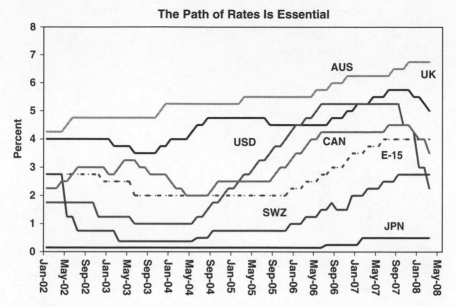

FIGURE 5.2 The path of relative interest rates is as important as absolute levels in currency markets.

Once the Japanese equity bubble burst in the early 1990s, the Nikkei-225 Index lost 40 percent in 1990 and 76 percent into 2001, erasing over US$7 trillion of wealth in a decade. When Japan's banking sector was brought to a virtual collapse, long-term interest rates tumbled from their 7.5 percent peak in 1990 to below 1 percent in 1998 as the central bank aggressively slashed its discount rate target from 6 percent in 1990 to 0.15 percent in 1999. Figure 5.3 illustrates the plunge in both Japanese equities and interest rates, which was followed by a multidecade deflationary spiral.

As Japanese interest rates plummeted near zero, the acceleration of carry trades out of the yen triggered a broad damage in the currency. For the USD/JPY exchange rate, the rally reached an eight-year high of 147.60, an 85 percent increase from the April 1995 low of 79.70 yen to 1 U.S. dollar. As yen shorts piled up, so did everything else financed with the carry trade, and the decline in the Japanese currency continued. Figure 5.4 highlights how Japan's ultralow interest rates fueled the carry trades into higher interest rate currencies of the United States, Germany, and the United Kingdom.

Of the most aggressively high yields were government bonds of emerging market economies such as East Asia and Russia. The Asian currency

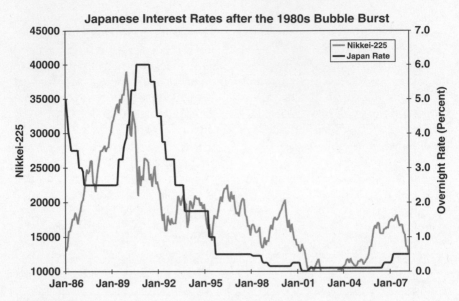

FIGURE 5.3 The 300 percent plunge in Japan's 1980s stock bubble proved to be coup de grace for equities and interest rates for the next 15 years.

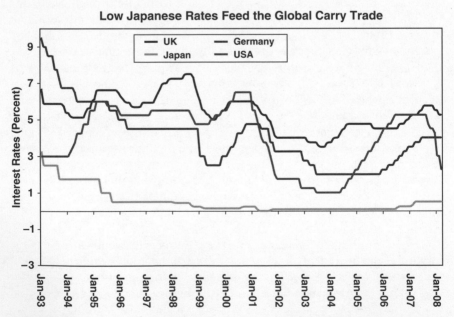

FIGURE 5.4 Tumbling Japanese interest rates prompted capital flows into higher-yielding foreign exchange trades.

crisis of 1997 did not dissuade investors from piling onto high risk economies with swelling current account deficits. In August 1998, Russia declared a moratorium on its $70 billion debt, accelerating the decline in the value of its bonds and triggering a freefall in its currency. Investors who had borrowed in low-yielding yen to exploit Russian interest rates as high as 140 percent stampeded back into yen, which consequently soared across the board. As holders of the dollar-yen carry trade risked having their +500 basis points differential eroded by a strengthening yen and a falling dollar, their unwinding operations accelerated the sell-off in the USD/JPY rate, prompting a decline of 6 percent, 3 percent, and 15 percent in August, September, and October respectively, to reach 115 yen from the August high of 147.60. On July 10, 1998, the dollar tumbled in one day from 130.70 to 118.90, a 7 percent decline that was greater than the 5 percent differential between the two currencies.

The episode of autumn 1998 was the first major example of the unwinding of yen carry trades. During most of 1999–2006, Japan's central bank maintained its zero interest rate policy, effectively keeping its overnight rate at zero percent. The result was an 88 percent plunge in households' interest income, which further dented an already damaged consumer purchasing power. The consequences were a repeat of 1998. Japanese savers hungry for yield and non-Japanese investors exploiting low yen borrowing costs used the yen as a funding means to invest in higher-yielding currencies, equities, and commodities. A relatively low risk environment between 2004 and 2007 emboldened investors to expand on their carry trades, magnifying the rally in those assets at the expense of the yen. In contrast, interest rates in the United States, the United Kingdom, the Eurozone, Australia, and New Zealand averaged a monthly rate of 3.7 percent, 4.8 percent, 3.0 percent, 5.4 percent, and 6.1 percent respectively. The interest rate deficit was too great to ignore by Japanese savers and investors.

The Japanese search for foreign yield had begun with foreign currency deposits, which fell out of favor due to their high commissions and fees. Investors then shifted toward foreign bond funds, which offered higher yields as well as monthly dividend payments aimed not only at enhancing interest income but also to offset any potential decline in the value of the bonds.

Notably, individual Japanese investors upped the ante on exploiting rate differentials in 2004 as G5 nations were in the midst of normalizing interest rates upward following the concerted rate cuts of 2001–2003. But this time it was through online-based foreign exchange margin trading, whereby speculators use leverage to control regular-size contracts with deposits 50 to 100 times less than normal size. With a 100 to 1 leverage, speculators can expand the 5 percent rate differential 500 times, magnifying the potential profit and risk of loss. The rate differential is then further enhanced or offset via the resulting currency fluctuations.

Yet the main players in carry trades remain hedge funds as they bet hundreds of millions of U.S. dollars in leveraged positions using the low-yielding currencies to fund not only higher-yielding currencies but also rising stocks, commodities, and even real estate. Their role of the yen carry trade was behind the biggest one-month decline in the USD/JPY exchange rate in October 1998, and proved its presence once again in 2007 and 2008. As yen selling was increasingly used in funding purchases of high-yield currencies, stock indexes, and commodities, the inverse relation between the Japanese currency and these assets grew more prominent.

Conversely, profit-taking in stocks and commodities was inversely related with a rebounding yen. The relationship was strikingly apparent starting in 2004, as global central banks began raising rates while the Bank of Japan kept its rates near zero. Figure 5.5 highlights the increasingly positive correlation between USD/JPY and the S&P 500 since the Fed began raising interest rates in June 2004. As the tightening cycle extended into June 2006, the two-year period was accompanied by a rise in the USD/JPY rate. The yen was also sold off against all other major currencies as the Bank of Japan was the last major central bank to join the global rate hikes, delivering the least amount of tightening.

FIGURE 5.5 USD/JPY, S&P 500, and global equities benefited from rising carry trades in 2004 as the Fed and other central banks began raising rates.

USING RISK APPETITE TO GAUGE FX FLOWS

The aforementioned cases illustrate the straightforward nature of carry trades. Borrowing in lower-yielding currencies to invest in higher-yielding currencies requires a sufficient interest rate differential and/or appreciation of the target currency. As will be seen later in this chapter, carry trades are also used to invest in higher-yielding assets, beyond interest-bearing accounts denominated in foreign currencies. Such alternatives can be equities, commodities, or even real estate. But, as we also have seen, regardless of the target investment, investors will always run the risk of sustaining a decline in the value of the target currency (currency risk), a rise in the funding currency, or a decline in the interest rate differential (yield risk).

As was seen in the first example in this chapter, Jane's purchase of the pharmaceutical firm's shares would have been riskier had it been via credit from a bank rather than using her own funds. Just as she bore the risk of a decline in the price of shares, carry trade investors bear the risks of a falling yield, a declining target currency, and/or a rising funding currency. In both cases, the investor exhibited a tolerance for risk in order to reap the rewards of an increase in the stock price, currency, and yield differential.

Understanding the various gauges of risk appetite is essential in grasping the dynamics dictating currency movements in the short and medium term. Once these dynamics have escalated near excess levels, one can become prepared for an unwinding of these positions and a potentially speedy unwinding of carry trades. The four measures most often used as yardsticks in assessing risk appetite shaping currency markets are (1) equity indexes, (2) the volatility index (VIX), (3) speculators' futures commitments, and (4) corporate bond spreads.

Equity Indexes

Equity markets can serve as a basic and straightforward yardstick of risk in financial markets during periods of sudden sharp losses, protracted declines, or frequently recurring selling. Such cases reflect eroding market confidence arising from worries about the economy, negative geopolitical events, and mounting systemic risk.

During the U.S. trading session, the S&P 500 Index is the preferred gauge of equity markets due to its broad coverage of the market. Although it focuses on companies with large capitalization, the index covers about 75 percent of U.S. equities, making it a suitable proxy for the total market. After 4 P.M. Eastern Time, traders can use equity futures as an indication, or Japan's Nikkei-225 equity index. Hong Kong's Hang Seng's index and China CSI 300 Index are useful for gauging sentiment in the Asia-Pacific area. The FTSE-100, DAX, and CAC-40 are the main benchmark indexes in the United Kingdom, Germany, and France, respectively.

Figure 5.6 shows the increasingly negative correlation between major equity indexes and the low-yielding yen after summer 2004. Being the most-sought currency in carry trades, the Japanese yen exhibited a near perfectly negative correlation with the Dow and the Nikkei as investors funded their equity positions with cheap yen loans. The correlation grew particularly strong in 2005 when interest rates increased in most G7 nations except for Japan. The result was a simultaneous decline in the yen versus most major currencies and a rally in major equities. Conversely, as these positions were unwound due to increased risk aversion (i.e., reduced risk appetite), yen currency pairs began to turn around (yen appreciated versus other currencies).

The strength of the yen-stocks relationship is especially highlighted by its near consistency over several time frames. Indeed, the relationship between stocks and equities has strengthened to the extent of becoming even an intraday phenomenon. Oftentimes, for instance, during the period between third quarter 2007 and first quarter 2008, the S&P 500 sold off sharply in the last 30 minutes of trading. Such moves were often in the magnitude of 25 to 30 points or the equivalent of 1.5 percent to 1.8 percent. Consequently

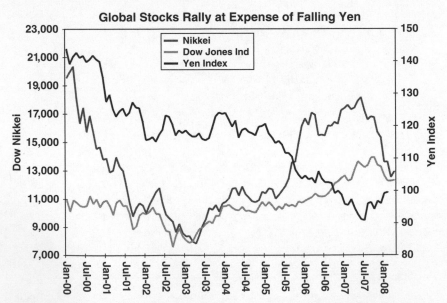

FIGURE 5.6 Yen weakness fuels advances in equities via heightened carry trades.

we would see notable gains in the Japanese yen against most currencies as risk reduction appetites dominate the market. Such currency moves are especially accelerated in the time period elapsing between the close of the U.S. equity session (4 P.M. EST) and the open of the Tokyo session (8 P.M. EST), when trading volumes are thinner than usual and movements more volatile. The existing move (the yen rally) may be further prolonged in the Tokyo session as the lack of confidence in the U.S. market spills over to Asian trade, prompting traders there to further unwind the carry trades and boost the yen.

Not every drop in equities implies rising risk. Aside from the magnitude, one must discern whether the sell-off is a result of factors confined to a specific company, or related to a macroeconomic/financial market issue, which is part of a concern with the economy. Thus, one must ask: Do the declines warrant a general rise in fear, or loss of confidence? In answering that question, we turn to a more appropriate measure of risk, namely the VIX.

The Volatility Index

The volatility index (VIX) measures the volatility of a wide range of options on the S&P 500 Index and is used to gauge the markets' expectations for volatility over the next 30 days. Quoted as a percentage, a VIX figure greater than 30 is associated with high volatility resulting from investors' fear of uncertainty, while values under 20 are associated with relatively low volatility or less anxiety about the market. Low values may also reflect complacency arising from overconfidence with a rising market, or exuberance. Accordingly, the VIX is known as the *fear* index. During the market crash of October 1987, the VIX shot up to a record high of 172 from the mid-20s in the prior week.

Figure 5.7 shows how the VIX shot up in periods of extreme volatility, which were accompanied by sharp declines in equities. The catalysts to such declines included geopolitical events, sudden declines in business confidence, or escalating worries about losses in companies or industries.

The advantage of using the VIX over stock indexes in gauging potential shifts in risk appetite is partly related to the components used in calculating the VIX index, namely the implied volatilities of various index options. As its name suggests, *implied volatility* is the variance or quantifiable risk of an individual stock or index option obtained via an option pricing model. Thus, sudden moves in stock indexes sometimes result from an aberration in a few selected stocks or simply profit-taking, in which case the impact may weigh on the broader index but is no indication of any shift in risk.

To the average trader or investor who may not have access to the intraday developments of the VIX index, following the intraday fluctuations of

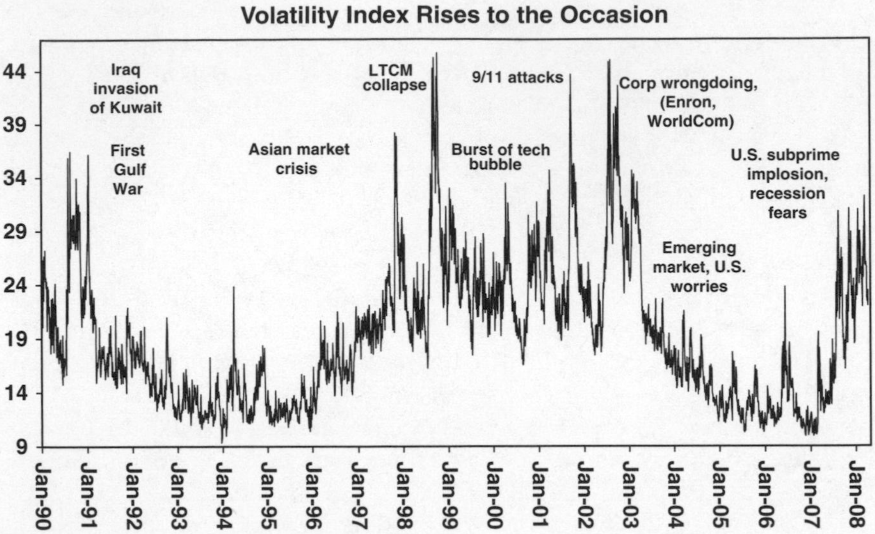

Volatility Index Rises to the Occasion

FIGURE 5.7 The VIX rallied during all major risk-triggering events.

the S&P 500 or the Nikkei-225 can be useful in detecting significant developments, which may trigger similarly important moves in currencies. But the main advantage of the VIX over equity indexes is its use as a benchmark reference for risk, hence offering a neutral perspective on market risk and appetite without referring to the price equities, and therefore the ability to pinpoint how sell-offs or rallies evolve.

Say, for instance, that stocks are falling across the board, down 2.5 percent. A greater and more useful perspective would be added to the moves in the event of a 2 to 3 percent jump in the VIX. But if the same equity developments are accompanied by more modest gains in the VIX, then there may be little inferred from the pullback in equities. The fact that the VIX is expressed in percentage terms allows it to be distinguishable and easily comparable to previous highs or lows regardless of time.

Using VIX in Exposing Complacency While much has been said about the efficacy of the VIX to expose rising fear in the market, the index also deserves at least the same amount of ink spilled for its ability to expose rising risk appetite, sometimes also known as rising complacency. Figure 5.8 illustrates how the most prolonged periods of relatively low volatility coincided with a phase of rising equities, characterized by rising bullishness and heightened investor confidence in the stock market. These phases are prominently identifiable in August 1998, January 1999 through February 2000, and May 2003 through January 2007.

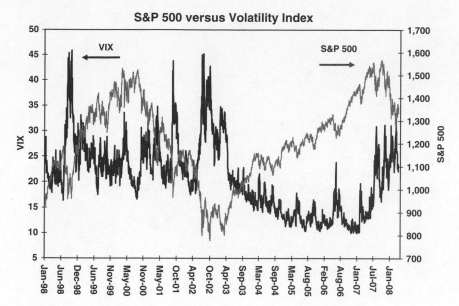

FIGURE 5.8 Falling VIX highlights excessive optimism in equities.

Phases of increased risk appetite are often accompanied by a rise in carry trades as improved confidence drives investors to borrow low-yielding currencies to buy higher-yielding currencies, equities, and commodities. Recall earlier in the chapter we addressed the strong positive correlation between high interest rates and current account deficits. Currencies of current account deficit countries are said to be riskier and hence pay high interest rates. Conversely, rising risk appetite is correlated with a decline in low-yielding currencies such as the Japanese yen and Swiss franc.

Figure 5.9 illustrates the relationship between risk appetite—as measured by the VIX—and the yen, as measured by the USD/JPY exchange rate. Note how investors exploited declining volatility between 2004 and 2006 by aggressively selling the yen against higher-yielding currencies as their confidence toward risk increased. Rising global growth and the corresponding run-ups in global equity markets from 2004 to early 2007 were instrumental in bolstering global investor confidence to the extent that the yen was used not only for funding purchases of equity indexes, but also for fueling gold, oil, and real estate.

Aside from improved risk appetite and intensifying advances in equities, the initial decline in the yen had been especially magnified by the prevailing interest rates landscape. By the end of 2004, all major central banks

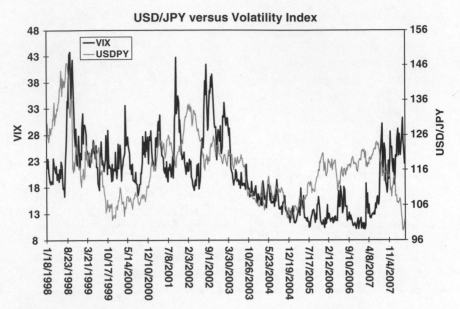

FIGURE 5.9 USD/JPY and VIX hand in hand as yen is sold against the dollar to scale up on risk appetite.

with the exception of the European Central Bank and Bank of Japan had begun raising interest rates following the easing campaign of 2001–2003. As they announced their rate hikes, the Federal Reserve, Reserve Bank of Australia, and Reserve Bank of New Zealand were signaling further increases as part of their commitment to contain inflation. This further emboldened investors to reap the widening interest rate differential relative to the paltry 0.25 percent in Japan.

By the end of 2006, interest rates in the United States, Canada, Australia, New Zealand, and the United Kingdom were raised to 5.25 percent, 4.25 percent, 6.25 percent, 7.25 percent, and 5.00 percent respectively. Even the European Central Bank and the Swiss National Bank had joined the global tightening campaign, lifting their rates to 3.5 percent and 2.00 percent respectively.

Eventually, in July 2006, the Bank of Japan delivered its first rate hike in six years, raising the benchmark overnight rate target to 0.25 percent from 0.15 percent, a decision that had minimal effect in staving off speculators from selling the yen after the central bank had widely telegraphed the rate change that was long overdue. Traders were especially enthusiastic in opening fresh yen carry trades as officials from the Japanese government and central bank talked down the currency extensively so as to counter the impact of any advances resulting from the rate hike. Attempting to end years of deflation, Japanese policy makers were loath in exacerbating the decline in prices via renewed yen strength. With a little help from the officials, the yen sustained renewed selling. Hedge funds, bank dealers, corporate treasuries, and even Japanese housewives saw little risk in borrowing in yen and placing the proceeds in the rallying aussie, greenback, loonie, kiwi, and British pound, as well as equities and commodities.

But every trend must reach its end, or at least a temporary reversal. The accumulation of yen carry trade flows was faced with periodic disruptions, triggered by sporadic bouts of risk-reduction episodes. These were brought about by a rising VIX as the increase in volatility and sell-off in equities prompted investors to unwind their yen carry trades, rushing out of high-yielding currencies, stocks, and commodities back into the low-yielding Japanese currency.

Volatility would later return with a vengeance in 2007, dealing U.S. and global markets punishing blows on increased evidence that the slowdown in U.S. housing had spilled over to the rest of the economy. On February 27, 2007, unsubstantiated reports of Chinese regulators planning to levy a tax on stock transactions were enough to destabilize an overheating and record-breaking Chinese market and send the Shanghai Composite Index falling by more than 9 percent. U.S. markets already reeling from Chinese markets and the rest of the Asian continent took a turn for the worse on reports that an attack on a U.S military base in Afghanistan had killed Vice President Cheney, and an unexpectedly large 7.8 percent decline in U.S. durable goods. Although VP Cheney emerged unharmed from the attacks, the volatility was enough to shed a 50.3 point loss in the S&P 500, or a 3.3 percent decline—its biggest one-day percentage loss in four years. The Dow Jones Industrial Average tumbled 416.02 points, its biggest one-day point decline since September 17, 2001—the day markets opened after the September 11 attacks.

On that eventful week of tumbling stock markets and sharp reduction in risk appetite, the yen rose 4 percent against the dollar and the euro, 5 percent against the Aussie and the pound, and 7 percent against the kiwi. Such violent unwinding in the yen carry trade was a short-lived version of the October 1998 jump in the yen, and a resounding premonition of what would take place later in the year.

The volatility-filled period of January 2007 to March 2008 is illustrated in Figure 5.10, focusing on the many spikes in the VIX and corresponding sell-offs in equities. The mirror image was reflected in the falling EUR/JPY as the unwinding of the yen carry trade meant rapid flows into the Japanese currency away from EUR and all other major currencies. Although we mentioned in Chapter 3 that the euro was known as the anti-dollar for its

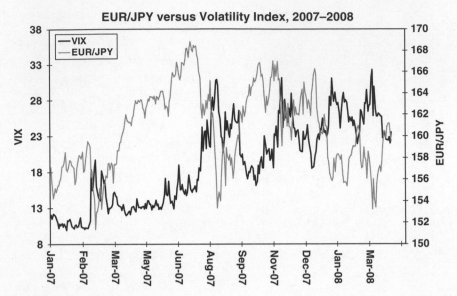

FIGURE 5.10 EUR/JPY reflects a mirror image of the VIX as soaring volatility drives capital back to JPY.

contrasting ways vis-à-vis the U.S. currency and the competitive edge between the currencies' economies, both currencies have shown generally similar trends against the yen. Thus, carry trades into the yen and their unwinding are not limited to USD/JPY but extend to EUR/JPY, AUD/JPY, NZD/JPY, GBP/JPY, CAD/JPY, and so on.

In July–August 2007, the crisis in the U.S. subprime market was no longer just a case of inappropriate selling of loans to unqualified home borrowers, but a catalyst to tens of billions of downgraded debt backed by unhealthy subprime mortgages, held by hedge funds, banks, and pension funds. Clients of hedge funds rushed to withdraw their money while money managers sold their existing holdings to meet clients' requests and meet margin calls. The result was accelerated selling in equities and a seized-up credit market. In the week ending August 17, 2007, the yen soared 6 percent, 8 percent, 15 percent, and 16 percent against the USD, EUR, AUD, and NZD, respectively.

The unwinding of carry trades also took place in currency pairs not involving the yen, such as the aussie, kiwi, and sterling, each of them falling against the USD amid squaring of positions that aimed at exploiting the dollar's interest rate disadvantage relative to the high currencies. Figure 5.11 shows various examples during August and November 2007 when tumbling stocks dealt a sharp blow to risk appetite, prompting sharp declines in the

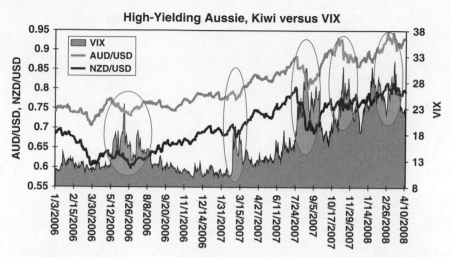

FIGURE 5.11 Spiking VIX dragged down high-yielding pairs such as AUD/USD and NZD/USD.

high-yielding currencies such as the aussie, kiwi, and sterling versus their lower-yielding counterparts.

The market swoon continued in November 2007 and into the first quarter of 2008 as U.S. banks piled up their write-downs from uncollected debt backed by subprime paper. Consequently, the Federal Reserve was forced to complete its about-face turn in policy priorities from containing inflation to reviving growth and slashing interest rates by 225 basis points in four months, 125 basis points of which were cut in nine days.

Speculators' Futures Flows

The weekly figures on traders' futures commitments obtained from the Chicago Mercantile Exchange's International Monetary Market shed valuable light on the developing flows pursuing one currency versus another. The data are broken down into commitments by commercial players (usually made up of businesses aiming to hedge currency risk) and speculators (traders buying and selling contracts purely for reaping the gains from price changes). The figures, expressed in number of contracts, show the buyers and sellers of futures' currency contracts and total open interest.

Considering that excessive yen purchases are a reflection of escalating risk appetite, one can discern the extent of carry trades via the trend in the yen shorts—the amount of yen-selling contracts versus the dollar. Figure 5.12 shows the clearly positive correlation between speculators' commitment in the yen and the value of USD/JPY.

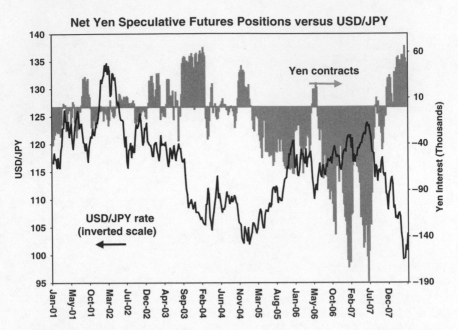

FIGURE 5.12   Fed hikes in 2004–2006 extended USD/JPY gains by lifting interest in short JPY contracts versus USD. As volatility surged in 2007, JPY shorts turned to net longs, dragging USD/JPY lower.

The low-yielding Swiss franc is another currency used for funding carry trades and is thereby subject to considerable gains during the unwinding of carry trades. Figure 5.13 highlights the deviation of commitments in the yen and the Swiss franc ("swissy") from commitments in other currencies between January and September 2007 as JPY and CHF were sold to finance the rise in equities and risk appetite. This explains why excessive gains in equities are accompanied by extensive shorts in the yen and swissy, which calls for cautiousness ahead.

The relationship between risk appetite and the low-yielding CHF and JPY stands out in Figure 5.14 with the two currencies plotted against the VIX. In 2004–2007, market volatility fell to multiyear lows, reflecting heightened investor confidence in global equities. As a result, both CHF and JPY were sold to finance carry trades in higher-yielding currencies and higher-return investments such as equities.

One drawback to using futures speculators' commitments report is the one-week lag of the data and, hence, the possibility of falling behind the trend and chasing a runaway market. Yet in fact what may be a drawback could be turned into an advantage if one were to look for a breaking point and a reversal in the trend. Say, for instance, that net yen shorts

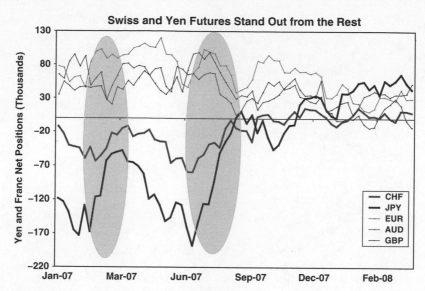

FIGURE 5.13 CHF and JPY futures fell in January–July 2007 as CHF and JPY carry trades boosted rising equities. But subsequent market decline unwound CHF and JPY shorts amid sharp reduction in appetite.

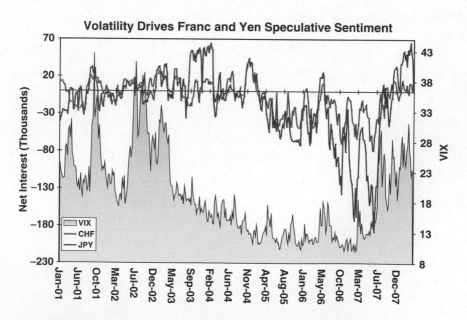

FIGURE 5.14 Falling VIX is positively correlated with falling interest in yen and franc futures due to heightened global investor confidence.

have risen to their highest level in four years and USD/JPY has hit multi-year highs. One could then conclude that the yen carry trades are reaching unsustainably high levels, possibly leading the way for someone to build a contrarian trade to buy the yen. But looking for clues from the VIX and equity markets as to whether risk aversion may have topped out could help signal the point of reversal. Once having reached levels judged too extreme, financial markets require little in the way of catalysts to trigger reversals. In the case of carry trade reversals, the fundamental triggers include negative economic figures from the economy of the high-yielding currency, instability in financial markets, or any positive news impacting the low-yielding currency.

Speculative futures' commitments are a fundamental gauge of sentiment in currency markets. In the case of the yen and Swiss franc data, these reports offer an important part of the carry trade puzzle, particularly the yen, due to extremely low interest rates. Combining futures flows in currencies with risk signals such as the VIX offers valuable insight on the prevailing currency trend. Whether traders are piling up on shorting low-yielding currencies, scaling down their carry trades, or simply selling the U.S. dollar across the board, this combination is paramount in determining the driving force behind current sentiment.

High-Yield Corporate Spreads

Another way to gauge the extent of market risk-taking and corporate confidence is via corporate spreads, which measure the difference between high-yield corporate bonds (also known as junk bonds) and U.S. government bonds of similar maturities. The higher the risk faced by a bond issuer, the higher the interest rate demanded by holders of the bond. With U.S. government debt considered to be the least risky from the perspective of credit risk (chances of default), yields on government Treasury bonds (Treasuries) are relatively lower than those on corporate bonds, especially as companies face credit, business, and inflation risk.

In times of robust economic growth and low business/economic risks, companies face generally lower probability of defaulting on their debt and incur lower yields on their bonds.

This means that the spread between corporate bond yields over treasuries yield is lower as the price of high-yield corporate bonds pushes higher. At times of economic uncertainty and higher probability of default or late payments, yields are pushed higher to compensate for the risk of default, and so is the spread over less-risky Treasury bonds.

Just as a rising VIX tends to reflect increased volatility (fear) in the general market, rising bond spreads are indicative of emerging worries with corporate finances, which is more likely to be the case during market uncertainty and/or economic slowdown. Falling or low bond spreads usually prevail during periods of healthier economic growth, falling risk, and increased bond market liquidity. And, similar to the VIX, excessively low spreads can be a sign of investor complacency and a disregarding of the risks associated with high-yield bonds.

This explains the positive correlation between corporate bond spreads and the VIX index in Figure 5.15. Note how a rising VIX index coincides with an increase in bond spreads as investors grow risk averse and the economy slows. Sometimes, market fear escalates and spreads rise while the macroeconomic fundamentals remain solid. Conversely, falling bond spreads are the result of rising prices of junk bonds due to increased demand in the extra yield of these risky securities. This is manifested in the chart between June 2004 and April 2007, a period of advancing U.S. and global equities, plentiful liquidity, and booming mergers and acquisitions.

As risk appetite intensifies, so does the use of carry trades as investors accumulate confidence in purchasing higher-yielding currencies, equities, and commodities with cheap funding from the yen and Swiss franc. Currency market participants therefore can pick up a few clues about the prevailing trends in bond spreads so as to determine the general state of confidence and risk aversion in the market. Say that risk appetite has risen

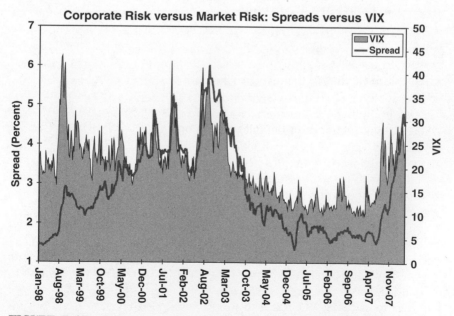

FIGURE 5.15 Corporate bond spreads measure credit risk while VIX measures market volatility.

alongside an increase in the VIX and a falling stock market without any pickup in bond spreads. In such a scenario, one could surmise that an eventual widening of bond spreads is near, which may fuel the existing increase in risk aversion once junk spreads begin to increase.

Interest rate differentials will always be around, moving as a function of traders' expectations, economic data, central bank action, and sentiment. But it takes more than yield differentials to prompt traders into borrowing in low-rate currencies. Rather than getting on the bandwagon and chasing a trend, it is imperative that one discern the drivers of the trend and the fluctuating dynamics behind the ups and downs of risk appetite.

TYING IT ALL TOGETHER: 1999–2007

When correlating risk appetite to currencies in a real-world scenario, we find a fairly strong correlation between rising risk aversion and a strengthening in the Japanese yen and the Swiss franc. As investors reduce their appetite for risk, so do the flows into carry trades diminish. An increasing level of fear causes carry trades to be unwound from high-yielding assets and back into the lower-yielding yen and franc.

Table 5.1 illustrates this relationship between 1999 and 2007 using stocks, VIX, and high-yield bond spreads as measures of risk, while the yen and franc are used to represent the funding currencies. By selecting the 13 periods with the most pronounced equity market declines in 1999–2007, we note a fairly consistent response in the VIX, bond spreads, and low-yielding currencies. Declines in the broad equity indexes, as measured by the S&P 500, are accompanied by increases in the VIX. They are also accompanied by widening in the corporate bond spreads and an increase in interest in the yen and Swiss franc's futures against the dollar. As risk appetite declines, traders scale down their shorts in the yen and the franc, prompting a strengthening in these currencies.

The exceptions were during events 3, 7, 8, and 9, when these currencies sustained a decrease in their futures contracts against the U.S. currency. In event 3, yen futures fell during September–December 2000 as markets continued unwinding the yen longs, which ensued during the preceding two months.

In event 7, January–March 2003 witnessed a slight divergence between equities and currencies, whereby the broad equity indexes had continued to weaken in the run-up to the Iraq war. Meanwhile, currencies had posted the bulk of their pre-Iraq war gains versus the U.S. dollar in September–December 2002 as U.S. and U.K. support in favor of an attack on Iraq intensified, rendering war a stronger probability. Although equities

TABLE 5.1 Risk Appetites and Carry Trades, 1999–2007

Event #	Date	Event Description	Stocks	VIX	High-Yield Spread	CHF	JPY
1	July–Oct. 1999	Fed hikes remove 1998 cuts	–13%	61%	30%	132%	184%
2	Jan.–Mar. 2000	Peak of tech bubble	–5%	42%	27%	53%	132%
3	Sep.–Dec. 2000	Burst of bubble	–18%	72%	25%	142%	–34%
4	Feb.–Mar. 2001	Start of U.S. recession	–22%	59%	36%	–278%	113%
5	Sep. 2001	Sep. 11 attacks	–18%	96%	29%	47%	29%
6	May–Oct. 2002	Stocks sell-off hits five-year lows	–25%	115%	73%	371%	191%
7	Jan.–Mar. 2003	Pre-Iraq war nervousness, WMD speculation	–16%	36%	–10%	–78%	–85%
8	Mar.–Apr. 2005	Rising U.S. inflation triggers rate fears	–8%	50%	69%	–516%	–356%
9	Sep.–Oct. 2005	Hurricanes Rita, Katrina	–6%	42%	11%	–3121%	–94%
10	May–June 2006	Fears of BoJ hike, emerging markets	–8%	100%	13%	174%	681%
11	Feb.–Mar. 2007	China stocks tumble, U.S. subprime	–6%	100%	13%	74%	59%
12	July–Aug. 2007	Losses in U.S. funds on subprime	–12%	147%	50%	66%	101%
13	Oct.–Mar. 2007	Rising write-downs in U.S. banks	–11%	94%	52%	272%	174%

had continued to sell off into the first quarter of 2003, yen and Swiss franc futures underwent an adjustment in the end of the first quarter following significant purchases between September and December 2002.

In event 8, the low-yielding yen and franc, along with most major currencies, fell against the U.S. dollar as the Federal Reserve vowed to prolong its rate hike campaign to contain rising inflation. Nervousness about further Fed tightening threatened to destabilize equities, lifted bond spreads, and boosted the dollar on the outlook of higher U.S. yields.

In event 9, both the yen and the franc sustained losses as part of a general dollar rally being prompted by prolonged Fed tightening. Indeed, the Fed's rate hikes continued in September 2005, despite the economic damage of hurricanes Rita and Katrina. Note how corporate bond spreads rose by a mere 11 percent as the market deemed the fundamentals of corporations' debt-paying ability to remain strong despite the hurricanes.

Aside from the aforementioned four exceptions, significant declines in equities are normally a reflection of falling risk appetite, thereby lifting the low-yielding currencies of Japan and Switzerland.

Interest rate differentials will always be around, moving as a function of traders' expectations, economic data, central bank action, and sentiment. But it takes more than yield differentials to prompt traders into borrowing in low interest rate currencies. Rather than getting on the bandwagon and chasing a trend, it is imperative that one discern the drivers of the trend and the varying dynamics of risk appetite.

Taking a glance at equity indexes, low-yielding currencies, and the VIX allows traders to figure out whether risk appetite is calling the shots, and hence whether carry trades are accumulating or unwound. In today's world, where currency fluctuations are increasingly correlated with equity market volatility, forex participants can no longer afford to look only at currencies. More than ever, risk appetite trades are assuming the lead in currency markets. Whether traders are piling up on shorting low-yielding currencies, scaling down their carry trades, or simply selling the U.S. dollar across the board, this combination is essential in determining the principal force behind current sentiment. Incorporating currency futures commitments with indicators of risk appetite such as the VIX and bond spreads will enable currency participants to gain a vital insight on the prevailing trend in currencies.

CHAPTER 6

Reading the Fed via Yield Curves, Equities, and Commodities

The relationship between foreign exchange rates and interest rates remains a principal force in determining currency trends and values. Interest rates continue to be a vital source of oxygen for economic activity, business sentiment, and financial market liquidity, all of which are key determinants of a nation's economic growth and the value of its currency. The ability to predict future moves in interest rates of the world's major central banks hinges on a strong grasp of a nation's economic pulse, of its most influencing macroeconomic variables and financial market indicators. Grasping each individual central bank's policy mandate—whether it is bound by an inflation target, ceiling, or a combination of growth and inflation targets—is as necessary as understanding the policy makers' statements regarding current and future economic direction.

The United States continues to be the world's largest economy as well as a major influence on global economic growth, despite a gradual waning in such influence as of late. And although several global central banks have reduced the U.S. dollar holdings of their currency reserves in favor of EUR, JPY, AUD, and GBP, over two-thirds of the world's total central bank reserves are denominated in U.S. dollars, compared to over one-fifth for euros. Meanwhile, as of 2007, the U.S. dollar accounted for 86 percent of the average daily foreign exchange market turnover, compared to 37 percent for the euro.

But each currency must be traded against another currency. And the EUR/USD pair continues to dominate currency trading, accounting for 27 percent of the daily turnover in global currency markets as of 2007. Thus, it is no surprise that during U.S.-specific developments, such as market-moving economic reports, Federal Reserve action, or even geopolitical events, EUR/USD tends to react considerably to such action. Other USD-related pairs also respond to U.S.-specific factors, but the popularity of the EUR/USD pair makes it a consistent mover to these events. Considering the vital role of interest rates, central bank action, and the strong relevance of U.S. economic developments to currency markets, the ability to grasp and predict the dynamics shaping the direction of U.S. interest rates is an invaluable advantage.

This chapter does not cover the determinants of interest rates and central bank decisions. Rather, it focuses on the relationship between short- and long-term interest rates, and how it enables us to understand and predict future interest rate decisions by the Federal Reserve, as well as to better assess the timing of such decisions. This chapter also explains how to use the relationship between gold and oil prices in gauging the direction of the overall economy and its implications for Federal Reserve policy.

YIELD CURVES AND THE ECONOMY

The yield curve is a snapshot of yields on bonds of similar credit quality and asset class, ranging from maturities of as little as one month to 30 years. Unlike the coupon interest rate, which is the fixed payment to bondholders, the yield to maturity measures the total return an investor receives by holding the bond until it matures, regardless of whether it pays a coupon rate. Yield curves are commonly a measure of bonds issued by national governments, and are therefore almost devoid of business risk. The governments of the United States and other countries with robust bond markets raise funds by issuing bonds with different time durations to banks and other national governments. These banks will then resell the bonds to other banks, pension funds, hedge funds, various institutional investors, and individual investors. The bonds, like any other IOU, promise to pay interest at a stated rate throughout the life of the bond, followed by the full principal at maturity.

The short end of the yield curve represents interest rates on short-term maturities, ranging from three months to two years. The middle of the curve includes interest rates on maturities ranging from 3 to 7 years, while the long end shows interest rates from 10 to 30 years. Since central banks control short-term interest rates via changes in the overnight interest rate, the short end of the yield curve is influenced by the central bank's monetary policy and market expectations of future policy. Monetary policy is primarily driven by interest rate announcements, open market operations (buying and selling of government securities to manage liquidity), and bank reserve requirements. The longer end of the yield curve is partly determined by the auctions that governments use to make the initial sale of 5- to 30-year bonds to banks. Once these bonds are resold in the secondary market, their supply and demand determines prices and yields.

Bonds are also determined by traders' assessment of the economy, with inflation being the main economic determinant of their price and yield. Rising expectations of inflation or an actual increase in inflation outstrips the fixed income of bonds' coupon payments, thereby reducing the value of the bonds and boosting their yield to maturity. The same applies during releases of stronger than expected economic reports, which increase the risk of inflation. Conversely, falling inflation and/or weak economic reports are usually favorable for bond prices and negative for their yields.

Since graphic illustrations of yield curves are not always readily available to investors, the shape or steepness of the yield curve can be easily determined by the difference between selected short- and long-term interest rates. A popular measure is the difference between yields on 10- and 2-year government securities, known as the 10-2 spread. In the case of the United States, another viable measure is the difference between the Fed funds rate and the 10-year rate, where the Fed funds rate is the overnight rate charged between commercial banks.

TYPES OF YIELD CURVES

Due to the time value of money, bonds with longer maturities pay higher interest rates than bonds with shorter maturities. Creditors willing to lend funds for longer periods of time will demand higher interest rates than those willing to lend for shorter durations. As a result, the shape of the yield curve is positively or upward sloping. Figure 6.1 illustrates an upward-sloping or normal shaped curve dated July 18, 2007, and a less steep or flatter yield curve on June 6, 2007. Upward-sloping yield curves have normally preceded economic expansions as bondholders demand a higher rate of return from the inflationary risks accompanying economic upturns. In this case, however, the buildup of the upward-sloping curve in July 2007 was a result of worsening economic conditions, which were priced in the flatter yield curve. As markets fell and the risks of an economic downturn accelerated, bond traders sent short-term rates lower, pricing incoming Fed cuts.

Flat yield curves usually signal an approaching economic slowdown or expansion, depending on which stage of the economy had initially prevailed. As the economic expansion prevailing over a steep yield curve takes hold and the Federal Reserve raises interest rates, the short end of the curve shifts upwards. Figure 6.2 shows such an example when a flat yield

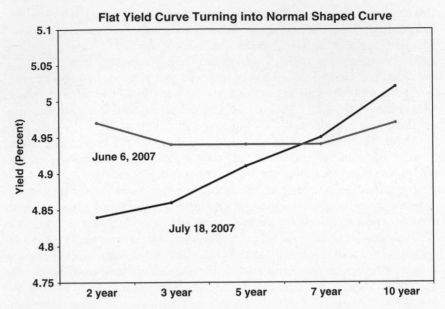

FIGURE 6.1 On June 6, 2007, the flat yield curve gradually turned steeper in the subsequent seven weeks due to worsening credit market turmoil and increased expectations of a Fed rate cut.

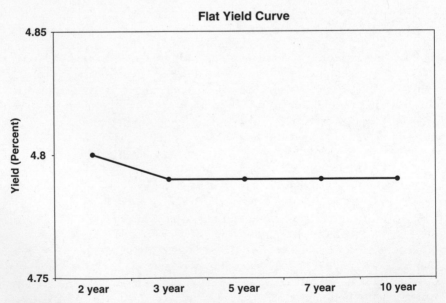

FIGURE 6.2 Yield curve moved from an inverting to a flattening formation in late March, 2006 as the cooling economy began to feel the Fed's 2004–06 rate hikes.

curve preceded an economic slowdown. On the long end of the curve, bond traders are no longer pricing the chance of rising inflation due to their anticipation of slower growth ahead. The role of the flat yield curve in signaling a slowdown was especially powerful in this example as it was clearly at odds with the record highs seen in U.S. and global stock indexes in May 2007. Followers of equity markets ended up being largely misled when the economy slowed later in the year and the Fed was forced to cut rates three months later.

Sometimes, however, yield curves emerge when the economy begins to recover from a slowdown or recession. At this stage, traders of 10- and 30-year Treasury securities are certain the economy has reached bottom and begin to project higher inflation and interest rates in the distant future, thereby raising long-term yields. It is rare that yield curves stay flat for more than a week as the economy emerges out of a downturn.

Inverted yield curves usually signal economic slowdowns and are often a harbinger of recession. The negative slope of the yield curve shows that short-term yields are higher than long-term yields as bond traders expect lower interest rates ahead. Historically, yield curve inversions have started about 12 to 18 months before a recession. Figure 6.3 illustrates the inverting formation in January 2007, suggesting that short-term rates were too high relative to the bond market's forward-looking interest rate outlook as seen farther down the curve.

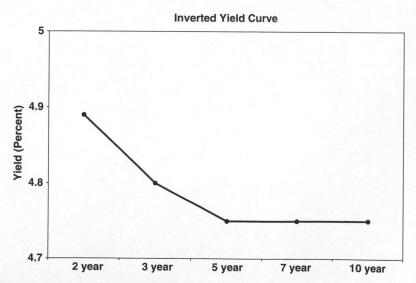

FIGURE 6.3 On January 18, 2007, yield curve inversion reflected further economic weakness and incoming Fed easing.

RATIONALE OF INVERTED YIELD CURVE IMPLICATIONS

The main reason inverted yield curves have presaged economic weakness is that they narrow the premium gained by banks between the short-term interest rates paid out to depositors and the longer-term interest rates earned on loans. But interest income has become a smaller share of banks' overall income amid the creation of several financial products, which have made non-interest-rate income a bigger share of banks' total profits. Asset managers selling short-term bonds and buying long-end bonds get squeezed out when the cost of their short-term debt increases relative to their longer-maturity holdings. And finally, rising short-term rates increase homeowners' interest costs on their floating-rate mortgages, thereby reducing demand for new and existing homes as well as weighing on the value of house prices against which home owners are borrowing. Negative-yield spreads then become self-enforced when long-term yields remain pressured by expectations of low inflation, slowing growth, or both.

EFFECTIVENESS OF YIELD CURVE SIGNALS' IMPLICATIONS

Many economists have disputed the validity of the yield curve as a predictor of recessions and economic slowdowns. Figure 6.4 shows the relationship between the 10-year Treasury yield and the effective Fed funds rate, which is a viable representative of short-term interest rates. Of the eight recessions between 1957 and 2008, only the first two recessions (1957–1958 and 1960) were not preceded by an inverted yield curve. And out of the eight occasions (including 2006–2007) when the yield curve was inverted since the 1950s, only twice were the inversions not followed by recessions: 1966 and 1998. The exceptions of the 1950s and 1960s may be discounted due to the relatively low levels of depth and size of financial markets 50 years ago, and the different mechanism by which the Fed managed monetary policy at the time. Nonetheless, in each of the aforementioned inversions, the Federal Reserve was forced to cut interest rates, which is the primary focus of this chapter. Recessions are extensions of economic downturns, which were signaled by yield inversions and consequently triggered interest rate reductions.

A more comprehensive view on the consistency of the yield curve's signaling of recessions and economic slowdowns over a more historical basis can be seen in Figure 6.5. The charts show how the recessions of 1990–1991 and 2001–2002 (shaded areas) were effectively signaled by the inversion of

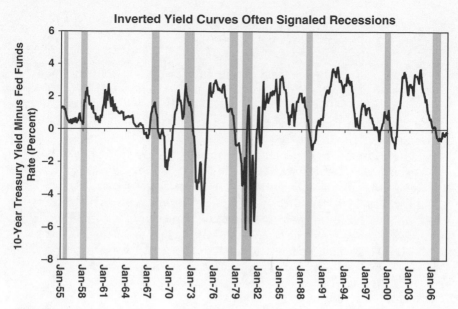

FIGURE 6.4 Yield curve's signal detection is also effective by 10-year Treasury yield minus Fed funds rate.

the yield curve, with economic activity stalling in services, manufacturing, and labor markets. The charts also show that in 1995 the yield curve was close to inverting but a series of Fed rate cuts that year quickly normalized the yield curve and averted recession. Nonetheless, the near inversion of 1995 did lead to a slowdown in GDP growth, employment, and services industry activity. The brief yield curve inversion of summer 1998 was the other example in the chart where no recession occurred, but the ensuing global market crisis did shed 20 percent off U.S. stock indexes, prompting the Federal Reserve to cut rates in three consecutive months. Each of these phases is revisited in more detail later in the chapter.

GREENSPAN'S "CONUNDRUM" PROVED BERNANKE'S PROBLEM

When the Federal Reserve normalized monetary policy by raising interest rates from their 1 percent low in 2003 to 5.25 percent in 2006, the yield curve began to flatten in late 2005, before inverting throughout most of 2006. Two-year yields rose from 1.25 percent to 5.27 percent in June 2006, while 10-year yields rose from 4.9 percent toward the 5.20 percent level, matching their two-year yield counterpart.

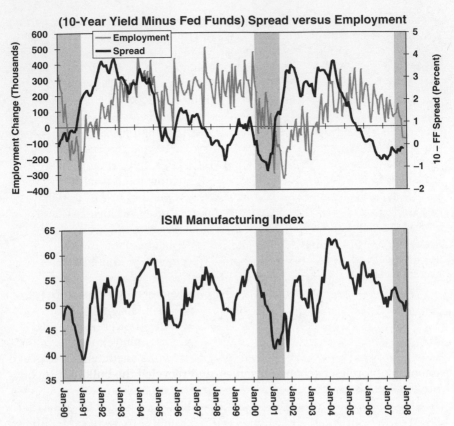

FIGURE 6.5 Yield curve's track record is validated by developments in employment and manufacturing.
Source: Federal Reserve Bank of San Francisco Economic Research Department (http://www.frbsf.org/publications/economics/et/index.pdf).

The relatively low rate of appreciation in long-term interest rates despite the Fed's rate hikes and aggressive talk against inflation was referred to by former Fed chairman Alan Greenspan as a "conundrum" during his late days in office before his departure in February 2006. Greenspan then introduced an explanation that was later expounded on by his successor, Chairman Ben Bernanke. They postulated that the decline in long-term interest rates stemmed from the global savings glut accumulated by developing nations as a result of the growing U.S. current account deficit, which was partly boosted by a deteriorating trade deficit, rising domestic consumption, and negative savings. As the U.S. current account deficit soared from $300 billion in 1999 to over $800 billion in 2006, the imbalance was increasingly translated into rising surpluses in developing countries. The surpluses grew due to surging oil prices, which lifted Gulf nations' account surpluses from $15 billion in 1999 to $233 billion in 2006. In the case of East Asian economies, the hard lessons of the 1997–1998 currency crises prompted these nations into rapid accumulation of exchange reserves and a higher rate of savings. Current account surpluses in developing Asia jumped from $38 billion in 1999 to $278 billion in 2006.

The bulk of these surpluses were channeled into U.S. and non-U.S. government securities, to the extent of depressing long-term global interest rates. The average weekly yield on U.S. 10-year Treasury notes fell from 6.04 percent in 2000 to 4.29 percent in 2005. In Germany, it fell from 5.25 percent to 3.38 percent; in the United Kingdom it fell from 5.25 percent to 4.42 percent; and in Canada it fell from 5.81 percent to 4.07 percent.

Bernanke also explained the low interest rates via lower volatility in capital markets causing holders of long-term bonds to require a lower compensation for the perceived risk. The other explanation for lower long-term rates was the surge in pension funds' investments in long-term bonds as long-term liabilities were prolonged by shifting demographics.

Most interestingly, however, when congressmen and reporters asked Greenspan and Bernanke whether the 2005–2006 flattening of the yield curve was a harbinger of economic slowdown, they both rejected the possibility, opting to give the aforementioned savings glut explanation. This made plenty of sense as Asian emerging economies accumulated massive amounts of foreign exchange reserves, and recycled the bulk of it by buying U.S. Treasuries to keep their currencies competitive. But the Federal Reserve's persistent refutation of the idea that the flat and inverted yield curves of 2005–2006 were a signal of an incoming slowdown proved to be a significant gap in the central bank's economic assessment vis-à-vis the effectiveness of a relationship with an 86 percent rate accuracy. The latter part of the next section demonstrates the early signs of disagreement between the apprehensive economic assessment of the bond market and the rosy assessment of the Federal Reserve and U.S. Treasury throughout 2006 and early 2007.

IMPLICATIONS FOR GROWTH, STOCKS, AND CURRENCIES

We will now go over the three most recent examples of yield curve inversions (1998, 2000, and 2006–2007) and how each fared in signaling shifts in the U.S. economy, the state of the markets, and the U.S. dollar. The charts in Figure 6.6 are a resounding illustration of the effectiveness of yield curve inversions in foretelling economic slowdowns, stock market declines, and ultimately Federal Reserve rate cuts.

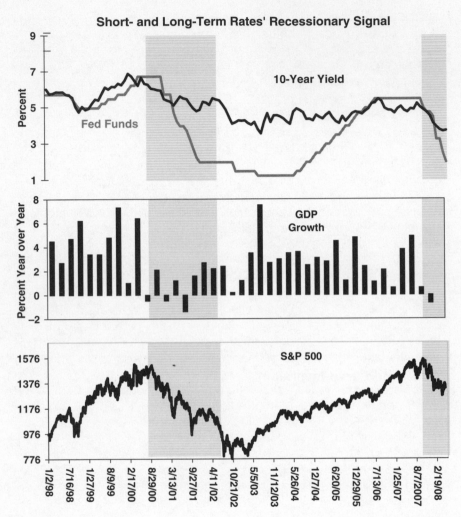

FIGURE 6.6 Trends in short- and long-term interest rates have served to predict turnarounds in stocks.

1998 Yield Curve Inversion

Starting with the top chart, we see how a brief flattening in the yield curve in summer 1998 saw the 10-year yield falling toward the level of the Fed funds rate, ultimately prompting a slowdown in GDP and an 18 percent decline in the S&P 500 in the three months ending October 1998.

Although no recession ensued in 1998, the emerging market crisis in East Asia, Russia, and Brazil had reverberated to stock markets worldwide, causing the collapse of the Long Term Capital Management hedge fund, which had lost nearly $5 billion of client funds. The Federal Reserve cut the Fed funds rate target by 25 bps in September, October, and November, bringing the rate down to 4.75 percent. The rate cuts were largely addressed at a sudden plunge in bond market liquidity and deteriorating global investor confidence, rather than slowing U.S. economic activity. Nonetheless, the rule of the flat yield curve predicting Fed rate cuts and falling stock markets did prevail.

For currency traders, the inversion of June 1998 had not only foretold the beginning of the autumn 1998 rate cuts, but also signaled the peak of the U.S. dollar in mid-August 1998. The currency lost more than 10 percent against the yen, British pound, and deutsche mark over the following six weeks. In trade-weighted terms, the dollar index peaked 11 days after the beginning of the yield curve inversion, falling 9 percent in the ensuing two months. But in bilateral terms, the dollar would make one of its biggest one-week losses against the yen, shedding more than 18 percent from October 5 to 10 as massive amounts of yen carry trades were unwound. Investors who had borrowed in low-yielding yen to invest the proceeds in higher-yielding emerging debt—including Russian government paper yielding as much as 140 percent—were knocked out of their positions when Russia chose to default in its debt and let its currency slide.

2000 Yield Curve Inversion

The next yield curve inversion shown in Figure 6.6 took place in the first quarter of 2000, when the decline of the 10-year yield was prolonged toward the 6.5 percent level of the Fed funds rate. Note that no period of flat yield curve prevailed prior to the curve inversion as the Fed's rate hikes of 2000 were relatively more abrupt than in other tightening phases when rate increases were well communicated. The yield inversion lasted for 11 months, before prompting the Federal Reserve to begin a three-year easing campaign, cutting the Fed funds rate from 6.5 percent to a 45-year low of 1 percent. The U.S. economy fell into recession in 2001–2002 and the major U.S. stock indexes fell into the longest postwar bear market, losing as much as 75 percent within three years.

The currency impact of the 2000 yield inversion materialized in late November 2000 when the Federal Reserve made a 180-degree turn in its policy bias. At the December meeting, the Federal Open Market Committee shifted its outlook on the economy from that of strength to weakness, paving the way for an unscheduled meeting on January 3, 2001, to cut interest rates by 50 bps. The rate cut marked the start of the 2.5-year-long easing campaign, which sent rates from 6.5 percent to 1 percent. From late November 2000 to mid-January, the dollar index fell more than 8 percent as the currency tumbled 16 percent against the euro, 13 percent against the aussie, 8 percent against the British pound, and 5 percent against the Canadian dollar. But the dollar, along with the rest of these currencies, strengthened against the yen as Japan's economy displayed another false awakening from its 1990s recession.

2006–2007 Yield Curve Inversion

The final yield curve flattening in Figure 6.6 began in late 2005, and turned into an inversion in 2006–2007 as bond traders sent long-term rates down on the expectation of slowing economic growth. Throughout 2006 and the first half of 2007, Fed Chairman Bernanke shifted the focus from the global savings glut theory toward stressing the risks of rising inflation, while addressing the emerging housing slowdown as merely an "adjustment" that was "unlikely to seriously spill over to the broader economy or the financial system."[1]

Figure 6.7 provides a more detailed look at the economic and market picture of 2005–2007, highlighting the disparity between soaring equity markets and an already weakening job market, recessionary manufacturing sector, and deteriorating housing story. Investors who heeded the speeches of Federal Reserve officials in 2006 and early 2007, warning persistently about the dangers of inflation while comforting the public about the housing correction, had every right to expect a rate hike in late 2007 or early 2008. U.S. and global stocks continued to surge to new record highs in the second quarter of 2007 after a brief scare in late February and early March that year, when a 9 percent decline in Chinese shares and a set of negative U.S. reports destabilized global investor confidence.

The Fed maintained with confidence that the overall economy would remain immune to the housing slowdown, which it described as being largely confined to the subprime lending market. Those pronouncements had taken place despite a slowdown in GDP growth from 4.6 percent in first quarter 2006 to subpar growth rates of 2.4 percent, 1.1 percent, 2.1 percent, and 0.6 percent in the ensuing four quarters. In the second and third quarters of 2007, GDP growth rebounded to 3.8 percent and 4.9 percent respectively, primarily due to rising exports and falling imports, prompted by a falling dollar, weak U.S. demand, and robust foreign growth. But the net increase in GDP overlooked the prolonged dislocations in the housing market and the resulting deterioration in market liquidity.

As the Fed went on to expect continued economic expansion in early second quarter 2007, private equity firms extended their deal makings to

---

[1]Ben S. Bernanke, 2007 International Monetary Conference, Cape Town, South Africa, http://www.federalreserve.gov/newsevents/speech/bernanke20070605a.htm.

FIGURE 6.7 Yield curve is more robust predictor of economy and helps detect stocks-economy divergences.

new heights, global investor confidence soared, and risk appetite pushed carry trades to new heights at the expense of multiyear lows in the Japanese yen. Meanwhile, housing-related indicators continued to deteriorate, with new home sales tumbling 25 percent over their prior year levels, monthly construction employment dipping under its three-month average, while building permits and housing starts tumbled 25 to 30 percent over their prior year levels to reach their worst levels in 10 years.

In July 2007, financial markets eventually gave in as credit rating agencies downgraded tens of billions of securities, which were backed by loans and mortgages with poor credit quality. Hedge funds announced losses of 30 to 40 percent in a single month, while others closed shop as they eroded clients' money. In August, market interest rates soared as credit institutions lacked the confidence to lend and borrow, bringing interbank lending to a virtual halt. Broad equity indexes registered weekly declines of 4 to 7 percent, while the VIX index soared to levels not seen in four years.

Just nine days after the Federal Reserve announced holding rates unchanged at 5.25 percent and described rising inflation as its "predominant policy concern,"[2] the Federal Open Market Committee called an emergency meeting, cutting its discount rate by 50 bps. Less than two weeks after it had stated that the "downside risks to growth have increased somewhat," it altered the qualifier to "increased appreciably," without mentioning a word on inflation. Deteriorating market conditions, increasing bank write-downs, and broadening signs of economic weakness forced the central bank to cut rates by 100 bps in 2007, followed by an unprecedented 125 bps of rate cuts in a span of nine days in January 2008, bringing the Fed funds rate down to 3 percent.

Once again the dollar had complied with the law of the yield curve inversion. After rebounding by as much as 15 percent in 2005, the U.S. Dollar Index peaked out in November 2005. The currency then consolidated during the first eight weeks of 2006, before cementing a peak in the second week of March 2006. That was also two months after the yield curve had inverted. What would later ensue was a gradual deterioration in dollar sentiment, accelerating in April and May 2006, when the Federal Reserve signaled the end of the two-year rate hike campaign. In fall of 2006, the euro regained the $1.30 level last attained in April 2005 as U.S. economic growth underperformed that of the Eurozone, the United Kingdom, Canada, Australia, and even Japan.

Currency traders with less than 15 years experience would witness something they had never experienced in their working lives. Markets began expecting interest rate cuts in the United States while the rest of the world was in the midst of raising theirs. In 2007, there was no longer any suspense in currency markets. The housing recession spread to all parts of the U.S. economy and corroded the normal functioning of credit markets. The U.S Dollar Index hit the lowest level in its 40-year history, reaching 74.48. The U.S. currency hit record lows against the euro, 32-year lows against the Canadian dollar, 25-year lows against the New Zealand dollar, 23-year lows against the Australian dollar, 14-year lows against the British pound, and 5-year lows against the Japanese yen.

Figure 6.8 illustrates the dollar impact of turnarounds in the U.S. yield curve, showing that curve inversions precede dollar selling by periods ranging from two weeks to nine months. The various time lags have been a function of the duration of the inversion as well as the speed with which the Federal Reserve shifted from a neutral policy to that of an easing policy.

Although there exists no clear-cut relationship between yield curve inversions and the U.S. dollar, recent history has shown a noticeable relationship between the latter stages of the inversion and the value of the greenback. These final stages of curve inversions take place amid

---

[2]See http://www.federalreserve.gov/newsevents/press/monetary/20070807a.htm.

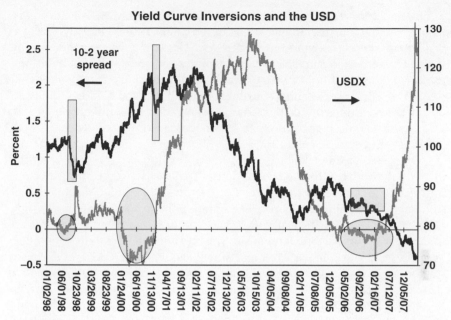

FIGURE 6.8 Yield curve inversions have generally signaled dollar weakness as short term yields weaken relative to long term yields.

markets' expectations for a looming Fed cut, which start to drive down short-term yields (two-year yields) toward longer-term rates (10-year yields). As these yield developments are manifested into the market, currency traders begin selling the dollar on the argument that lower U.S. rates will erode the dollar's yield differential with other currencies.

Table 6.1 dissects the currency and stock market impact of yield curve inversions from a timing perspective. The U.S. economy slipped into

TABLE 6.1   Timing of Dollar Peak, Stocks Peak, and Rate Cuts from the Start of Yield Curve Inversions

Yield Inversion	Time Elapsed for Peak of USDX after the Inversion	Time Elapsed for Peak of S&P 500 after the Inversion	Time Elapsed for Start of Rate Cuts after the Inversion
January 1989 to January 1990	5 months	18 months	18 months
June to July 1998	11 days	1.5 months	3 months
February to December 2000	9 months	2 months	11 months
January 2006 to June 2007	2 months	18 months	19 months

recession in third quarter 1990 but the yield curve had begun inverting in January 1989. Five months later, the dollar index peaked at 104.30 before losing 8 percent in the ensuing 17 months. The Fed inaugurated its easing campaign 18 months after the curve inversion and 13 months after the start of the dollar sell-off. The Fed's rate cuts also coincided with the sell-off in the S&P 500, which shed 20 percent of its value in three months.

The 1998 inversion resulted from a drying up of global market liquidity rather than domestic U.S. economic concerns. The one-month-long yield curve started in early June 1998, two weeks after which the dollar reached its peak. The currency lost 9 percent in the ensuing two months, while the S&P 500 dropped 17 percent in two months. It wasn't until the implosion of the LTCM hedge fund in September that the Fed headed off its interest rate cuts, three months after the beginning of the inversion.

The 2001–2002 recession officially began in March 2001, 14 months after the yield curve had inverted. The 9 percent sell-off in the dollar materialized in late November 2000 and into mid-January, while the Fed's easing campaign began in January 2001. The burst of the equity bubble was triggered in March 2000, under the measure of the S&P 500, leading to a 50 percent sell-off that lasted into October 2002.

In January 2006, short-term yields breached above longer-term yields to start a curve inversion that lasted over 18 months, including brief bouts of normalizations. But it took the dollar only two months from the January inversion to descend into a two-year slump in the magnitude of 18 percent. Throughout the currency sell-off, rising liquidity greased the wheels of a record-breaking equity bull market in 2006 and 2007, obscuring the deepening cracks of a faltering housing market. It wasn't until 18 months after the January 2006 inversion that the S&P 500 hit a peak. One month later, the Fed was forced to cut its discount rate, initiating an aggressive easing campaign in its Fed funds rate.

The aforementioned cases served as powerful illustrations of the consistency of the yield curve's effectiveness in predicting rate cuts by the Federal Reserve, when other indicators have pointed otherwise. In summer of 1998, the flattening yield curve signaled a series of Fed rate cuts in September, October, and November 1998 at a time when nonfarm payrolls were growing by a monthly average of 248,000 in the first half of the year, and GDP growth surged from 2.7 percent in the second quarter of 1998 to 4.7 percent and 6.2 percent in the third and fourth quarters, respectively. Had investors paid attention solely to those macroeconomic indicators, they'd have hardly been able to see those rate cuts coming and the equity indexes tumbling. By the end of 1998, the U.S. economy rode on the coattails of rising productivity, low inflation, and a surging stock market, all of which created the longest uninterrupted period of postwar economic expansion.

But when the 1990s tech bubble came to an end, the yield curve was there to signal its culmination two months prior to the peak in equities. Perhaps it was no big feat by many to have expected the burst of a bubble that was largely founded on exuberant price targets when several companies had shown no profits on their books. The two-month lag between the inversion of the yield curve and the peak of the broad indexes did help signal that the days of the Fed rate hikes were numbered and that a shift to easier Fed policy was not far away.

TYING INTEREST RATES TO THE GOLD-OIL RATIO

The ever-increasing role of commodity prices in global financial markets and its impact on world economies cannot go unnoticed. Record prices in energy, metals, and agricultural commodities have introduced a new element to aggregate demand, enriching the revenues of exporting countries and casting a pall on the trade balance of importing economies. Record prices in gold and oil have left forecasters rather challenged as these commodities attain unprecedented levels. Rather than simply looking at these commodities individually, examining their interrelationship can offer valuable clues about the global economy in general, and the U.S. economy in particular.

During the days of the gold-backed U.S. dollar regime of $35 per ounce, oil prices held up at $1.00 to $1.50 per barrel. But after the dollar broke free of the gold standard due to the United States' inability to back its currency at the corresponding rate of $30 per gold ounce, the dollar tumbled in value and gold shot up from less than $40 per ounce in 1971 to more than $60 in 1972.

As the devaluation of the U.S. currency eroded the value of oil producers' exports, the oil cartel was forced to lift prices from less than $2 per barrel in 1971 to $13 per barrel in 1974. These dynamics rebalanced the price relationship between oil and gold, sending the gold/oil ratio to 34.0 in 1973, more than tripling its value from the preceding two years. But as soaring U.S. inflation, prolonged dollar declines, and escalating geopolitical tensions boosted the price of gold, the gold/oil equation was subsequently rebalanced and the gold/oil ratio brought down toward a historic monthly average of 15.0.

Measuring the price of oil against gold offers a valuable perspective on the true value of these commodities as it provides a different and useful alternative to measuring them solely against the currency at which they are normally priced. The overall similarity in the price trend of gold and oil against the U.S. dollar often leaves traders with little indication as to which of the two commands more secular strength and leads the way in commodity dynamics. Just as oil prices are influenced by their own specific fundamentals (supply decisions by OPEC, inventory data, weather, geopolitics, and global growth), gold prices have their own supply and demand factors (production, central bank purchases/sales, inflation, monetary policy, and geopolitics). Figure 6.9 demonstrates that the relationship between gold and oil since 1972 has remained generally robust. The monthly correlation stood at a robust 78 percent between 1972 and 2007.

But more can be gleaned from the close relationship between gold and oil. Since 1972, prolonged declines in the gold/oil ratio have proven to be a drag on the U.S. economy, causing recession in the majority of cases. The rationale of such causality postulates that oil prices have increased sufficiently relative to gold to the extent of slowing world oil demand and impacting global growth. Thus, in many cases, both gold and oil may be on the rise, but figuring out the pace of increase of one relative to the other is essential in determining the possible implications to economic growth.

During economic expansions, rising demand for industrial metals and energy boosts both oil and gold prices, which leads to a rising or steady gold/oil ratio. But in cases where substantial advances in oil are the result of supply factors (political risk, wars, acts of God, labor union action,

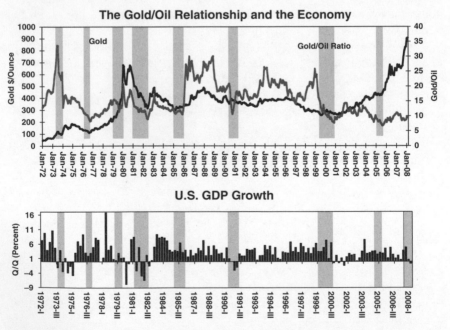

FIGURE 6.9 In addition to high monthly correlation between gold and oil, bottoms in the gold/oil ratio have predicted economic downturns.

OPEC action/rhetoric, refinery shutdowns, and falling inventories), oil prices tend to chart significant advances, clearly outpacing any gains in gold in relative terms and ultimately thereby weighing on the gold/oil ratio. We will see such examples later in the next section.

Ever since the dollar-gold convertibility was suspended in 1973, each of the last five U.S. recessions was preceded by 20 to 30 percent declines in the gold/oil ratio from its recent highs. Although the financial media usually defines a recession as a period of two consecutive quarterly declines in GDP growth, the U.S. National Bureau of Economic Research (NBER) maintains its definition of recession as a "significant decline in economic activity." The NBER uses indicators such as employment, industrial production, real income, and retail and wholesale sales. Thus, although the recession of 2001–2002 did not qualify under the definition of back-to-back quarters of negative GDP growth, it qualified under the NBER's definition because GDP growth declined in three out of five quarters.

1973–1975 Recession

As the dollar prolonged its decline in the aftermath of the 1973 breakdown of the dollar-gold convertibility, oil prices increased fourfold to nearly $12 per barrel in 1974, triggering sharp run-ups in U.S. gasoline prices and a subsequent halt in consumer demand. Gold also pushed higher during the same period, gaining about 15 percent. But the faster appreciation in the fuel dragged down the gold/oil ratio from a high of 34.0 in July 1973 to 23.2 in October of the same year, before extending its fall to12.2 in January 1974. By 1974–1975, the U.S. economy as well as the major industrialized economies had fallen into recession.

The 1973–1975 recession was followed by a period of economic recovery lasting from second quarter 1975 to first quarter 1976 and prevailing over a fall in gold and oil prices. Throughout, the gold/oil ratio dropped from 16.2 to 11.0 as gold fell to a two-year low, losing 20 percent while oil remained steady at around $11 per barrel. Although no recession ensued, growth slowed by more than threefold during the second half of 1976.

1980–1982 Recession

A tumbling dollar and record oil prices were the main culprits in the 1980–1982 recession. The gold/oil ratio dropped from 15.3 in January 1979 to 11.4 in August 1979 due to a doubling in oil to $29 per barrel and a more modest 30 percent increase in gold. The 1977–1979 dollar crisis was already forcing OPEC to hike prices in order to offset the eroding value of its oil revenues. But an increasingly unstable political environment in Iran was endangering the fate of oil supplies; thus ensued a 200 percent increase in oil prices between 1979 and 1980, giving rise to the second oil shock within less than 10 years.

Note the temporary spike in the gold/oil ratio from 12.5 in autumn 1979 to 21.0 in winter 1980 due to a $400 jump in gold from September 1979 to January 1980, resulting from the Soviet Union's invasion of Afghanistan. The invasion struck a turn to the worse in the Cold War between the United States and the Soviet Union, triggering an exodus into the safety of gold. Oil prices, meanwhile, had posted a more modest 33 percent increase to $38 per barrel than did the invasion-fueled oil, pushing the ratio higher.

But the gold/oil ratio fell once again from early 1981 to mid-1982 as oil remained around the mid $30s per ounce level while gold plummeted from the $830s territory to $400 over the same period as the price impact of the Soviet-Afghan war began to wane. In summer 1981, the gold/oil ratio dipped to a four-year low of 11.4 amid plummeting gold and stable oil, while interest rates stood at a postwar high of 19 percent, resulting from Paul Volcker's war on inflation. Rates eventually peaked at 20 percent in October 1981 before plummeting to 12 percent in January 1982. The ratio would later reach a fresh five-year low of 9.0 in summer 1982, in line with the deepening 1981 recession which extended into mid-1982. After the initial declines of the gold/oil ratio between the second and third quarters of 1979, their renewed tumble in 1980 and 1981 reflected the pullback in gold and industrial metals relative to high energy prices, thus correctly foretelling the second leg of the 1980s recession.

1985–1986 Slowdown

In autumn 1985, the gold/oil ratio bottomed at 10.6 after declining from a 16.9 high in February 1983 in the midst of relative stability in both the metal and the fuel, coinciding with a peaking Fed funds rate of 8 percent. The dollar was in the midst of a 10 percent correction, while GDP growth slowed in fourth quarter 1985 before bottoming to a four-year low in the second quarter of 1986. Unlike in the prior cases of falling gold/oil ratios, GDP growth avoided a contraction, partly due to the offsetting positive effects of the 1986 oil price collapse following OPEC's decision to lift production. But the 35 percent decline of the gold/oil ratio over the two-year period proved a successful signal to the 1985–1986 slowdown and the resulting Fed rate cuts during February through July 1986. The war, the slowdown, and the rate cuts prolonged an already falling U.S. dollar, which was initiated by the joint interventions between the United States and major industrialized countries.

1990–1991 Recession

Upon Iraq's fateful invasion of Kuwait on August 2, 1990, oil prices surged from less than $21 per barrel to $31 per barrel in less than two weeks, before extending to a record $40 per barrel in October. The oil price jump dragged the gold/oil ratio by 50 percent to a five-year low of 10.6 in less than three months. That autumn, the Fed accelerated its interest rate cutting campaign, slashing rates from 8 percent in August to 7.25 percent in December before pushing them down to 3 percent into autumn 1992. The recession started in fall 1990 and continued until the end of the first quarter of 1991. The currency impact was largely negative for the dollar in the eight weeks following the invasion, as escalating oil prices hampered a U.S. economy already reeling from the banking failures of the savings and loans crisis of the late 1980s. Soaring oil prices of summer 1990 exacerbated the slowdown and pushed the economy into recession from third quarter 1990 to second quarter 1991.

2001–2002 Recession

In December 1998, oil prices plummeted due to OPEC's decision to increase supplies, combined with the break of Asian oil demand in the midst of the 1997–2008 market crisis. OPEC's miscalculation cut oil prices by more than half to $11.00 per barrel in December 1998, their lowest since the glut of 1986. The combination of cheap oil and rising investment spending fed into a powerful rally in asset prices (stocks and real estate), thus resurrecting global appetite for the fuel throughout 1999 and 2000. Oil prices more than doubled in 1999, breaching $28 per barrel before extending past the $37 mark in 2000, the highest since Iraq's invasion of Kuwait 10 years earlier.

But the effect of higher oil and rising interest rates from second quarter 1999 to second quarter 2000 transitioned from that of an economic cooling to a prolonged stock market sell-off lasting three long years. The 10-year economic expansion was declared officially over in March 2001 by the National Bureau of Economic Research. The Fed began its easing campaign in January 2001 and was forced to reduce rates from 6.5 percent to 1 percent in June 2003. The ensuing recession and broadening bear market was predicted by many market strategists, analysts, and reporters. From a commodity standpoint, the sharp decline in the gold/oil ratio from a four-year high of 26.0 in 1998 to a nine-year low of 11.1 in 1999 served as an effective signal for the ensuing recession, almost 10 years to the month from the 1991 recession.

Despite the recession of 2001–2002 and the prolonged bear market in equities, the dollar maintained a predominantly strong run, with the exception of a relatively brief retreat from late November 2000 to mid-January 2001. The dollar index had fallen more than 8 percent as markets anticipated a looming rate cut. But the dollar decline proved limited as traders rewarded the currency due to the Federal Reserve's aggressive easing, which was seen as a means for the U.S. economy to lead the world economy into recovery mode.

2007–2008 Slowdown: Recession?

After the outbreak of the second Iraq war in March 2003, oil prices began their multiyear bull market, rising from $30 per barrel in March to over $50 per barrel in March 2005. Oil ended that year at $61 per barrel, up more than 100 percent over the prior two years, compared to a 54 percent increase for gold over the same period. The price moves dragged the gold/oil ratio to 6.7 in August 2005, its lowest level over the past 35-year history. The global economic expansion had broadened into emerging markets, and China had displaced Japan as the world's biggest oil consumer behind the United States. China's demand was also notable in heavy industry commodities, especially in copper and gold.

As the gold/oil ratio fell nearly 50 percent, the negative implications of its decline began to surface in the U.S. economy. By the time more stable oil prices and faster gold appreciation in first quarter 2006 lifted the ratio off its lows above the 10.0 level, U.S. GDP growth fell from 4.8 percent that quarter to 2.4 percent, 1.1 percent, and 0.6 percent for the following three quarters of the year. The S&P 500 lost more than 7 percent between May and June and the USD Index shed 8 percent between March and May. Reduced risk appetite in global equity markets led investors to seek safety in the low-yielding yen and Swiss franc. Although the 2005 decline of the gold/oil ratio was not followed by a recession or Fed rate cuts in 2006, the U.S. central bank did halt its three-year-long tightening campaign in June 2006 due to the broadening housing slowdown. It took another year for a reluctant Federal Reserve to finally cut interest rates and push aside its much-touted inflationary risks.

Just as the yield inversion beginning in January 2006 correctly signaled the ensuing decline in the U.S. economy, the 2006 decline of the dollar, and the 2007 rate cuts, so did the slide of the gold/oil ratio in 2005. After a brief rebound in 2007, the gold/oil ratio tumbled anew in July of 2008, dipping to a new all-time low of 6.5. By then, the signal of an economic slowdown in the U.S. and the rest of the world proved too clear.

CONCLUSION

The most cogent conclusion to be drawn from the preceding dynamics is that a bottoming in the gold/oil ratio has most often accompanied a peak in short-term interest rates, which was later followed by interest rate cuts.

The other prominent aspect of the relationship is the subsequent growth slowdown. Recessions were triggered in four out of the five cases, with the exception of case 3 (fourth quarter 1985) due to the positive growth implications of the 1986 oil price collapse.

Rather than simply focus on the price of oil and gold separately, investors ought to follow the interaction of these two important commodities. Such interaction is more appropriately measured by the gold/oil ratio rather than, say, comparing the percentage increase of both. In the case of interest rates, the yield curve indicator continues to exhibit a convincingly strong effectiveness in signaling economic downturns and rebounds via curve inversions and steepening.

The tremendous multiplicity of market- and economic-related materials inundating investors has generally helped them improve their grasp of the main drivers of financial markets as well as the functioning of basic macroeconomic relationships. But with Federal Reserve policy makers often echoing the long-term policy preferences of the central bank rather than signaling the future outlook for the economy, investors are left with little direction. The increased tendency for divergence between equities and the economy has also challenged the understanding of prevailing and future developments. Integrating the analysis of short- and long-term interest rates into relative trends of commodities offers a forward-looking view into the trend of interest rates, economic growth, and equities to the extent of reading important shifts in central bank policy.

CHAPTER 7

U.S. Imbalances, FX Reserve Diversification, and the U.S. Dollar

O ver the past 10 years or so, it has become impossible to discuss the present or future value of the U.S. dollar without addressing the deficits in the U.S. current account, trade, and budget balances. Each of these items represents part of what is known as the structural imbalances implanted in the world's biggest economy and the world's reserve currency. Until the new millennium, these imbalances filled the editorials of financial and mainstream media and dominated the conversation among investors, economists, and politicians, yet failed to derail the U.S. dollar from its position as the world's top reserve and invoicing currency. In 2006–2007, however, the U.S. deficits began shifting from a mere set of economic statistics to a gradually threatening dynamic to the U.S. economy.

The progression of these imbalances has given rise to two opposing schools of economic thought. One postulates that the U.S. deficits have been around for most of the past 30 years and that foreign investors will continue to show faith in the strength of the U.S. economy and its financial markets by financing these imbalances. The other school of thought warns that foreign investors could soon stop financing these deficits, thus triggering a shortage of capital flows, a jump in interest rates, a plunge in the dollar, and ultimately a severe and prolonged recession.

The more optimistic view proved its validity between 2003 and 2005 when the U.S. economy appeared to stage a solid recovery despite the twin deficits having reached a combined record 9 percent of GDP. But the unfolding developments of the US economy in 2007–2008 and the resulting deterioration in the value of the dollar have significantly impaired the overriding assumption behind this view that foreigners will maintain their zeal for U.S. assets, regardless of the strength in economic growth and the value of the currency. The spreading of the U.S. housing crisis and credit market turmoil into a full-blown recession has forced the Federal Reserve to slash interest rates at unprecedented speed, corroding the dollar's interest rate advantage relative to the world's major currencies. The dollar's 85 percent and 30 percent declines against the euro and the yen from its 2002 peak to early 2008 have rendered the current slide the biggest uninterrupted loss of value in the currency since it became freely floated in 1971.

This chapter demonstrates how the evolving trends in global economic growth and the secular bear market in the dollar could reshape the makeup of U.S.-bound capital flows and reshape the foreign financing of U.S. imbalances. The impact of such developments on the U.S. dollar and overall global currency reserve composition could be significant, especially as the rally in commodities continues to unfold at the expense of the greenback, and the euro accumulates further credibility in global markets.

THE U.S. TWIN DEFICITS

Since 1980, the U.S. economy bore witness to a highly visible set of economic imbalances, namely the current account and budget deficits. The former is a reflection of increased U.S. spending on foreign products and services and the latter a result of excessive federal spending relative to tax revenues.

To better understand the current account balance, one must grasp the concept of the balance of payments, which is an account of a nation's transactions with the rest of the world. The balance of payments records a nations' spending and receipts of all types of flows and transactions. These transactions are divided into three major categories: the current account, the financial account, and the capital account. An account called net errors and omissions is used to attain the final balance.

The current account has three main subcomponents:

1. Trade balance between imports and exports of goods and services—often referred to as the trade balance.

2. Income payments from inbound and outbound investments, including net income from paid and earned interest on domestic and foreign financial assets as well as net income from foreign direct investment.

3. Net unilateral transfers of money flows, which do not involve a counterclaim, such as gifts and grants.

Due to the large component of the international trade balance in the current account, both balances are often used interchangeably by the public when referring to the trade gap. Since 1995, the exports-imports balance has accounted for about 90 percent of the overall current account.

Figure 7.1 compares the U.S. current account deficit as a percentage of the world GDP to that in the Eurozone, Japan, emerging Asia (EmAsia), and oil-exporting nations. Aside from the United States, only the Eurozone has a modest current account deficit. The rest of these nations enjoy substantial surpluses due to substantial exports revenue (in the case of oil-producing nations and emerging Asia) and due to relatively higher savings (in the case of emerging Asia and Japan).

The financial account measures a nation's investment position, balancing all transactions between domestic and foreign residents involving a change of ownership of assets. It is the net result of private and public international investment flowing in and out of the country, including foreign direct investment (ownership of lasting interest in companies, such as at least 10 percent of total capital), portfolio investment (minority ownership of stocks or bonds), and other investments. A positive investment position means a nation is a net creditor, while a negative position means the nation is a net debtor. The financial account is discussed further in the next section.

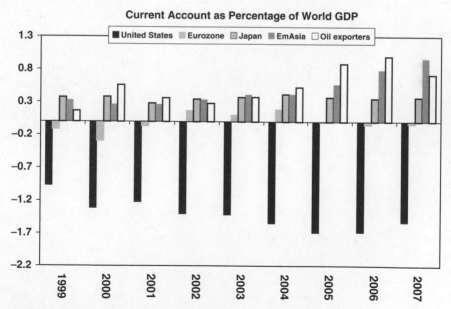

FIGURE 7.1 High current account deficit nations are characterized by lower savings and higher interest rates.

Figure 7.2 compares the U.S. international position as a percentage of the world GDP to that of the Eurozone, Japan, emerging Asia, and oil-exporting nations. Both the United States and Eurozone are net debtors as they attract substantial global capital flows into their equity and capital markets. By contrast, Japan is the biggest net lender to the world as Japanese investors are major providers of capital to world financial markets. The yen carry trade has played a vital role in channeling capital from Japan to global markets in search of yield, with 15 trillion yen in Japanese funds estimated to be used overseas. Due to the surge in oil prices since 2002, net foreign assets in oil-producing nations have more than doubled, propelling them to a close second behind Japan.

The capital account measures the international payments and change of ownership of capital goods, such as factories, equipment, property, and other tangible assets.

A nation's fiscal balance must also be taken into consideration as a catalyst to the current account. As Federal spending and borrowing exceed receipts and tax revenues, an expanding budget deficit must theoretically be financed by increased domestic saving via investors' purchases of government treasuries, or be met by borrowing from abroad through the sale of U.S. treasuries to foreign investors. Notably, the latter case has

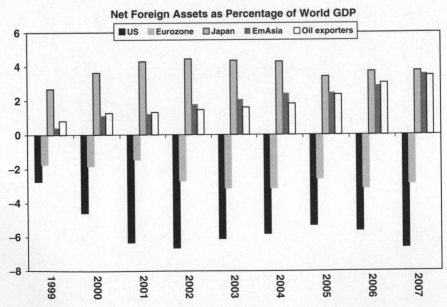

FIGURE 7.2 Trade deficit countries are net debtors, as borrowed capital makes up for their trade gap.

accounted for the bulk of the financing of the budget deficit. Since these flows are considered international investments, they are recorded in the financial account of the balance of payments. Thus, while a rising budget deficit increases the financial account surplus, it also helps to offset the increase in the current account deficit component of the balance of payments. A higher financial account increases the value of the dollar.

U.S. CURRENT ACCOUNT DEFICIT: OLD PROBLEM, NEW CHALLENGES

International economics theory states that depreciating currencies reduce current account deficits as they make exports cheaper to the rest of the world while weighing on import demand via rising prices. Conversely, prolonged periods of dollar strength led to an escalation in the current account deficit. For the U.S. dollar, this relationship has worked with varying time lags.

Figure 7.3 shows that out of the five major directional cycles in the dollar index since 1971, four cycles managed to make a difference in the current account. The 83 percent rise in the dollar between 1980 and 1984 dragged the current account balance from a surplus in 1981 to a deficit in

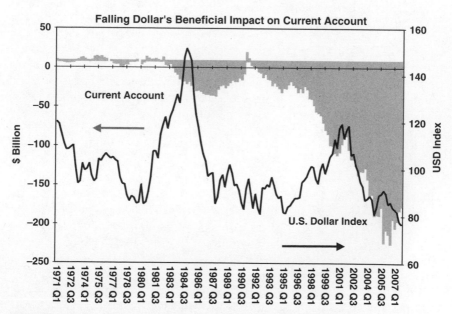

FIGURE 7.3 Is the falling dollar finally reducing the current account deficit?

1982, which then posted six consecutive annual increases. The 47 percent decline in the dollar between 1985 and 1994 reduced the current account deficit for 4 consecutive years between 1988 and 1991 before producing the first surplus in 10 years. The 47 percent increase in the dollar between 1995 and 2001 coincided with the longest increase in the current account deficit, which quadrupled to $46 billion from $11 billion or, to 4.8 percent of GDP from 1.5 percent of GDP. The rapid run-up in the trade deficit of the late 1990s was not all about the strong dollar, but also a fast-spending U.S. consumer bolstered by an expanding wealth effect from an eight-year economic expansion of soaring equities and housing prices.

As for the current dollar bear market, which is in its seventh year and losing 48 percent since its 2002 high, it is finally starting to stabilize the widening trade gap and the current account deficit. After peaking in third quarter 2006, the trade deficit fell 14 percent between August 2006 and December 2007, the biggest decline in any six-quarter period since the 2001 recession. While the impact of the current recession has played an important role in curtailing U.S. imports, it is the role of the depreciating dollar that helped bring about an improvement in the trade deficit. During the two years ending in December 2007, U.S. exports had only three declining months, while imports had a period of eight declining months. Again, slowing U.S. economic growth and more robust economies in Europe and Asia were effective in these U.S. trade developments, but the 18 percent decline in the value of the dollar was paramount in increasing the affordability of U.S. exports to the rest of the world.

While much has been discussed about the currency's influence on the trade and current account balances, relatively little emphasis has been given to the role of economic growth as a driver of these balances. As imports outpace exports and the trade gap deteriorates, the negative trade is reflected in overall growth, dampening the final calculation of GDP. But the causality also works in reverse. As economic growth falters, consumer demand weakens and import growth slows.

Figure 7.4 illustrates the relationship between the current account balance, budget balance, and interest rates since 1980. Both accounts are measured as a percentage of GDP. We note that both imbalances evolved largely in synch, with the exception of 1992–2002, when the Clinton administration's fiscal policies eliminated the budget deficit via higher taxes and lower spending, despite a rising trade deficit. The inclusion of the interest rate graphs for the Fed funds rate and the 10-year yield is aimed at showing the state of the economy as seen through monetary policy. Note how the declines in the current account deficit have coincided with periods of falling interest rates as slowing growth prompted a decline in demand for imports. The shift from a current account deficit to a surplus in 1980–1981 and 1991 coincided with the prevailing recessions at the time, hence the

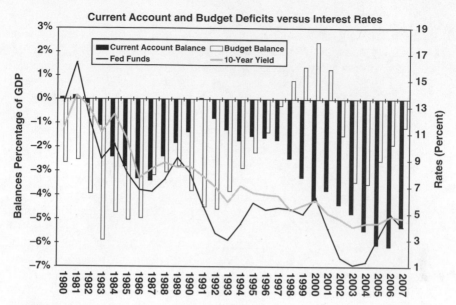

FIGURE 7.4 The positive correlation between U.S. budget and current account imbalances broke during the 1990s as the former went into surplus and the latter surged to record deficits.

periods of bottoming interest rates. In 2007–2008, this relationship is again emerging as the deepening U.S. slowdown had eroded U.S. imports, while the resulting fall in the dollar has boosted exports.

The falling dollar does not come without its disadvantages. As the bear market in the currency intensified between 2003 and 2008, so did the rally in oil prices. With the dollar losing 50 percent against the euro and 20 percent against the yen between 2003 and early 2008, oil producers faced the danger of seeing their dollar-denominated receipts eroded significantly. Whether it was geopolitical developments, weather factors, or simply the general bull market in commodities behind the oil rally, oil producers largely welcomed rising oil as a compensation for the corroding value of the dollar, especially those whose imports are largely non-USD-based. As long as U.S. dependence on foreign oil shows no retreat, rising oil prices will continue to boost the overall cost of imports, diluting the benefits on exports from a falling dollar. Figure 7.5 shows how the U.S. current account deficit carved out a bottom in late 2006, while petroleum imports' share of total imports has remained on the rise, pushing to more than 17 percent in early 2008, from 6 percent in 2002.

Such is the reality of the oil-dollar relationship. A simultaneous decrease in the dollar and increase in oil has prevailed since the start of the

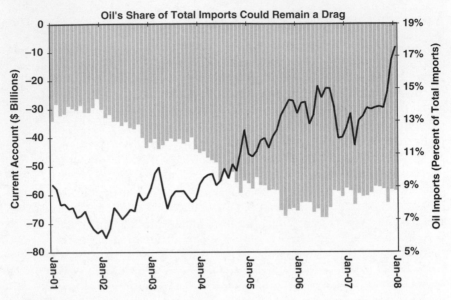

FIGURE 7.5 Rising share of U.S. oil imports as a percentage of total imports is the downside to weak dollar on trade gap.

dollar bear market in 2002. The only recent exception was in 2005, when a temporary dollar rebound emerged alongside high oil prices due to accelerating oil demand from China. That scenario represented the worst of both worlds for the United States, as a rising dollar weighed on U.S. exports and higher oil pushed up imports. Conversely, the combination of falling oil and the dollar would be an optimally beneficial development for the U.S. trade balance. But such an occurrence has proven extremely rare and short-lived over the past 30 years.

While the current account deficit has been around since 1981, fading and reemerging in the financial fabric of the U.S. economy, its presence will take on new meaning in the evolving global marketplace. Subsequent sections in this chapter will show that the U.S. financial markets are no longer the gold standard for global investors, just as the U.S. dollar is no longer unfettered in world currency markets. The current account deficit may have been around for nearly three decades, but its reaction to the shifting global market and economic challenges is already giving rise to reverberations not seen in at least six decades. Currencies are overshooting to record highs, commodities stretching to soaring heights at lightning speed, and developing economies reaping a bigger share of the world's capital movements. Before moving on to the state of the financing of the current account deficit, let's shed light on the domestic imbalance: the budget deficit.

ADDING THE BUDGET BALANCE TO THE MIX

Although the correlation between current account deficit and the dollar has been predominantly negative, no definitive conclusion may be reached about the relationship between the budget deficits and the greenback. The theory postulating that growing budget deficits push up interest rates has had a mixed record in the real world.

In the late 1990s, Democrats claimed credit for achieving budget surplus for the first time in three decades, but the resulting decline in interest rates remained debatable. Interest rates eased in the late 1990s before recovering due to strengthening economic growth and rising inflationary pressures. Republicans have attributed the disappearance of the surplus to mounting spending related to Homeland Security and the wars in Afghanistan and Iraq. The resulting erosion in the fiscal balance from a surplus of 1.3 percent of GDP in 2001 to a deficit of 3.5 percent of GDP in 2004 failed to drive up long-term interest rates. Escalating foreign purchases of U.S. treasuries in 2002–2006 were instrumental in boosting bond prices and dragging down their yields. But when these flows diminished in 2007, long-term interest rates remained pressured by traders' expectations of an economic downturn.

While the correlation between the current account balance and the dollar has been considerably positive, the relationship between the budget balance and the currency is negligible. Some economists have postulated a direct relationship between budget deficits and the dollar on the rationale that swelling budget imbalances have fueled up interest rates, causing the dollar to gain on higher yields. But the empirical evidence is inconclusive. Figure 7.6 shows no lasting correlation over the past 37 years. In 1970–1976, a positive correlation between the deteriorating budget deficit and the falling dollar emerged, before the relationship broke down in the remainder of the decade when a reduction in the deficit was accompanied by continued dollar declines.

The correlation turned negative in the first half of the 1980s when double-digit interest rates increased the dollar's yield foundation, propelled borrowing costs, and lifted the deficit to a record 5.9 percent of GDP. The relationship remained negative in the second half of the 1980s when the budget balance and the dollar reversed course. A falling deficit prevailed alongside a tumbling dollar after major economies intervened to reverse the soaring dollar. Between 1992 and 2002, the substantial transition from budget deficit to surplus emerged alongside a strengthening dollar rally as the technology equity boom combined with higher taxes sent federal finances into the black. The low inflation growth pushed

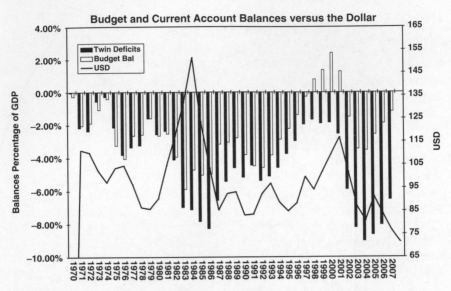

FIGURE 7.6 Fiscal balance and USD relationship has proven mixed.

the dollar to its highest level in 15 years. The correlation remained positive after 2002 when the dollar entered a seven-year bear market and the Bush tax cuts as well as rising budget spending produced swelling deficits.

FINANCING THE DEFICITS: THE PATH TO UNSUSTAINABILITY?

As was mentioned earlier, a nation's balance payment includes three major components: the current account, the financial account, and the capital account. The current account deficit means the United States is a net consumer of goods and services, and the financial account surplus shows the United States to be a net seller of assets such as stocks, bonds, and equity stakes in companies. While in the previous section we examined the current account, this section tackles the financial account and its position vis-à-vis the current account as well as the implications for the dollar and the U.S. economy.

Figure 7.7 shows the United States' financial account, illustrating a net external debt of more than $2.5 trillion in 2007. This is represented by the excess of foreign-owned assets in the United States over U.S.-owned assets abroad, as seen by the dotted line. This figure fell below zero in

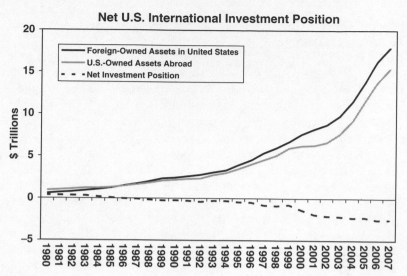

FIGURE 7.7 U.S.-bound foreign purchases of stocks and bonds key to U.S. debtor position.

1986, rendering the United States a net debtor, receiving more in capital flows than it is sending out. Soaring foreign purchases of U.S. stocks and bonds in the mid-1980s, in contrast to negligible interest by U.S. residents abroad, were instrumental in swaying the net investment balance into the red.

Net foreign inflows are therefore positive because they help finance the current account deficit, but they also render the United States dependent on foreign capital, making it a net borrower from the rest of the world. The main question to be raised later in this chapter is whether the United States will continue to draw sufficient capital in order to finance its current account deficit. Asked differently, will the rest of the world continue to be willing to lend to the United States through buying its assets, considering the challenges facing the economy, its currency, and the expanding investment alternatives in other world markets?

With over $2.5 trillion in net borrowed assets, the United States has had no difficulty in attracting the required capital to finance its budget and trade deficits which, combined, have risen to nearly $900 billion. But with the U.S. Treasury estimating that the budget deficit will nearly triple to $500 billion in 2009 from its 2007 level, the necessary inflows from abroad will need to pick up in pace. The next section examines the key components of these flows and how their recent evolution tells us something about the future trend.

DISSECTING U.S.-BOUND FOREIGN CAPITAL FLOWS

When tracking foreign flows in any country it is important to distinguish between flows and gross positions. The former reflects interperiodic analysis and the latter reflects gross amounts held in a given year or month. As mentioned earlier, the United States is a net borrower of over $2.5 trillion in assets, reflecting the excess of foreign-owned assets in the United States (more than $17 trillion in 2007) over assets held abroad by U.S. residents (about $15 trillion in 2007). One way to better gauge the progress of the flows is to track the change of the net financial position stemming only from the increase/decrease in investment flows, rather than changes such as prices, capital gains, and exchange rates of assets. These investment flows include both portfolio and direct investments.

Figure 7.8 shows the annual difference between foreign-owned assets in the United States and U.S.-owned assets abroad. The decrease in 2007 to $657 billion from $804 billion means that the excess of foreign-owned assets in the United States over U.S.-owned assets abroad has fallen by $147 billion, or 18 percent in 2007. While the decline means a reduction in net capital inflows into the United States, it also suggests a reduction in net foreign debt. Such a decline may reflect a reduction in net foreign purchases of U.S. securities, or of U.S. company ownership, or an increase

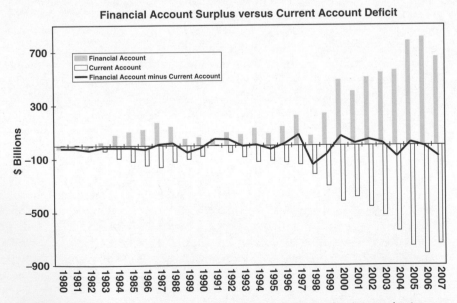

FIGURE 7.8 A slowing U.S. current account deficit translates into slowing net foreign purchases of U.S. financial assets.

in net purchases of foreign assets by U.S. residential investors. We will see later how U.S. interest in foreign investments is increasingly playing an important role in determining net international capital flows.

It is also worth noting the currency element in gauging these net financial inflows. Holding other factors constant, such as equity prices and the economy, the value of the dollar has played a key role in determining foreign flows into U.S. assets. Figure 7.9 shows that the sharp increase in net foreign holdings in 1999 and 2000 may have been partly fueled by the dollar's climb to 15-year highs. It is more plausible that substantial foreign inflows into U.S. assets, such as the 1999–2000 tech bubble, were a cause of dollar strength, rather than an effect of it. But as the dollar began its prolonged decline in 2002, 2003, and 2004, net foreign holdings formed a plateau, before lifting 40 percent in 2005 on a one-time dollar rally that year. As the greenback resumed its decline in 2006 and 2007, net inflows again peaked out before heading lower.

U.S. STOCKS AND BONDS VIE FOR FOREIGN MONEY

This section examines foreign inflows into the United States, breaking them down by asset class. According to the data on net foreign capital

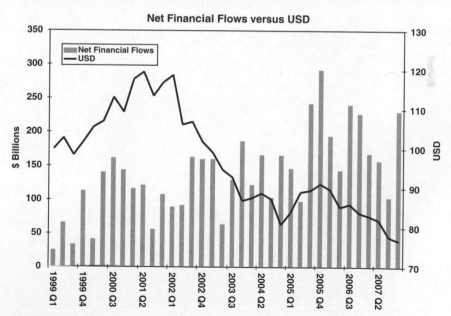

FIGURE 7.9 Foreign capital flows were a key component to the dollar's 1990s rally.

flows from the U.S. Treasury Information Capital System (TICS), the flows of 2005–2007 have shown an emerging pattern that could spell trouble ahead for the financing of the swelling budget deficit and the trade gap. Figure 7.10 shows net foreign inflows into U.S. securities since 1989, breaking down the purchases by three asset classes: bonds issued by the U.S. Treasury and government-sponsored agencies (such as Fannie Mae and Freddie Mac), corporate bonds, and corporate stocks. The analysis applies only to portfolio flows and excludes foreign direct investment stakes.

Figure 7.10 illustrates that U.S. equities were the only asset class to have amassed an increase in net foreign buying in 2005, 2006, and 2007. This asset shift by foreign investors can easily be explained by the global market recovery of 2005–2006, which led to record high equities in 2007. The question becomes whether a prolonged bear market in global stocks will keep foreign investors on the sidelines in general, and out of U.S. markets in particular, considering the broadening slowdown across all segments of the U.S. economy.

In contrast, net foreign purchases of agency and Treasury securities fell 4 percent, 14 percent, and 11 percent in 2005, 2006, and 2007 respectively, while net purchases of U.S. Treasuries alone fell 4 percent and 42 percent in 2005 and 2006, before rising a mere 3 percent in 2007. These

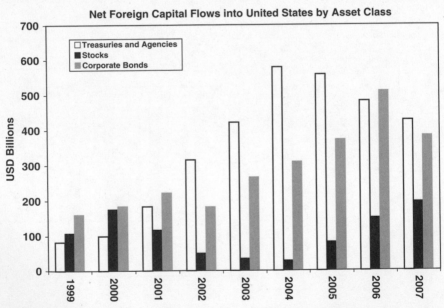

FIGURE 7.10 U.S. equities were the only asset class receiving increasing foreign purchases since 2004.

growth rates are a far cry from the 548 percent and 121 percent increase seen in 2002 and 2003. Considering the crisis in home mortgages and the downside pressure sustained by these debt-dependent agencies, foreign investors may continue to shun these going forward into 2008 and 2009.

The 2007 decline in net flows going into corporate bonds was the first since 2002. With credit spreads widening as a reflection of an increasingly challenging macroeconomic environment and heightened pressure on credit rating agencies to make up for the tens of billions in defaults, interest in corporate debt will lose the zest of the 2003–2005 period. And if the underlying credit crisis expands into corporate balance sheets and/or the appetite for deal making continues to dry up, then foreigners will continue to shy away from the corporate debt market, which took 60 percent of total foreign net inflows in 2006.

Figure 7.11 shows the changing trend of each asset class as a share of total net inflows into U.S. securities. Treasuries sustained the most volatility, drawing a negative share of total flows in 1999 and 2000 as foreigners were net sellers of government debt, shifting toward the bull market in equities. A recovery in Treasuries purchases was under way during 2002–2004 as bond prices rallied following the Federal Reserve's interest rate cuts, which took down the Fed funds rate to a four-decade low of 1 percent in 2003. But Treasuries once again lost favor among foreigners in 2005, 2006,

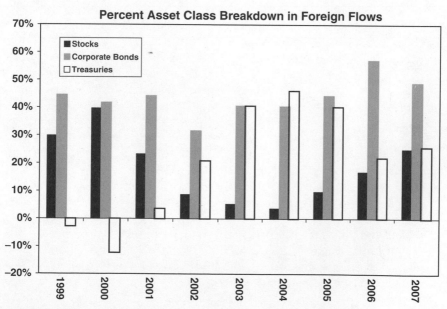

FIGURE 7.11 Decline in foreign purchases of U.S. Treasuries and corporate bonds has partially shifted to U.S. stocks.

and 2007, dropping to less than 30 percent of total net inflows from over 45 percent in 2004, amounting to a $151 drop in flows in three years. In the current Fed cycle, U.S. Treasuries face the possibility of a similar rebound demand to that of the 2001–2004 easing period, but the current erosion of the U.S. dollar and the search for yield in today's volatile equity and capital markets may lead to a wider aversion to holding U.S. dollar-denominated fixed-income securities, especially given falling yields.

The share of U.S. equities as a percentage of total net foreign purchases rose from 4 percent in 2004 to 25 percent in 2007. But such interest among foreign investors risks encountering the same fate as in 2001–2003, when the burst of the stock market bubble dragged the equity share of net foreign purchases from 40 percent in 2000 to 4 percent in 2004, a net loss of $147 billion from U.S. markets. The emergence of commodity-rich sovereign wealth funds in the Middle East and East Asia is widely expected by several analysts to act as a partial buffer against protracted declines in U.S. and other equity markets as these funds aim to snap up stakes in fundamentally healthy banks and companies at attractive valuations. But the concept of "dumb money" has also emerged as these funds seek to buy beaten-down companies largely due to the lower price element, disregarding the negative conditions surrounding the company, the industry, and the economy. Substantial losses in multibillion-dollar stakes in U.S. banks and private equity concerns have already been incurred by sovereign wealth funds in the Middle East and China.

Considering the increasing role of U.S. equities in attracting more than $160 billion in net foreign purchases between 2005 and 2007, the outflows may be at least just as great as those inflows as we approach the latter third of the decade, due to ongoing global portfolio reallocation into emerging markets. These shifts of capital aim at profit from the global boom in commodities. Assets in emerging market funds have doubled to $800 billion in 2007.[1] Global investors have also started to retain their money in safe money market funds to shield against systemic risk in global markets.

More ominously, with U.S. stock indices down having fallen more than 20 percent in summer 2008 from their 2007 highs, any added losses in U.S. stocks could jeopardize foreign demand into U.S. securities. The importance of U.S. equities is underlined by the fact that they were the only asset class to have consistently drawn increasing net flows from abroad between 2005 and 2007, providing 25 percent of total net flows in 2007. Their importance is also highlighted following the credit troubles surrounding mortgage lenders Fannie Mae and Freddie Mac, whose bonds fall under the Government Sponsored Enterprise category of U.S. assets. Foreign purchases

---

[1]*Source:* Emerging Market Portfolio Funds Research.

of GSE debt fell from 44 percent of total net inflows in 2006 to 35 percent in 2007. Foreigners are expected to further scale down their purchases of GSE securities following the losses at Fannie and Freddie. But to what extent will they fill the void by moving to equities remains a key question.

CAPITAL FLOWS SHIFT IDENTITIES

In order to better gauge the future sustainability of U.S. external debt financing, it is as essential to determine the origin of this financing as it is to break down the destination by asset class. The previous section showed that U.S. equities had received a growing share of foreign capital during 2003–2007 as government and corporate bonds began to ease off. But since net foreign inflows into Treasuries and agency securities have accounted for an annual average of 62 percent of total net purchases between 2003 and 2007, their role remains paramount.

Figure 7.12 charts the gross foreign holdings of U.S. Treasury securities (bills, notes, and bonds) as a share of total U.S. public government debt. In the fiscal year ending September 2007, total public debt reached $5.1 trillion, 44 percent of which was held by foreign gross holdings of U.S. government securities. In a matter of six years, the foreign share of total

FIGURE 7.12 Foreign ownership of U.S. public debt remains on the rise.

public debt rose by more than 50 percent, with emerging Asia accounting for the lion's share of that increase.

The top holders of U.S. treasuries continue to be Japan, China, and the United Kingdom at $581 billion, $478 billion, and $157.4 billion respectively, as of December 2007. When including Hong Kong's Treasury holdings, China's total Treasury stock becomes $548 billion, further closing the gap behind Japan. A major reason for the United Kingdom's substantial holdings is the custodial role of UK-based banks and asset management funds holding U.S. Treasuries on behalf of private investors and even governments from countries seeking to keep their holdings under the radar. In the case of Japan and China, these two largest holders of Treasuries are undergoing an important evolution in their holdings.

Although Japan remains the largest holder with at $581 billion of Treasuries by end of 2007, its holdings have declined by over 16 percent since their 2005 peak. Figure 7.13 shows the contrasting picture between Japan's shunning of U.S. Treasuries and China's accumulation of these securities. These opposing trends are a reflection of the monetary and currency policies adopted by the People's Bank of China and the Bank of Japan. Ever since the Bank of Japan ceased from intervening in currency markets by

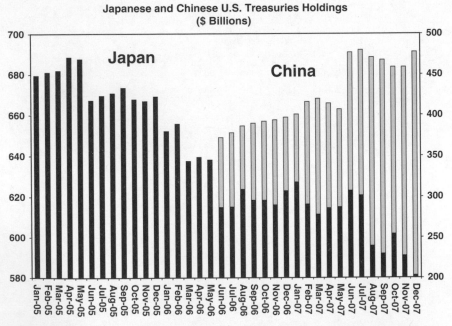

FIGURE 7.13 China's accumulation of U.S. Treasuries may have peaked but Japanese holdings remain on the decline.

buying Treasuries and selling yen to prevent excessive yen strengthening, Japan's holdings of Treasuries have begun to dwindle. Reducing Japan's excessive exposure to an increasingly falling U.S. dollar was also a currency decision. For China, the escalating buildup in U.S. Treasuries stemmed from China's intervention in currency markets to contain excessive yen strength.

FOREIGN DIRECT INVESTMENT AND M&As

The preceding section focused on portfolio investment flows, which involve the ownership of minority stakes in companies, without taking controlling interest or securing a lasting ownership in these assets. The financial account also includes foreign direct investment (FDI), which is the ownership of lasting interest in companies such as more than 10 percent of total capital. Foreign direct investment in the United States can take two forms: (1) *greenfield* investments involving the building of plants and companies; and (2) mergers and acquisitions (M&As) between U.S. and foreign existing businesses. Since the late 1980s, M&As have accounted for nearly 90 percent of all new FDI in the United States.

Figure 7.14 shows that U.S.-owned direct investment abroad exceeded foreign direct investment in the United States by more than $800 billion in

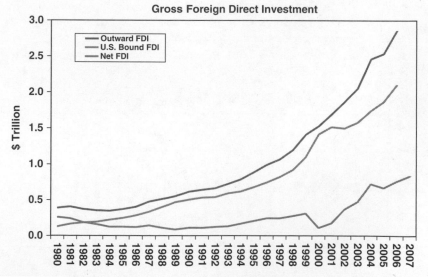

FIGURE 7.14 Outward gross U.S. foreign direct investment continues to exceed inbound investment from abroad.

2007, with U.S. gross investments abroad totaling about $3 trillion or 22 percent of GDP. Since U.S. FDI flowing abroad has consistently exceeded U.S.-bound FDI, the net balance is considered a positive because a net credit is recorded in the financial account of the balance of payments, reducing the overall net external debt.

In order to better discern the changes in foreign direct investment in and out of the United States, the picture must be examined from a flow perspective. Thus, even though gross U.S. FDI outflows continue to outpace inflows, the pace has varied throughout the years. Figure 7.15 illustrates the net FDI flows into the United States, with negative figures in 2006 and 2007 showing the pace of outflows exceeding inflows into the United States. As the dollar drifted near record lows against the euro and 13-year lows against the yen in 2007, its affordability may have further emboldened accelerating investments into U.S. companies. Nonetheless, increased U.S. scrutiny of foreign interest in U.S. assets on the grounds of national security have thwarted U.S.-bound investments by foreign companies. But U.S. scrutiny has quickly turned into urgent need as sovereign wealth funds purchases of U.S. stakes jumped 153 percent to $48.5 billion in 2007 as U.S. banks and finance companies desperately needed fresh capital to help them recover from hundreds of loan write-downs. Aside from the seemingly cheap valuations of these companies, the falling dollar played a major role in spurring these foreign purchases.

The situation already carries reminders of the second half of the 1980s when Japanese investors poured nearly $300 billion into U.S. properties such as the Rockefeller Center, Columbia Pictures, and Pebble Beach Golf Club. A near tripling in Japanese equities and a 50 percent appreciation in the yen against the dollar between 1985 and 1989 were behind those spectacular investment flows. The present situation is characterized not

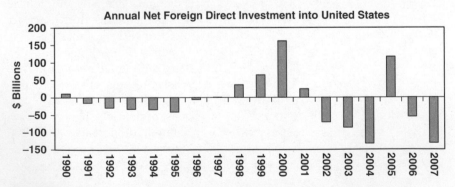

FIGURE 7.15 Net U.S.-bound direct investment falls in the red as increased U.S. scrutiny slowly repelled foreign interest in U.S. companies.

only by a weak dollar but also by a far stronger economic position amid exporters of oil, gas, iron ore, and outperforming commodities.

But a major difference from the 1980s or the 1990s is the multiplicity of investment opportunities beyond the United States and Europe. Oil-rich Gulf states are already earning big dividends from channeling oil wealth into diversifying their economies into global hubs of financial services, high tech, and even entertainment. East Asian economies have used their hard-earned armory of vast currency reserves to further invest mostly at home, but have yet to transform their consumption capacity into a global investment vehicle. Later in this chapter, these emerging markets' holdings of individual U.S. securities are broken down by country.

HOW LONG WILL FOREIGN CAPITAL BE AVAILABLE ON THE CHEAP?

An integral element to the sustainability of the growing U.S. current account deficit has been the cost of financing it. The rate of return on U.S. investors' direct investment abroad has continued to exceed the rate of return on foreigners' direct investment in the United States. This renders the United States a net creditor from a cost-of-capital basis, despite being a net debtor in its overall investment position. In other words, the United States is paid for borrowing from abroad. Interest rates are a major driver of this cost differential. Falling U.S. interest rates reduce interest payments to foreign investors, thereby raising the net interest expense flow in the United States' favor.

Figure 7.16 illustrates that periods of falling U.S. interest rates generally provide a boost to net interest rate income, which is the return received by U.S. investors from foreign investment minus the return to foreign investors from their U.S. investments. Conversely, falling net interest income has prevailed during monetary policy tightening, such as in 1979–1981, 1994–1995, and 2004–2006. The sharp rebound in net income receipts in 2007 was a result of the Fed's aggressive interest rate cuts. Note that total income also includes flows from foreign direct investment.

In addition to having an implicitly lower cost of debt, the United States has the luxury of printing the currency of denomination of its own debt, a rare privilege enjoyed by a country whose gross external debt stands at more than $17 trillion. Thanks to this privilege, which is a result of the currency's world reserve status, the United States seems to face no difficulty in extending its twin deficits. But, as will be seen later on, this assumption is increasingly being challenged.

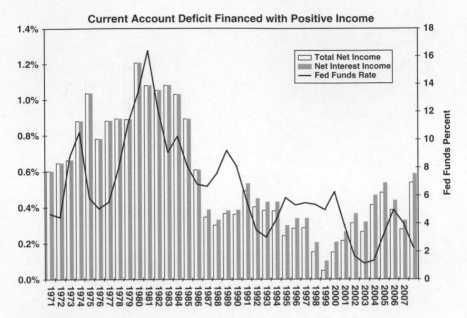

FIGURE 7.16 The United States has been able to finance its current account deficit at lower rates than those received by U.S. investors in foreign investments.

The effective cost of foreign capital is also transmitted via exchange rates. A falling dollar enhances the return received from foreign-currency-denominated assets held by U.S. residents. Thus, periods of dollar weakness caused by Fed easing tend to reduce the effective cost of U.S. debt and improve the net return to U.S. investors.

DON'T IGNORE U.S. INVESTORS' FLOWS ABROAD

While the emphasis of this chapter has largely focused on foreign investment into the United States, attention must also be given to U.S. residents' purchases of foreign assets. Aside from the globalization of investing and the broadening of investment choices made by U.S. fund managers, the falling dollar has also played a role in improving the returns of foreign-currency-denominated assets. The concept of diversification has been effectively preached to individual investors, whether through direct investing or their pension funds. Figure 7.17 shows the increasing monthly net outflows from U.S. investors into foreign stocks and bonds, which reached

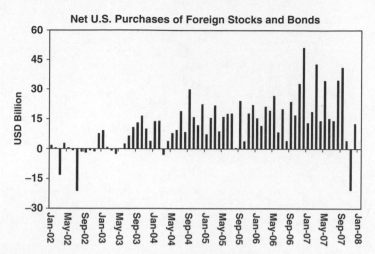

FIGURE 7.17 U.S. investors' net purchases of foreign portfolio assets have exceeded net foreign purchases of U.S. assets since 2003.

a total of $25 billion in net outflows for all of 2006 before stabilizing at $22 billion in 2007. The chart illustrates how the intensification of outflows emerged in 2002–2003, which coincided with the beginning of the dollar decline.

Figure 7.18 breaks down U.S. net purchases of foreign stocks and bonds, illustrating the persistence of outflows in both asset classes as the search of yield reaches out internationally. The climate for international investing has improved markedly from an economic, regulatory, and diversification perspective. Rising commodity prices, improved political stability, and executive accountability have all played a role in ameliorating investor confidence in international assets in both the industrialized and developing world.

The United States' current investment position shows no immediate threat of any sudden discontinuation of foreign capital. Despite $17 trillion in gross external debt, the U.S. continues to attract sufficient foreign capital to finance $2.5 trillion in net foreign debt, or 20 percent of GDP. But given the 17 percent average annual growth in net external borrowing, the balance could reach 30 percent of GDP in less than 10 years. Such a development may be especially threatening considering the 35 percent decline in the dollar, the increasing availability of foreign markets, and the robustness of the euro as a store of value. The single European currency's share of allocated world central bank reserves has risen from 17.9 percent in 1999 to 26.4 percent in 2007, while that of the U.S. dollar has dropped from 71.1 percent to 63.9 percent.

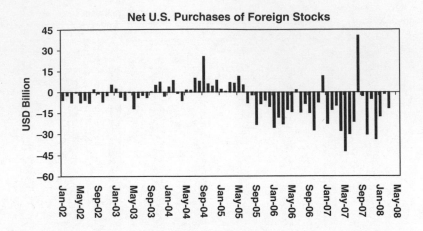

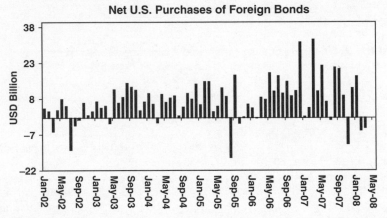

FIGURE 7.18 U.S. investors have increasingly turned to foreign stocks and bonds since 2003 in search of growth and diversification opportunities. Negative figures reflect purchases by U.S. residents of overseas assets because they denote outflows from the U.S.

Without a doubt, the dollar continues to be the reserve currency of choice as well as the most popular invoicing tool for international commerce. (See Figure 7.19.) Despite its 80 percent increase against the dollar from its 2000 lows, the euro has charted modest progress in its share of the world's currency reserves. But these statistics include only those reserves reported by global central banks, and exclude the +$1.7 trillion in reserves held by the People's Bank of China. And as we shall see in the next section, currency rebalancing decisions by the central banks of the Gulf could trigger a sea change in FX proportions.

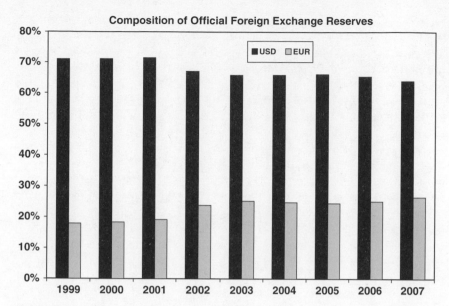

FIGURE 7.19   Share of euro-denominated currency reserves at major global central banks has shown minor progress relative to U.S. dollar.

CURRENCY RESERVE DIVERSIFICATION: OPEC AND THE MIDDLE EAST

Preserving currency strength is an increasingly vital factor to the Gulf Cooperation Council (GCC) group of nations as they plan a unified currency for 2010. A steady foreign exchange rate and price stability are vital prerequisites to any currency union as they encourage participating economies to contain inflationary pressures and attain monetary policy uniformity. This was seen in the late 1970s when the currencies of the European Community were pegged to an artificial currency called the ECU—the European currency unit—in the European Exchange Rate Mechanism as a precursor to the 1999 creation of the euro.

Germany's currency, the deutsche mark (DEM), was first used an anchor currency for the ECU and later the euro as Germany's economy was the region's largest, characterized by low inflation and steady growth. The Bank of England had to maintain the pound at the high exchange rate of 2.95 deutsche marks per pound. The costs of economic disparity culminated in 1991–1992, when a struggling British economy suffering from slowing growth and rising unemployment was further stifled by the Bank of England's policy of keeping interest rates near Germany's 10 percent.

In 1991, German GDP grew 5 percent in contrast to a 2 percent decline in the United Kingdom. As the growth disparity escalated, the Bank of England was forced to spend over tens of billions of USD per day to support the pound at the 2.95 DEM rate. On what was called "black Wednesday," September 16, 1992, the Bank of England threw in the towel, allowing the pound to fall off the ERM as currency speculators spent massive amounts selling the currency. Currency trader George Soros made $1 billion in profits after spending double the amount in selling the British currency.

In the Gulf countries, currencies pegged to the falling dollar are suffering the opposite problem of the British pound in 1991–1992. Currency speculators have been buying local currencies, betting that the central banks will allow a break away from the dollar peg or a revaluation against it. Prior to its 2007 decision to depeg its currency from the dollar, the Central Bank of Kuwait had faced mounting speculative pressure and was forced to cut interest rates three times in less than two months to prevent its currency from appreciating as speculators bet that the central bank would end its peg to the dollar. Inflation surged to 5 percent, well above its historical average of less than 2 percent. Allowing the currency to be tied to the falling dollar would have stirred further inflationary pressures for Kuwait, not only via the declining purchasing power of the dinar, but also through the obligation to maintain Kuwaiti interest rates in line with those of the United States. The central bank eventually abandoned its regime of 100 percent peg to the dollar in favor of a basket of multiple currencies.

In Saudi Arabia, record inflation rates had prevented the Saudi Arabian Monetary Authority from mimicking the interest rate cuts of the Federal Reserve, as has been the case over the past 20 years. The other reason for the reluctance to cut rates is the negative impact on the value of the kingdom's mostly dollar-denominated investments in its central bank and sovereign wealth funds, totaling over $300 billion. There is also the political element as Saudi Arabia continues to obtain concessions in arms deals with the United States. As the oil-rich Gulf nations are paid in an increasingly falling U.S. dollar, their purchasing power diminishes while their imported inflation surges. As long as U.S. interest rates remain at their lows and the dollar under pressure, portfolio losses in these central banks' holdings will become an issue.

The UAE and Kuwait have already discussed reducing the proportion of their dollar holdings in their currency reserves. As of this writing, Qatar and Bahrain are expected to follow suit within the next six months. The strong political and trade relationship between the Gulf nations and the United States played a key role in Saudi Arabia's maintaining of dollar-based investments, but local pressure and economic realities are making the current arrangement increasingly untenable.

Market analysts and media commentators have repeatedly wondered at what point the dollar's decline is considered to be at crisis level. This point is drawing near as the powerful group of oil producers begins mulling plans to receive payments in currencies other than U.S. dollars for their oil. While the presidents of Iran and Venezuela have made aggressive calls for terminating the dollar pricing of OPEC's oil, such remarks have also borne a degree of hostility to the United States. Instead, the real influence lies with Saudi Arabia, which produces 9.2 million barrels per day, well above the aggregate 6.7 million barrels produced by both Iran and Venezuela. Saudi Arabia and other Arab Gulf nations have already set up committees assessing pricing alternatives to the dollar, such as a basket of currencies that includes the dollar and the euro. The currency composition of such a basket would likely reflect the currency breakdown of the Gulf nations' largest export customers.

Despite OPEC's surging wealth from soaring oil, the implications of a price pullback and continued dollar declines could be significant. OPEC made more than $370 billion in 2007 from rising oil prices alone. Assuming a $15 decline in the price of oil and a 5 percent decline in the dollar—half the decline of 2007—the estimated revenue would amount to nearly $170 billion. The risks are particularly high for Arab Gulf nations suffering from higher inflation resulting from pegging their currencies to a falling dollar. Rising inflation and falling oil receipts would not only be economically damaging to these economies, but would also prove to be politically unsustainable as prices of everyday commodities continue to surge relative to personal incomes. In light of the impending U.S. recession and the resulting impact on global oil demand, the likelihood of this double whammy—falling oil and lower dollar—is considerable.

FURTHER CURRENCY DIVERSIFICATION IS INEVITABLE

In order to reduce their currency dependence on the falling dollar, the Gulf nations could take the Kuwait route and tie their currencies to a basket of international currencies (EUR, GBP, JPY, and the USD) while revaluing the dollar portion. Alternatively, they could revalue their currency against the U.S. dollar while maintaining a full dollar peg. Moving toward a basket of currencies as well as reducing the dollar would be appropriate for these nations, which are major importers of European products. A currency basket would also reduce upward speculative pressures on the local currency that would result from a revaluation. Common solutions for alleviating the problem of surging prices have been increases in salaries and subsidizing food items. But Gulf states cannot afford to continue giving short-term Band-Aids to deepening structural problems.

The unfolding commodity environment shows no signs of halting the ensuing dollar damage. On the oil front, the falling currency is at risk of eroding the dollar-denominated revenues of oil producers, driving even some of the staunchest U.S. allies this week to consider cutting output. OPEC has certainly learned from its disastrous decision to raise output in 1997, which sent prices plunging to 13-year lows at $10 per barrel as increased supply saw little demand in the midst of the Asian economic crisis of the past decade. Today's global economic slowdown risks triggering similar consequences for OPEC, particularly due to the tumbling value of the dollar.

The potential for OPEC to price oil in a currency other than the dollar is at its closest point of materializing as Arab Gulf oil producers may no longer be able to sacrifice the eroding purchasing power of their dollar-pegged currency regimes to the benefit of their mutually advantageous arrangements with Washington. Regardless, OPEC is already in the process of exploring the creation of basket-type currency for pricing oil. Such an occurrence would be a key landmark in the declining path of the U.S. dollar, thereby allowing little choice for global central bankers to further reduce their accumulation of dollars in favor of euros, sterling, and even gold.

Several market participants have countered that central bank diversification of dollar reserves would be offset by the expected accumulation of dollar-based assets from commodity-rich sovereign wealth funds (SWFs). Last year, investment funds from the Middle East and the Far East injected nearly half a trillion dollars worth of capital into U.S. corporations, providing them with an essential source of funding in shaky market conditions.

Aside from pressure from Washington, the hefty amounts of U.S. dollar denominated holdings in SWFs are the main reason to the Gulf States' reluctance to revalue their currencies against the U.S. dollar. The foreign exchange currency loss from any revaluation has been a major obstacle to adjusting these increasingly unsustainable currency regimes. At the end of the day, the Gulf nations will have to choose between surging domestic inflation (resulting from pegging to a falling dollar and following the Fed's monetary policy despite double digit inflation rates) and the currency hit.

Rising purchases of U.S. corporate stakes will surely extend into the rest of the decade, exploiting a cheap dollar and fallen prices. But the increased availability of attractively valued investment opportunities around the world reduces the likelihood of SWFs remaining tied to U.S. stakes to the point of losing their bargaining power. As a result, any gain in protectionist momentum from the presidential hopefuls will easily deter SWFs from U.S. borders. These funds have already demonstrated their invest-ment aloofness to requests of further injections from the likes of Citi-group. SWFs from Kuwait and Qatar have already started diversifying into Japanese, East Asian, and European investment opportunities. Without a doubt, the diversification trend will continue and U.S. assets are no longer the only game in town. Any further escalation in protectionist rhetoric from the new administration will not only deflect vital doses of capital from U.S. companies, but also further weaken an already unstable flow of foreign fi-nancing of the $800 billion current account deficit. Weak foreign financing of the deficit drives up long-term interest rates and exacerbates the costs to home owners and buyers.

THE VIEW AHEAD

These are the realities of the new global economy. Rising commodities prices may not be a new development to those born before the 1960s, but it is the first time in more than 60 years that soaring commodities are emerging simultaneously with the presence of an increasingly viable alter-native currency to the U.S. dollar. The advent of the euro as an increasingly reliable and robust medium of exchange run by a highly respected cen-tral bank is posing the first real threat to the dollar's global reserve status since World War II. Although the euro accounts for less than a third of the world's foreign exchange reserves—compared to nearly two-thirds for the U.S. dollar—the growth of its composition has risen by about 50 percent since 1999.

The underlying assumption that the United States will continue bor-rowing cheap capital to finance its deficits is facing stiff resistance. At the time of this writing, the United States is navigating through rough eco-nomic currents, and although it hasn't fallen into a technical recession, the economy bears an ominous combination of the worst of the past three re-cessions, namely rising inflation, surging oil prices, a deepening housing slump, and falling equity markets.

The six-year decline of the dollar has finally begun shrinking the trade gap by making U.S. exports more affordable abroad. But it has also dou-bled the oil-portion of our imports over the same period. Unlike the past three recessions of the 1980s, 1990–1991, and 2000–2001, which prevailed during a period of a strong dollar, the current economic slowdown has presented exceptional challenges due to the inflationary consequences of the falling currency. U.S. consumers are running out of alternatives as they face escalating debt servicing costs, falling home equity values, and contin-ued erosion of their purchasing power. These woes could be exacerbated in the event of renewed erosion in the dollar.

The causality between a falling dollar and rising oil has resurfaced just as it did at the turn of the decade. Besides the oil-driven element of a weak dollar, this time the greenback is in the midst of a prolonged down cycle, dogged by the simultaneous existence of credible alternatives for currencies and yield. The lessons have yet to be recognized and the opportunities have yet to unfold.

CHAPTER 8

Commodities Supercycles and Currencies

The commodities price rally at the turn of the decade has helped redraw the financial market landscape and broaden investment and speculative opportunities for institutions, money managers, and individual investors. No longer are investors limited to speculative oil wells or mining projects in order to seek higher rates of return at the risk of losing all of their capital. Commodities have branched out into a multifaceted asset class, enabling investors to exploit the growth opportunities in just about every component of the production process of the global economy.

The end of the 1995–2001 bull market in the U.S. dollar and the beginning of a new secular bear market in 2002 was an integral force in shaping the advance of the commodity boom, particularly as the majority of the world's resources are traded in U.S. dollars. The burst of dot-com bubble in U.S. equities throughout 2000–2002 and the resulting Fed easing policy slashing interest rates to 45-year lows dealt a severe blow to the dollar's yield foundation relative to other currencies. By mid-2002, it became clear that the Bush administration preferred a weak dollar to support the ailing steel industry despite its reiteration of what it called its "strong dollar policy." A swelling trade deficit, an increasingly lax fiscal policy, and an unpopular war in Iraq all drew parallels with the economic and foreign policy realities of the early 1970s.

The falling dollar has been among the many catalysts to a commodities supercycle. A powerful confluence of supply and demand dynamics easing the way for the economic advancement of key emerging nations, as well as the surfacing of new rules in international economics and financial markets, helped create the broadest and deepest rally in commodities since the late 1970s. Accelerating growth rates in developing nations have created a vital demand source of energy, metals, and agriculture commodities, off-setting slower demand in the industrialized world.

Increased integration of commodities into the investment plans of institutions and individuals has also helped boost price appreciation of most commodities. Corporate and government pension funds, sovereign wealth funds, and university endowments are all including commodities in their portfolios for their risk-return attributes, whose paths have diverged away from traditional equity and bond instruments. The creation of new investment vehicles such as exchange-traded funds (ETFs) has facilitated individual investors' shifts into commodities, thereby enhancing liquidity and information flow.

Figure 8.1 highlights the extent of the rise in the various commodity groups since January 2003, illustrating that metals were the fastest-gaining group into early 2007, followed by energy and food items. As will be seen later in the chapter, the 460 percent increase in copper prices between January 2003 and March 2008 helped lift metals above energy products as the top-performing commodity group despite the 250 percent increase in crude oil over the same period.

As the emerging economies of Asia, the Gulf, and Latin America further participate in the global economy and fortify their foreign exchange reserves via stronger export revenues, their spending powers shift toward expanding infrastructure and feeding their growing populations. That means

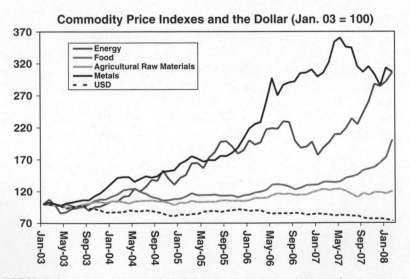

FIGURE 8.1 Energy and metals led the present commodities cycle.

demand for copper and aluminum for building and wiring cities; corn and soy for nourishing a growing population and dependable livestocks; oil and gas for transporting people and generating power for factories; and finally, surging demands for all of these as the self-feeding mechanism persists, regardless of whether the industrialized economies are slowing or growing.

Another powerful element helping to speed up the price moves of most commodities has been investor interest in commodities-oriented funds. Investors poured about $142 billion into commodities funds in 2007 from less than $10 billion in 1998. By June 2008, that amount is estimated to have reached $250 billion. Speculation has also been instrumental in adding to the liquidity of these funds, permitting short-term traders to push up prices to record highs, compounding the favorable supply and demand factors among producers, suppliers, and consumers.

THE CURRENT COMMODITY CYCLE VERSUS PREVIOUS CYCLES

The broadening decline in the value of the dollar combined with the aforementioned dynamics of growing demand and eroding supplies have shaped up one of the broadest rallies in commodities, encompassing oil, metals, and major food crops. Table 8.1 shows that the rally in each of these commodities groups surpassed the average advances of the past 60 years in both price and duration. Crude oil and copper started their ascendance as early as 2001, before being joined by the rest of commodity groups in 2004–2005.

The breadth of commodities rally can also be measured in the number of individual commodity booms, whereby a boom is defined as an increase lasting for at least one year. Figure 8.2 shows that the number of large commodity booms surged to 17 as of December 2007, outpaced only by 1974. The price decline in beverages and beef was behind the shorter price boom. The International Monetary Fund found that out of 74 months of broad-based boom periods between 1960 and 2007, about half started in 2005. The current supply and demand factors underpinning the various commodity groups are likely to prolong the duration of the prevailing rallies.

The timing of the current commodities bull market is another distinct attribute from other previous price booms. While major price rallies emerged at the end of relatively long periods of economic expansion, the current boom started earlier in the cycle of the global economic and industrial expansion. The 1973 oil-led rally emerged at the end of 1962–1965 expansion, which fed into other fuels, metals, and agricultural products. The 2000 rally in commodities was another example of surging prices at

TABLE 8.1 The Current Commodity Boom: Longer and Broader than Most Previous Booms

	Commodity Phase in 2008	Start	Price Change (Percent)	Average Price Change of Past Booms	Duration (Months)	Average Duration of Past Booms
Crude oil	Boom	Dec-01	210.1	54.0	73	18
Metals	Boom	Mar-03	104.8	43.0	58	22
Aluminum	Boom	Apr-03	29.0	41.0	57	22
Copper	Boom	Oct-01	212.5	61.0	75	21
Nickel	Boom	Oct-05	74.9	84.0	19	29
Food	Boom	Nov-04	30.4	21.0	38	18
Corn	Boom	Nov-04	62.2	39.0	38	19
Wheat	Boom	Apr-05	124.1	38.0	32	20
Soybeans	Boom	Jan-05	83.9	42.0	36	18
Palm oil	Boom	Jan-05	116.8	61.0	36	20
Soybean oil	Boom	Jan-05	100.9	50.0	36	18
Beef	Slump	Sep-04	−25.0	35.0	—	20
Agricultural raw materials	Boom	Dec-04	2.2	28.0	37	20
Rubber	Boom	Jan-05	77.2	56.0	36	21

Source: International Monetary Fund.

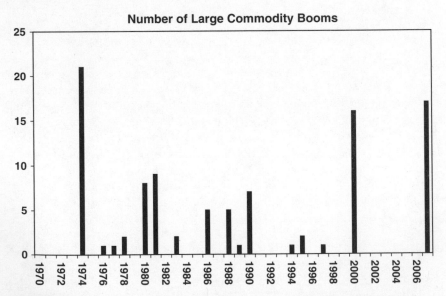

FIGURE 8.2 The number of commodity booms is nearing the 1970s record.

the end of major economic expansions. The burst of the dot-com equity bubble coupled with widespread revelations of corporate malfeasance and credit downgrades pushed the U.S. economy into recession, dragging down the industrialized world with it. In the current price boom, copper and oil prices started rallying in 2001, but the acceleration in those rallies wasn't stepped up until 2004–2005 when the world economy had fully emerged from the 2001–2002 economic downturn.

The fact that the current commodity boom has coincided with the beginning of a strong world recovery rather than at the end of it as in previous cases reflects the unique confluence of mutually reinforcing demand and supply factors, as well as the manifestation of vital interrelationships among commodities. Whether it is the price impact on oil and food from the increased production of biofuels, or the depreciation of the dollar and falling real interest rates, commodities have benefited in ways not seen before.

Figure 8.3 illustrates the annual price change in the U.S. producer price index for metals and farm products since 1914, and for all commodities together since 1927. Two main dynamics stand out from the chart: (1) Each of the rallies in the 1930s, 1940s, and 1970s was sharp and relatively short-lived, and (2) those price moves prevailed during periods of surging

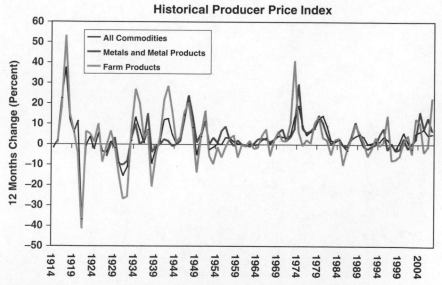

FIGURE 8.3 Despite their recent ascent, U.S. producer prices index remain lower than in previous historical advances, implying that current price strength is greater in real terms.

inflation rates, ranging from 5 to 20 percent annually, compared to the over
4.0 percent as of July 2008. This means that in inflation-adjusted terms, the
current price escalation must be at least twice as rapid as that in the 1970s.

DISSECTING COMMODITY CLASSES

In order to better understand the current commodities cycle, it is essential
to break price trends down into the various commodities classes and examine the supply and demand forces underpinning them individually. Thus, it
is no longer enough to speak about "metals" and "energy" in general terms
when comparing these two classes because some individual fuels and metals have grown two to three times as much as others within the same commodity class.

Figure 8.4 shows the price performance of crude oil, gold, copper,
corn, soy, and the Reuters/Jefferies-Commodities Research Bureau Index
(CRB), the most renowned index of commodities prices, consisting of
28 commodities. The chart measures the five commodities and the CRB
over four different periods: January 2000 through May 2008, January 2002
through May 2008, January 2005 through May 2008, and January 2007
through May 2008. In all but one of the four periods, oil was the best-
performing commodity, closely followed by copper prices. The rationale

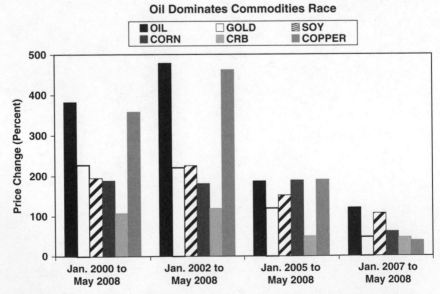

FIGURE 8.4 Oil leads commodities price rise in all four measurement periods.

of these price developments suggests that the current commodities cycle began on the heels of the two commodities used most widely in construction, power generation, and transportation.

Oil Fueled by Unique Demand and Supply Forces

What makes the latest spikes to record highs in oil prices stand out from previous rallies is the combination of supply realities and prevailing economic climate. Despite the accelerating slowdown in the U.S. economy, global oil demand is anticipated to post a small increase, rather than a decrease, as was the case in past periods of slowdown in the United States. Robust economic growth in emerging countries such as Brazil, China, and India has filled in the demand gap anticipated in the United States. The economic decoupling in select emerging economies is playing a significant role in filling the slack in demand for oil and other commodities, such as agriculture, metals, and other fuels. It is this crucial component of global demand that has contributed to maintaining the run-up in oil prices.

Just as gold is powered by speculators, so is crude oil. Figure 8.5 shows the volatile activity among speculators' interest in oil. Speculative activity has long been attributed to the price surge in oil. But as will be seen later, the fundamental forces prolonging the fuel's rise have become more cyclical (related to economic growth) and structural (supply and technology) in nature and therefore more durable than those resulting from speculators.

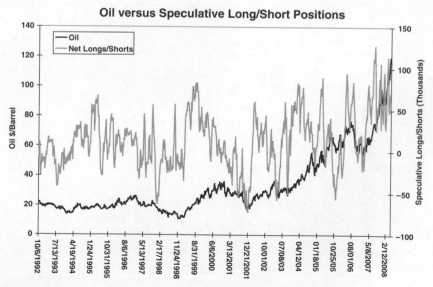

FIGURE 8.5 Speculators have helped fuel oil run.

Supply Realities   Barring robust demand from Brazil, China, and other emerging economies, the International Energy Agency (IEA) has made sharp downward revisions to estimates of overall global demand. Despite the risk of projected slowdown in global oil demand, the underlying supply realities continue to provide vital support for prices going forward. Oil production has been impacted by a series of disruptions, such as pipeline sabotage in Nigeria, the Iraq war, strikes among oil workers in Nigeria and Gabon, as well as confrontations between the Turkish army and Kurdish guerillas in the oil-rich region of northern Iraq.

Unlike in the 1970s, when most oil fields were located near consumption centers, the concentration of most current reserves is located in countries that are far away from large consuming markets, thus involving escalating shipping costs and sometimes delays. Surging exploration costs have also reduced the real value of oil companies' investments. U.S.-based international companies have seen their development costs increase fivefold to about $22 per barrel between 1995 and 2007.

In addition to transportation costs and supply disruptions, oil prices will likely remain underpinned by slowing production outside OPEC. Russia, Mexico, and the North Sea have all struggled with faltering production.

Is Russian Oil Peaking?   Russia expects its oil output to have peaked out at about 10 million barrels per day in 2007, an amount that is unlikely to be surpassed for the rest of the decade. In fact, Russia may have its first output decline since 1998 due to eroding production in western Siberia. Growth in the nation's oil production began to slow in 2003. Russian oil executives estimate that over $1 trillion a year will be needed to invest in exploring new fields in order for current production levels of 9 to 9.5 million barrels/day to be maintained over the next 20 years. This may augur badly for future supplies as most official estimates place Russia as third top contributor to the 2.6 million barrels/day of non-OPEC oil, behind Brazil and biofuels.

With the possibility that acreage expansions devoted for biofuels are likely to be untenable due to surging food prices, a decrease in biofuels and Russian supply may leave Brazil, Canada, and central Asia as the remaining non-OPEC sources of oil.

Mexico's Oil Days Are Numbered   At 2.9 million barrels per day, Mexico is the world's sixth-largest oil producer and provides 8 percent of U.S. supplies. It is also the biggest producer of oil from shallow waters. Its Cantarell field in the Gulf of Mexico is the world's second-largest so-called super-giant field but its output has been falling at an annual rate of 15 percent since production peaked in 2004. The country's overall crude oil production dropped to 2.9 millions barrels per day in March 2008 from its peak of 3.38 million barrels per day in 2004. Underinvestment and misallocation of capital have rendered Mexico's drilling equipment mostly obsolete, leaving the country with less than 15 billion barrels in proven reserves in 2008.

At the current pace of production, Mexico's reserves will near depletion by 2018. Larger oil reserves are believed to be located in the deep waters of the Gulf of Mexico, as far as 10,000 feet below surface. But unlike other oil producers, Mexico's constitution prevents the national oil company from signing contracts with international players that would compensate them in oil or cash for the amount of oil extracted. As a result, the laws reduce any incentive for oil companies to invest hundreds of millions of dollars to share their know-how with the national oil company and obtain proven reserves on their books.

Due to concerns with slowing global oil demand stemming from the economic slowdown, primarily in the U.S. and other industrialized economies, OPEC began cutting output by about 350,000 barrels per day in the first quarter of 2008. The 20 percent decline in the U.S. dollar during 2006–2007 has also signaled the red flag amid OPEC nations, raising the possibility of further currency declines in the event of prolonged deterioration in the U.S. credit crunch and on the macroeconomic front.

The oil cartel is too careful to avoid repeating the fateful error of late 1998 when oil prices tumbled below $10 per barrel after its decision to increase output coincided with falling demand from the Asian currency crisis. Ten years later, OPEC's rising economies have enabled it to maintain output even in the face of a slowing global economy in the event that conditions take a turn to the worse. Consequently, as of this writing, the forward oil curve, which projects oil prices into the long-term horizon, suggests prices are likely to remain well above $100 per barrel into 2016.

Gold's Multifaceted Shine

The price escalation in metals has broken away from previous trends, prominently shrugging off the 2007–2008 credit crunch and economic slowdown in the United States, Canada, Europe, and Japan. Indeed, metals have responded to surging energy and commodity demand from the emerging economies of Brazil, Russia, India, and China (BRICs) as these mobilize their budgets to improving their infrastructure via swelling demand for steel. China alone consumes 35 percent of world iron ore versus 8 percent for the United States.

From the Gulf to the Far East, construction of highways, bridges, factories and airports have filled up the rural landscape, while escalating energy demands have rendered superior infrastructure a basic requirement for handling the increased capacity. China's estimated net electricity use between 2003 and 2030 stands at a rate of 4.8 percent, versus 4.6 percent for India, 3.2 percent for Brazil, and 3.0 percent for the Middle East. This compares to 1.6 percent, 1.5 percent, and 1.2 percent for the United States, Canada, and OECD Europe. Figure 8.6 shows gold's performance against silver, oil, and the Commodity Research Bureau's commodities index from January 2001.

The most commonly listed causes of the latest gold bull market have been the accelerating pace of the dollar's decline, rising inflation, and increased jewelry purchases by the rising middle class in emerging economies such as India. Jewelry makes up about 68 percent of the world's gold demand and India is at the top of that list. As in other commodities, China and India have shown relentless appetite in their demand for gold and iron ore products. Together they account for 40 percent of global demand.

Before addressing supply factors, there is one more demand-related reason behind the surge in gold. Investments and speculation make up about 11 percent of demand for gold. A relatively novel but powerful component of such demand has been exchange-traded funds specializing in gold. These funds allow institutions, hedge funds, pension funds, and household investors to snap up gold at face values that are as small as a tenth of the bullion price. Gold ETFs have been instrumental in mobilizing large amounts of investors' capital into the precious metal to the extent of

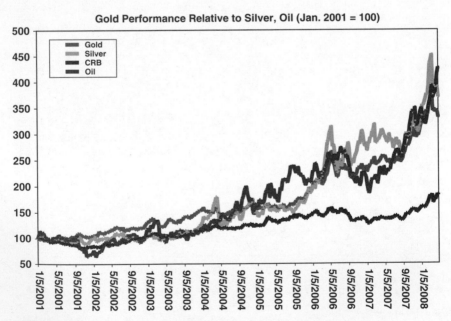

FIGURE 8.6 Gold at the core of the commodities rally.

rendering it a mainstream asset class. As of early 2008, investors in gold ETFs held over 870 tons of the metal, more than 7 percent of outstanding world gold. Gold ETFs now rank as the world's seventh-largest holder of physical bullion, surpassed by the United States, Germany, the International Monetary Fund, France, Italy, and Switzerland. According to the *Wall Street Journal*'s ranking of 140 ETFs in March 2008, StreetTRACKS' gold ETF ranked fourth by order of assets at $19.3 billion.

Prior to the creation of ETFs and similar investment funds geared toward gold, investors' main gold route was via speculating in the futures market. Figure 8.7 illustrates the net purchases/sales of gold futures contracts at the Chicago Mercantile Exchange. These positions are known as the *commitments of traders* as each contract represents an outstanding position to buy or sell. The positions are charted against the price of gold, thus exposing the role of speculators in boosting the price surge.

The supply side of gold has also contributed to the run-up in prices. Global mine production fell 6 percent between 2002 and 2008, mainly due to power shortages and miners' stoppages demanding better safety rights in South Africa. The world's top gold producer has seen output plummet to 70-year lows. Meanwhile, the top gold mining companies have also gradually reduced their hedge books designed to cover them against falling prices. As the upward price trend accelerated markedly between 2005 and

FIGURE 8.7 The number of contracts net long/short gold in futures markets closely tracks the price of bullion.

2008, companies closed their forward and options hedging positions so as to maximize the value of their outstanding positions. As of April 2008, gold producers' hedge books fell to their lowest since 1992.

Copper Is Preciously Vital

While the role of gold as a hedge against inflation and falling paper currencies gives it its prolonged allure, copper remains the most sought metal in the broader phases of manufacturing, construction, and electrical development. These attributes have rendered copper prices a leading indicator for economic growth. But given China's steady role as the world's largest copper consumer since 2002, its appetite for the metal has overshadowed any signs of a slowdown in the industrialized world. In 2007, Chinese copper consumption made up more than a fifth of the world's total, with a per capita consumption of 6.2 pounds, well below the 30 to 40 pounds per capita for developed countries. Leading the world with a 26 percent share of copper consumption, China has yet to take a bigger share as it meets the construction and infrastructure demands of its urbanization program.

As in the case with gold, copper is also supported by an array of supply-related dynamics such as power shortages, strikes, and underinvestment. Chapter 9 takes a closer look at these factors.

Figure 8.8 illustrates copper's superiority relative to gold, stemming from its vital role as an industrial metal in the midst of soaring global

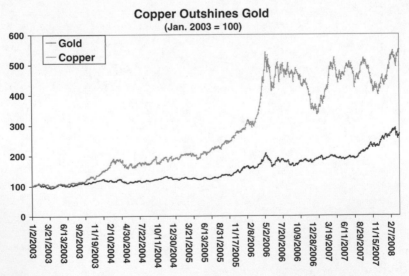

FIGURE 8.8 Copper's industrial usefulness outshines gold's luster.

demand. The fact that copper grew by more than twice the rate of gold suggests the price boom may lie further ahead.

Food and Grains Feed on Global Appetite

The durability of the current commodity supercycle is rendered especially potent by the rise in grains, crops, and food. Once again, the confluence of supply and demand forces has conspired to produce the longest and highest rally since the 1970s, lifting corn, soybeans, wheat, and coffee by more than 140 percent between 2003 and 2007. The main factors underpinning the rise in food are the following.

Rising Middle Class   Improved incomes in the emerging economies of China, India, Latin America, and the Middle East have lifted populations out of poverty and into the middle class. Consequently, large supermarket chains and discount stores have increasingly catered to consumers from this emerging socioeconomic class, offering a wider range of imported foods. In Asia, food spending accounts for a far bigger portion of shopping baskets than in the industrialized world. Figure 8.9 shows that as a percentage of the typical consumer price index, food makes up 59 percent, 57 percent, 55 percent, and 30 percent in Bangladesh, India, the Philippines, and China respectively. This compares to 10 percent, 14 percent, and 21 percent for the United Kingdom, the United States, and the Eurozone.

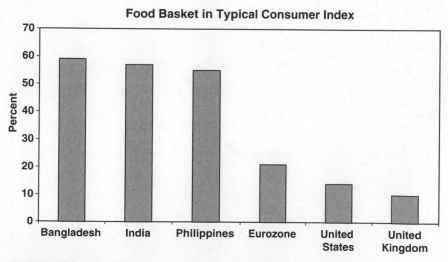

FIGURE 8.9   Food spending is a higher proportion of overall spending in Asia than in Europe and the United States.

Shifting socioeconomic dynamics have not only influenced spending patterns but also dietary trends (Figure 8.10). People in India are eating out more often, opting for Chinese cuisine and pizza. Asian meat consumption has risen 40 percent over the past 15 years, thereby boosting demand for wheat and corn for feedstocks.

Biofuels Revolution   U.S. energy legislation has encouraged the use of biofuels such as ethanol in an attempt to reduce dependence on foreign oil. President George W. Bush's decision to raise the use of biofuels to 15 percent of the nation's road fuels by 2017 has led to a shift in corn usage for biofuels such as ethanol, away from food production. As a result, U.S. corn production nearly doubled to 4 billion bushels in two years, driving prices up by 50 percent to $6 a bushel within one year. Ethanol production in the United States has more than doubled from less than 3 billion gallons in 2003 to over 6 billion gallons in 2007.

As corn is shifted away from foods and syrups to biofuels, neither hunger nor escalating food prices will be contained. Ethanol could be imported from Brazil, where it is produced more efficiently from sugarcane, but its import is restricted by a 25 percent tariff in order to protect the powerful U.S. agricultural lobby. Thus, while U.S. import tariffs on ethanol are designed to protect local growers of sugarcane, such protection raises the burden on local consumers. The growing use of biofuels also means many farmers have shifted from soybeans to corn, causing an upward run

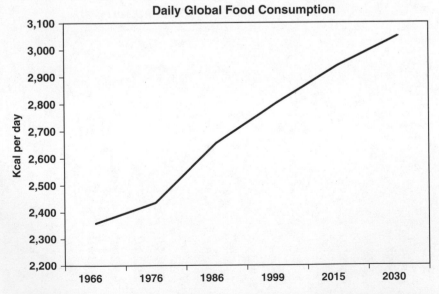

FIGURE 8.10 Surging global food consumption will challenge limited supplies.

in soy due to eroding supplies. The price action has since prompted many back to soy. Such shifts are bound to continue as long as demand for biofuels is sustained, especially in Brazil, which is the world's biggest producer of both crops. Figure 8.11 shows the inverse price action between corn and soy in 2008 as a result of these dynamics.

The speculative element is also present in grains. Figure 8.12 shows how speculators have responded to the U.S. administration's biofuels

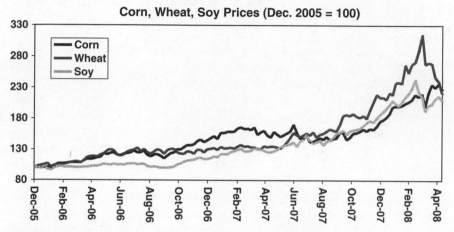

FIGURE 8.11 Corn battles it out with soy.

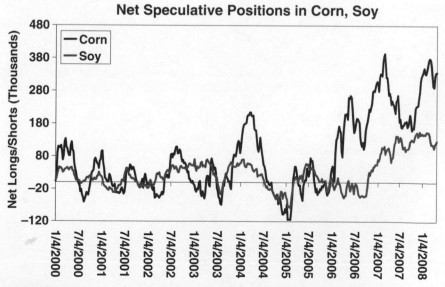

FIGURE 8.12 Corn speculators maneuver around farmers' planting trends.

policy by betting on price surges in the futures market. As farmers rushed toward corn, soybeans lost in favor and so did their price. This explains the weaker trend in speculators' net long positions in soybeans relative to corn futures.

Rising Fuel Prices   Higher oil prices have driven up the cost of agriculture inputs, such as tractors and other farming equipment, while rising natural gas prices have boosted the price of fertilizers. Farm-related machinery also becomes more expensive due to higher costs of steel and raw materials, as well as surging demand from China and other developing nations.

Nitrogen fertilizers, used in enhancing farm productivity, are largely dependent on the price of natural gas. Rising energy prices have driven up prices of natural gas, which in turn lifted prices of fertilizers by 120 percent between 2005 and 2007. Farmers in the developing world face the double whammy of soaring fertilizer prices from abroad as well as higher prices of grains used for animal feed. Escalating shipping costs have also added to the burden of importing nations. The Baltic Dry Index measuring freight rates for most commodities quadrupled in value between 2005 and 2007. These costs were mainly faced by countries whose costs are denominated in weakening U.S. dollars or whose currencies are tied to it.

Elevated Dairy Products   Rising dairy prices have been a result of the emerging middle class frequenting the surge of supermarket chains, where imported cheese and ice cream have become popular dairy products. India is the biggest producer of milk but its farmers struggle to meet demand due to weak infrastructure. As a result, milk prices are hiked in the export market. Dairy prices rose 200 percent in 2007 alone.

The shift of corn toward biofuel production and away from cattle feed has also contributed to the elevated price of dairy cows and dairy products. In 2007, New Zealand, the world's largest maker of dairy products and the fourth-largest milk producer, has seen farm wages rise 20 percent while the average price of a dairy cow doubled to $1,900. The resulting impact on New Zealand's currency has been noticeable.

Tariffs   While tariffs on imports designed to protect domestic industries are more common in international trade, many countries have adopted another form of food-trade protectionism. Barriers on exports were imposed as a way to contain food prices domestically and preserve self-sufficiency. The matter of urgency became figuring out how to limit foreign demand of local grains and crops and preserve limited resources, rather than how to encourage the selling of local crops. In the case of rice, supplies fell to 25-year lows, prompting India to ban exports of non-basmati rice. Egypt discontinued rice exports for six months as of April 2008 after a 50 percent surge in the price of cereals and bread led to fatal riots. Governments in Argentina, Kazakhstan, India, and Vietnam have taxed imports heavily to keep markets well supplied. The main problem with these restrictions is that they prevent farmers from enjoying high prices to the fullest at a time when they are facing mounting costs of transportation, equipment, fertilizer, diesel, and seed.

Weather Droughts and floods have impacted agricultural production by eroding crops, thus driving up crop prices. In 2007, droughts in Australia cut the wheat harvest period by half. In the United Kingdom and northern Europe, floods retarded agriculture production, as did the drought in southern Europe.

COMMODITIES AND THEIR CURRENCIES

Before moving on to a closer look at the various commodities and the currencies most dependent on them, we take a glance at the correlation between the U.S. Dollar Index and the various commodities groups since 1980. Figure 8.13 shows the biggest negative correlation with the U.S. dollar to have occurred with oil in the 1990s and with gold in 1980s.

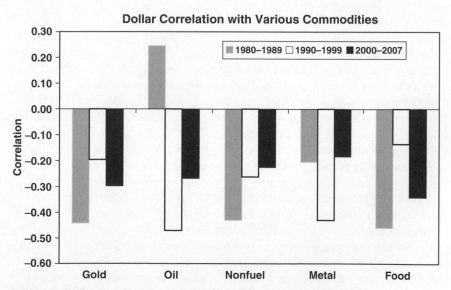

FIGURE 8.13 Negative correlations between commodities and the U.S. dollar have grown dominated by food recently, but oil and gold are expected to maintain their historical closeness to the greenback.

The geopolitical events of the 1980s, such as the Soviet invasion of Afghanistan—which triggered a $320 jump in gold in less than one month—were accompanied by equally sharp moves in the currency. The clear-cut paths charted by the greenback also helped to explain the higher negative correlations with commodities. The dollar soared 94 percent in the first half of the decade, before the coordinated interventions of the Plaza Accord helped drive it back down by 50 percent into the rest of the decade. In the 1990s, the greater USD negative correlation occurred with oil, the bulk of which emerged in the second half of the decade as the strengthening U.S. economy and escalating equity bull market boosted the dollar at the expense of the oil. In 1999, the dollar index surged to 10-year highs, coinciding with 14-year lows for oil at $12 per barrel and 20-year lows for gold at $253 per ounce. The 2000–2007 correlations for oil and gold were weaker than those in prior decades due to the fact that the dollar moved in tandem with oil in 2000–2002 and with gold in 2005. Nonetheless, the price developments in the first five months of 2008 have shown USD correlations between gold and oil to have resurged back into the range of −0.80 on a four-week rolling basis in gold and oil.

DEVELOPING WORLD TO MAINTAIN RIPE OUTLOOK FOR FOOD AND GRAINS

Unlike in the past when food, feedstocks, and fibers were the dominant uses of grains, fuel is now becoming a major end product for grains, hence the surging demand and soaring prices for the crop. As the United States plans to meet 30 percent of its transport fuel demand through biofuels by 2030, the resulting demand for corn and maize means that these valuable grains could virtually disappear from the international food markets.

In 2007, U.S. farmers planted more corn than in any other year since World War II after U.S. legislation encouraged the increasing use of corn for biofuels to reduce dependence on foreign oil. The legislation, combined with escalating imports from abroad, drove up corn prices by more than 50 percent within a year. U.S. ethanol production has also more than doubled, reaching over 6 billion in 2007 from less than 3 billion, with further expansion expected to push production above 12 billion gallons by 2010. The Renewable Fuel Standard (RFS) from the U.S. Energy Independence and Security Act of 2007 calls for total renewable fuel in the United States to reach 36 billion gallons by 2022 from 5.7 billion gallons in 2007. This means that ethanol derived from corn is to double to 15 billion gallons over the same period. If ethanol production is to accelerate at such a pace mainly from corn production, the question becomes how to speed up corn production at such a pace for so long?

The shift to corn by U.S. farmers has reduced the production of soybeans, the price of which has soared to new record highs but which remains cheaper to grow than corn. Against the backdrop of rising prices for wheat and soybeans, U.S. farmers face a few alternatives to growing corn, which may complicate the task of doubling ethanol production. To produce the necessary amount of ethanol, the United States may need to reduce the 54 cents per gallon tariff imposed on imported ethanol. Brazil's vast sugarcane fields allow it to produce and export ethanol relatively cheaply, but such a decision will have to bypass the U.S. farm lobby.

Aside from the classic forces of supply and demand, agricultural prices have been boosted by demand from new end-importer clients such as China and developing East Asia. Adding to the biofuels-driven price escalation of grains is emerging Asia's soaring meat consumption. China's per capita annual meat consumption has more than doubled since 1980 to 242.5 pounds in 2008. Figure 8.14 shows the doubling of Chinese urban consumption and expenditure for beef and poultry from 1982 to 2007. As the demand for meat surges, so will the demand for feedstocks for cattle and poultry. It takes two pounds of corn and soybean meal to produce one pound of chicken, while seven pounds of corn are required to produce a pound of beef, and nearly the same amount for a pound of pork. The grains implications of China's changing beefy diets are significant.

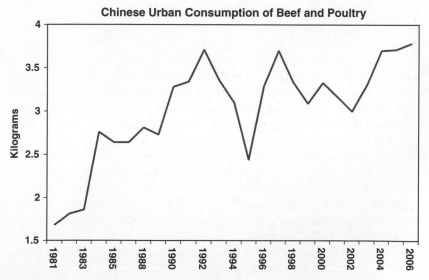

FIGURE 8.14 Chinese move toward beef means more demand for corn.

At odds with these demand factors in China are the supply constraints of arable land (Figure 8.15). As China's population becomes more urban and the rural areas are steadily converted to industrial and residential use, the future outlook for agriculture appears highly uncertain. In 2007, China's arable land fell to 470,000 square miles, nearing the 463,000 square miles level considered by the government as the bare minimum required for feeding the country. Aside from cracking down on unauthorized land expansion projects, Chinese authorities have not reached any solutions for the eroding land problem. China's soaring appetite and shrinking agricultural land shall remain a textbook example of dual supply and demand drivers of rising corn prices.

As long as these demand and supply constraints continue to lift agricultural commodities higher, export tariffs are expected to remain a long-term reality, further driving up prices. China, Egypt, India, Indonesia, and Vietnam have all stated they will not export any rice surpluses cultivated in 2008. Such restrictions on the global flow of rice will be one of the many underpinnings for higher commodity prices.

Currency Plays in Food and Grains

The aforementioned dynamics underpinning the rally in agriculture and food products has brought about a boom in commodity currencies of

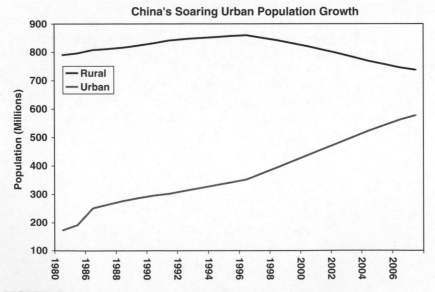

FIGURE 8.15 China's rising urbanism threatens arable land.

major food and grain exporting nations. The Australian dollar, New Zealand dollar, Canadian dollar, and Brazilian real are the principal commodity currencies traded in the freely functioning global currency markets. Despite Argentina's position as the world's third largest exporter of soy, number two exporter of corn, and fourth-largest provider of corn and beef, the Argentinean peso is not included in this section as the currency trades at a prefixed band of 2.90 to 3.10 pesos per U.S. dollar.

Brazilian Real   Brazil's currency has reaped the benefits from its position as the world's largest exporter of ethanol and soybeans at a time when these two items loom large at the top of commodity league. Increased energy efficiency and environmental awareness has spurred world demand for biofuels. Brazil's vast sugarcane fields make its sugarcane-based ethanol cheaper and more energy efficient than the corn-based ethanol produced in the United States. Despite its cheaper and cleaner attributes, Brazil's ethanol faces export tariffs in both the United States and the European Union as they protect their local farming industry. Brazil competes with the United States for the number one slot in soybean exports and was number one in 2008, exporting 25 million tons of soy, or 39 percent of the world's total. Accelerating production of biofuels and soybeans as well as a promising future for crude oil have all helped bolster solid advances in Brazil's equity markets and currency.

New Zealand Dollar   New Zealand is the world's leading maker of dairy products and the fourth-largest milk producer. Despite the negative impact of soaring agricultural input costs, such as the doubling of cow prices in 2008, the New Zealand dollar benefited tremendously from rising prices of cheese and milk. The resulting impact on its currency has been noticeable. Figure 8.16 shows the predominantly positive relationship between milk prices and the New Zealand dollar.

Australian Dollar   The aussie has been known for its high correlation to copper and gold, but Australia's position as the world's third-largest wheat exporter has also helped the aussie deepen its gains as commodities broadened their rally into grains and foods. Australia produced an estimated 15 million tons in the 2008 season, but the record droughts of 2006–2007 may push the country to speed up its crop production and possibly displace Canada in second position.

Canadian Dollar   The Canadian dollar is better known for its close relationship with oil than grains, but Canada is also the world's second-largest wheat producer, with 55 percent of its agro-food exports going to the United States in 2007. Considering the breadth of the latest

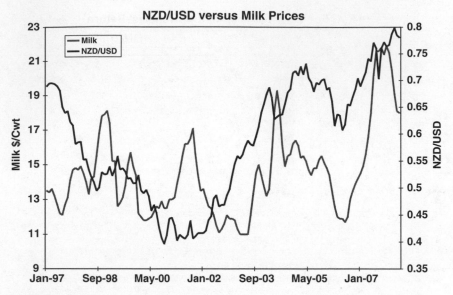

FIGURE 8.16 New Zealand's dairy production is behind the high positive kiwi-milk correlation.

commodities rally and the fairly robust relationship between grains and oil, the loonie's uptrend is expected to be sustained despite downside risks from its southern neighbor.

Figure 8.17 illustrates the performance of the aussie, real, loonie, and kiwi over the four different periods: January 2000 to May 2008, January 2002 to May 2008, January 2005 to May 2008, and January 2007 to May 2008. The charts show that both the aussie and the kiwi dominated over the longer measuring periods (i.e., since January 2000 and January 2002), largely due to the aussie's responsiveness to the rally in copper and gold, which preceded other commodities, and to robust demand from the Asia-Pacific region. But note how the performance changed in the more recent measurement periods when the strengthening rally fed on a 152 percent and 106 percent increase in soy and a 189 percent and 60 percent increase in corn from January 2005 to May 2008 and from January 2007 to May 2008. The Canadian dollar's performance is more likely to be a result of rising oil prices rather than food due to its higher correlation to the fuel, but the concentration of Canada's agro-food exports to the United States qualifies it as a food/grain-dependent currency.

Figure 8.18 illustrates that the rally in the Brazilian real intensified in 2005, at the same time most grains began their multiyear advance. Between 2006 and May 2008, prices of soy and corn rose more than 130 percent,

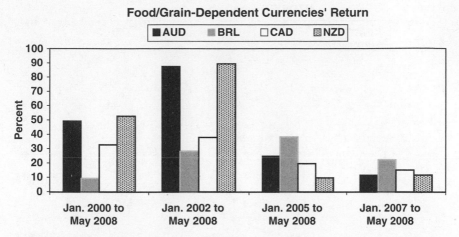

FIGURE 8.17 Brazilian real becomes powerful food-and-grain-dependent currency since beginning of agro-food price rise in 2005.

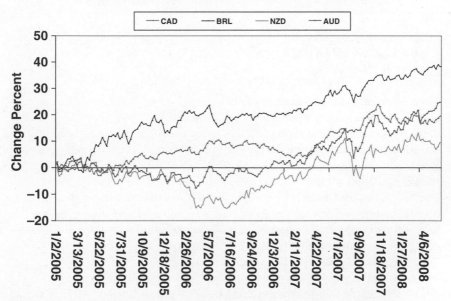

FIGURE 8.18 Brazilian real rally coincides with 2005 start of bull market in soy and corn.

while wheat soared more than 215 percent over the same period. While the role of commodities was instrumental in bolstering the real between 2005 and 2008, the inclusion of Brazilian securities in most international portfolio benchmarks and the record-breaking gains in Brazilian stocks were vital in propping the currency. Between January 2002 and April 2008, Brazil's Bovespa equity benchmark index rose 440 percent, while gaining 106 percent from January 2007 to April 2008. As a result, a large number of mutual funds and exchange-traded funds are offering opportunities to capitalize on Brazilian stocks and currency.

Finally, one currency that may be worth considering as a viable commodity play in the food business is the Polish zloty. Agriculture makes up nearly 5 percent of Poland's GDP, the third-highest proportion in Europe, after Portugal's 8 percent and Ireland's 5.5 percent. Polish food and live animal exports make up more than 8 percent of total exports, which is even higher than New Zealand's 4 percent. The zloty's future outlook may be underpinned by Poland's intention to join the European Monetary Union, which requires the country to meet strict fiscal and inflation control criteria. In the event that currency traders expect Poland to qualify for joining the euro area in 2012, the zloty will likely further appreciate during 2009–2011.

ENERGY EFFICIENCY NOT ENOUGH TO HALT HIGH OIL

Although the surge in oil prices has been increasingly compared to the dot-com bubble and other demand-oriented bubbles, the solidity of the current rally is characterized by supply-specific dynamics whose existence feeds price escalation despite any demand slowdown in the industrialized world. This does not necessarily mean that global oil demand has fallen across the board. Chinese appetite has been instrumental in filling the slack during the economic slowdown encountered in the United States and Europe, taking over 9 percent of the world's consumption. Indeed, the International Energy Agency (IEA) estimates that the world will need 55 percent more energy in 2030 than in 2005 in order to meet the projected needs of rising populations, and 45 percent of that energy demand will emerge from India and China. This means China's oil imports will jump fivefold from its current 3.5 million barrels per day, and India will become the world's third-largest net importer of oil by 2025.

The supply realities have also shaped the oil price environment. While world oil demand estimates were curtailed by 310,000 barrels to 87.2 million barrels in 2008, supply forecasts were trimmed to 815,000 barrels per day. The IEA says global oil demand will grow by 1.3 million barrels per day, with non-OPEC supply increasing by about 800,000 barrels per day. OPEC's share of world oil supply is expected to rise from 42 percent in 2007 to 52 percent by the end of 2030.

This raises the question as to how OPEC output will fill the gap, when even Saudi Arabia has difficulties surpassing its maximum capacity. The natural follow-up question is: Why is it in the interest of OPEC to raise output and risk a price decline when the world's largest consumer is facing a prolonged downside of economic risks? Furthermore, when the dollar's general weakness is factored in, the incentives for OPEC to raise output become less tenable. Indeed, unlike in the previous years of high oil such as 1999, 2003, and 2004, when speculation was the only main explanation OPEC could offer as a reason for high oil, today's rising price environment is largely shaped by tangible factors that are likely to endure for quite some time. Thus, each time Saudi Arabia has yielded to U.S. demands to raise oil output, prices found their way lower. But prices would quickly rebound at the mere mention of the U.S. credit crunch and the falling dollar being the cause of prolonged oil strength. Each of these factors presents a stark reality supporting OPEC's reluctance to bring down prices, regardless of U.S. demands.

Even if OPEC were able to increase output significantly, the cartel will grow cautious due to increased energy efficiency in the industrialized world. The 2007 U.S. Energy Independence and Security Act aims at reducing the United States' foreign oil dependency from 60 percent in 2007 to 50 percent in 2015. As the popularity of fuel-efficient cars increases and the use of ethanol enters the mainstream, the need for new but environmentally controversial drilling will abate. The proportion of diesel cars to total autos is expected to rise to 15 percent in 2030 from 1 percent in 2008, while overall auto fuel efficiency is expected to improve by 40 percent by the year 2020. Rising oil prices and increased efficiency have prompted the IEA to cut its forecast of overall U.S. fuel demand, predicting it will grow from about 20.7 million barrels per day in 2007 to 22.8 million barrels per day in 2030, rather than to 26.9 million barrels per day. But as we have seen throughout this chapter, any future slowdown in U.S. demand for oil or for any other commodity will likely be offset by demand from fast-growing economies in Asia.

And finally, the infrastructural realities of the world's top producing oil fields are rather sobering. Of the oil fields discovered since the late 1970s, none has produced more than 1 million barrels per day. As for the leading oil fields, they're either maintaining their present rate (Saudi Arabia's Al Ghawar field), peaked out (Russia's Western Siberian fields), or experiencing declines (Mexico's Cantarell Field). One must also not assume that OPEC will open the flood gates of supply at the first sign of accelerating demand from China or India. In 2008, Saudi Arabian officials stated that present demand forecasts did not justify expanding beyond the 12.5 million barrels per day projected output for 2009. Or, as King Abdullah put it more clearly: "I keep no secret from you that, when there were some new finds, I told them, 'No, leave it in the ground, with grace from God, our children need it.'"

Currency Plays in Energy

As in the previous section, only currencies that are freely in the global foreign exchange market are listed, while currencies that are in a managed float or set by a trading band are not included.

Norwegian Krone   The Norwegian krone has remarkably outperformed all other freely traded currencies of major oil-exporting countries between 2000 and 2007. The petroleum sector contributes more than one-half of total export revenue, while crude oil, natural gas, and refined petroleum products account for two-thirds of total exports. Norway is the world's third-largest exporter of crude oil behind Russia and Saudi Arabia and also the third-largest exporter of natural gas behind Russia and Canada. Surging oil prices pushed up Norway's merchandise trade surplus to a record US$61.3 billion in 2007, and lifted its current account surplus to 16 percent of GDP, the second highest of the industrialized world after Switzerland's 17 percent.

While the similarities between the Norwegian Krone and the Canadian dollar make it relatively difficult to pick which currency is most apt to benefit from rising oil, one large difference is the nations' export market. Eighty percent of Norway's exports go to the European Union, with as much as 26 percent and 13 percent destined for the United Kingdom and Germany, respectively. As we see in the following section on the Canadian dollar, 80 percent of Canada's exports are destined for the United States, thereby rendering the loonie vulnerable to any downdraft from that country, as was already manifest in 2008.

Canadian Dollar   The Canadian dollar has long been amid the top commodity currencies of choice due to its high correlation with oil prices, especially considering that the current oil price rally has preceded the gold rally in the commodities league. Canada sends 80 percent of its total exports to the United States, and over 90 percent of its oil is sold to that country. Canada's oil- and energy-related exports make up 20 percent of its total exports, and it is the world's seventh-largest exporter of crude oil at 2.27 million barrels per day as of 2008.

Canada's proven oil reserves amount to 179 billion barrels, which is second behind Saudi Arabia's 267 billion barrels and 14 percent of the world total. About 97 percent of Canada's proven reserves are in the form of bitumen oil, which account for 47 percent of total production. Most of the bitumen is located in the oil sands of Alberta, where vast amounts of oil are yet to be extracted, environmental considerations permitting. In fact, the environmental leaning of the next U.S. president after the 2008 elections may help shape the fate of future U.S. projects and gear future capital to Canada.

Russian Ruble The Russian ruble may not be the first to currency to come to mind when thinking about commodity currencies, but Russia's position as world's largest gas exporter and second-largest exporter of crude oil behind Saudi Arabia explains the currency's robust performance since 2003. As of May 2008, half of Russia's main stock market index consists of energy and oil companies.

Russia's exchange rate system is a managed float against a currency basket comprising 55 U.S. cents and 45 euro cents, whereby the central bank regularly intervenes to contain the currency within an informal band. Oil's 479 percent increase from January 2002 to May 2008 bolstered Russia's external trade position but also spurred inflation, which surpassed 14 percent in the second quarter of 2008. Currency speculators have had little choice but to bet on further strengthening in the ruble. Although the central bank intends to add some uncertainty to speculators' expectations of further ruble appreciation by intervening less in the currency markets, persistent increases in energy and grains prices will further bolster Russia's external trade position and underpin its currency. Oil's ascent has brought Russian companies to the typical internationally geared stock portfolios and led to a surge in Russia-only funds, which improved liquidity in the nation's capital market.

Mexican Peso Mexico is the world's sixth-largest exporter of crude oil and the provider of 14 percent of U.S. oil needs. But Mexico's Cantarell oil field, one of the four largest in the world, has already peaked and is now losing a quarter of its production capacity annually. Mexico's economy has also been boosted by the *maquiladora* industry (importing materials and equipment for manufacturing and then reexporting products for U.S. companies) as well as benefited by agriculture. But with oil accounting for 16 percent of total exports, the peso's outlook as a commodity currency remains doubtful. More than 80 percent of the country's exports go to the United States. This means the combination of a temporary decline in oil coupled with further slowdown in the U.S. economy could pose a drag on the currency.

The performance chart in Figure 8.19 illustrates the Mexican peso's underperformance relative to the krone, loonie, and ruble during the four different measurement periods: January 2000 to May 2008, January 2002 to May 2008, January 2005 to May 2008, and January 2007 to May 2008. Interestingly, the Mexican peso ended lower against the USD during the periods spanning January 2000 to May 2008 and January 2002 to May 2008, during which oil surged 382 percent and 479 percent respectively. The krone led all three currencies against the USD in all but one period (January 2005 to May 2008) where it was surpassed by the loonie by a difference of 2 percent.

Brazilian Real   Brazil is known as home to the world's largest sugarcane fields and the cleanest and most energy efficient type of ethanol, but it may also become a major player on the crude oil scene. One year after the world's biggest oil discovery since 2000 was made in Brazil's Tupi field in 2007, a new discovery emerged in Brazil, estimated to raise the number of discovered reserves to as much as 33 billion barrels. Full exploitation of these reserves could lift Brazil to the top-five list of oil producers from its current 19th position. Combining these future-looking oil-specific issues with Brazil's current strengthening fundamentals in ethanol, soybeans, defense technology, and information technology, the prospects for the currency remain promising. Separately, Brazil's partially state-owned oil company Petrobras has become the third-largest publicly traded company in the Americas as of April 2008, with a market value of US$295.6 billion. The company has even surpassed Microsoft, which has a market value of US$274 billion.

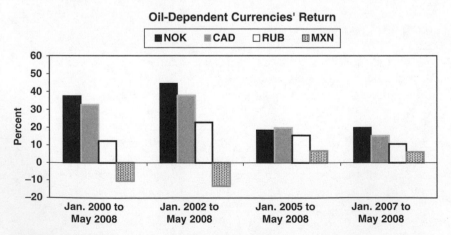

FIGURE 8.19   Norwegian krone proves its superiority as an oil currency while Mexican peso reflects the country's eroding oil output.

Figure 8.20 illustrates the performance of the four oil-dependent currencies against the U.S. dollar between January 2002 and May 2008. January 2002 was selected as the base date as it coincided with the beginning of oil's bull market.

COPPER AND GOLD TO SHINE ON LONG-TERM FUNDAMENTALS

As in the case of energy and grains, supply considerations have supported and are likely to continue to support copper and other metals into at least the rest of the decade, due to the following factors:

- Underinvestment in the mining sector, resulting from the price slump of the 1990s, hampered the creation of large capacity-enhancing projects.
- Prolonged power shortages in Chinese and South African mines are proving to be a structural and long-term impediment, in mines that are further burdened by escalating use and underinvestment.
- Mining companies are experiencing continuous strikes and mounting contract negotiations by mine workers demanding a higher share of windfall profits from surging metals prices.
- The lack of skilled labor is an acute problem for the mining sector.
- Environmental restrictions add to existing delays and lag time.

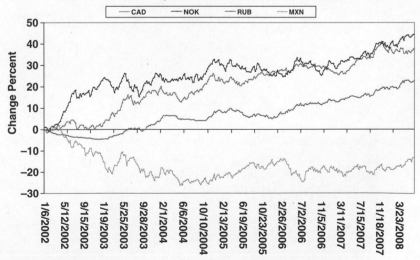

FIGURE 8.20 Norwegian krone and Canadian dollar performance battle it out, leaving peso and ruble behind.

Currency Plays in Gold and Copper

Currency opportunities emerging from gold and copper producers have long reached far beyond South Africa. The emergence of Australia as a powerful copper producer has been instrumental in elevating the aussie among the most heavily traded currencies in the foreign exchange market today. Yet there remain other golden opportunities for currencies in the metals arena.

Chilean Peso   Chile is the world's largest exporter of copper, which makes up nearly 55 percent of its total exports, with overall mining accounting for 8 percent of the nation's GDP. But the world's largest copper producer is also facing energy challenges hitting the mines as prolonged droughts threaten the required supply of water from hydroelectric reservoirs. The demand equation is also bolstered by China's surging copper demand, aimed at rebuilding its faltering power grid. China's power capacity and relatively thin electricity supplies are giving rise to continued forecasts estimating widespread shortages to take place by 2009, thereby reducing regional output in copper, zinc, and aluminum mines.

The 358 percent advance in copper between January 2000 and May 2008 is the second-biggest increase in a single commodity class, second only to the 382 percent increase in oil. Surging copper prices and robust demand have helped lift Chile's current account surplus to 4.4 percent of GDP.

Australian Dollar   Besides an aggressively hawkish monetary policy from the Reserve Bank of Australia prevailing since 2002, the Australian dollar has been remarkably underpinned by soaring copper and gold prices. Australia is the world's fourth-largest exporter of copper, and a leading producer of gold, iron ore, and aluminum. It is also the world's sixth-largest exporter. The 358 percent increase in copper from January 2000 to May 2008 and the near tripling in wheat have helped the economy avoid the strains of a soaring aussie, despite its surge to 24-year highs against the U.S. dollar.

The operational independence of the Reserve Bank of Australia has also brought about an inflation-vigilant central bank, pushing interest rates to a 12-year high of 7.25 percent in spring 2008. This prompted currency traders into opening hundreds of millions of dollars in carry trades, buying the higher-yielding aussie at the expense of the lower-yielding yen, franc, and U.S. dollar. The share of the AUD/USD pair's trading volume as a percentage of daily reported turnover rose to 6 percent in 2007, from 5 percent and 4 percent in 2004 and 2001 respectively. Australia's share of the world's average daily currency turnover rose from 2.4 percent in 1998 to

3.2 percent, 4.2 percent, and 4.2 percent in 2001, 2004, and 2007 respectively, ranking fourth behind EUR/USD, USD/JPY, and GBP/USD.

Peruvian New Sol   Peru's position as the world's second-largest exporter of copper has been a boon to the Peruvian new sol and the overall economy, as the metal makes up 25 percent of total merchandise exports. One way to assess Peru's promising copper future is via the concentration of its exports destined for China, which account for 11 percent of total exports. Having a tenth of its exports sold to China's demand machine helps the economy stave off any potential downturn in demand from the United States, which accounts for 24 percent of total exports.

Prospects remain solid after the government handed out exploration concessions covering 12 million hectares (45,000 square miles), which it estimates will draw about $11 billion in investment between 2008 and 2012. Despite the intensity of supply-side constraints emerging from power outages, labor unrest, and environmental opposition to building new mines, metals analysts have propped their price forecast for copper to increase by nearly 20 percent during the course of 2010–2020, thereby further underpinning the supercycle in the metal.

South African Rand   Although South Africa remains the world's largest gold producer, the once-robust relationship between the South African rand and gold has largely dwindled as a result of South Africa's plummeting gold production. Power shortages, labor unrest, and violence-related disruptions have led to a 73 percent decline in gold production from 1970 to 2007. Gold exports as a percentage of the total fell 50 percent since the 1980s. As a result, the rand fell 10 percent in 2007 despite gold's 100 percent increase over the year. Chronic energy shortages have also forced mines into rationing until new power is brought on line in 2012, thereby depriving miners from exploiting soaring gold prices. This is the opposite case from Australia, whose developed mining companies have the capacity to step up copper production and sell the high-priced metal in the export market.

The shortage situation ultimately dragged South African GDP growth to an annualized 2.1 percent in the first quarter of 2008 from 5.3 percent in fourth quarter 2007. Mining output tumbled 22.1 percent in the first three months of 2008, the biggest decline since 1967. As long as gold prices remain on their ascent and South African mines lose ground on high margin opportunities, the rand is likely to sustain its downward path.

Finally, it is worth noting that unlike the other metal-producing nations in this category, South Africa's exports are concentrated toward Japan and the United States, which together make up nearly 11 percent of total South African exports. Such exposure to the struggling U.S. economy and the lack of exposure to China's anticipated demand surge places South African trade at relative disadvantage to Australia, Chile, and Peru all of which derive a far greater share of exports from China.

Figure 8.21 shows the aussie's performance against the U.S. dollar relative to the rest of the currencies whose nations are large producers of copper and iron ore. Peru's currency, the nuevo sol (PEN), stands as the true emerging currency due to the upside potential for its copper production and yet-to-be-developed mines. When copper prices surged 84 percent between October 2007 and May 2008, the aussie rose 7 percent against the USD, versus 11 percent for Peru's new sol. The Chilean peso also fared positively due to Chile's unchallenged position as the world's top copper producer and exporter. The figure also shows that the once-robust relationship between the South African rand and gold has largely dwindled as a result of South Africa's plummeting gold production. As a result, the rand fell 10 percent in 2007 despite gold's 100 percent increase over the year.

Figure 8.22 charts the remarkable contrast between the South African rand and the rest of the four metal-dependent currencies during 2000–2008. Currency traders are no longer impressed with South Africa's position as world's biggest gold producer, especially as power shortages eroded overall economic output and employment, beyond just the precious metal. Consequently, the rand failed to keep up with gold's 100 percent rise between

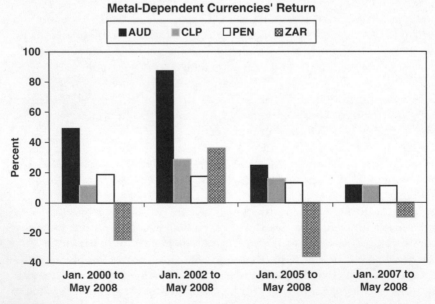

FIGURE 8.21 Aussie leads metal-dependent currencies, while Chilean peso follows closely.

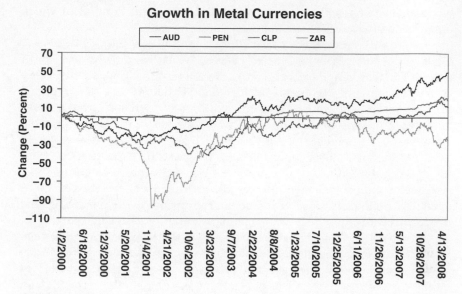

Growth in Metal Currencies

— AUD   — PEN   — CLP   — ZAR

FIGURE 8.22 South Africa's falling gold production takes the shine off the rand.

2005 and 2007 as the currency lost 14 percent before hitting five-year lows against the USD in early 2008. South Africa's leading position as the world's top gold producer may not matter to the markets as much as the gradual diminishing of that position to producing and exporting nations of gold and copper.

COMMANDING HEIGHTS OR COMMON BUBBLES?

After drifting in the shadow of prolonged bull markets in equities, bonds, and real estate for the past two decades, commodities are back in full force, feeding on the appetite of more affluent populations, robust developing economies, and demanding infrastructures. The latest commodity boom has repeatedly been dismissed as a speculative bubble in the making as pundits make flawed comparisons to previous asset bubbles and manias. But not all price surges are the same. Unlike the dot-com bubble of the late 1990s, which was founded on a combination of misperceptions of stock valuations, inexistent corporate profits, outlandish price targets by analysts, and unrealistic expectations by individual investors, the current price cycle in most commodities classes reflects real demand and supply requirements for actual products that are instrumental in the nourishment of growing populations, building infrastructures, and technologies.

On the oil front, China's inevitable path to becoming the world's biggest oil importer combined with peaking supplies worldwide is an integral component serving to maintain prices in their upward trajectory. The growing use of biofuels and increased demand from China and India ties into the growing demand for corn and other grains, thus bolstering the foundation of higher prices for grains and agricultural products. That is why the Organisation for Economic Co-operation and Development (OECD) and the United Nations' Food and Agriculture Organization (FAO) officially declared that world food prices have undergone a paradigm shift and will maintain their high plateau for at least 10 years. On the metals front, gold will likely preserve its secular rally as rising world inflation challenges the role of fiat money. Meanwhile, copper prices remain supported by a virtuous circle of power outages restricting supplies and increased mine construction, and increasing demand for the metal.

Further underpinning these powerful supply and demand forces is the thirst of investors. Index funds specializing in commodities have accumulated $260 billion at end of first quarter 2007, nearly 20 times that in 2003. In the first 10 weeks of 2008, demand for commodity funds grew by more than $55 billion, or nearly $1 billion a day. Rather than catering for short-term speculators, these index funds have helped shape international acceptance of investing in commodities, and made it a new asset class among pension asset managers, insurers, and endowment funds.

The currency implications of these compelling price trends are significant. The broadening of the commodities rally across energy, metals, foods, and agricultural raw materials has increased the share of trading activity in commodity-led currencies such as the aussie, kiwi, loonie, krone, real, and ruble. The Chilean peso and Peruvian new sol have yet to draw the awareness of the average individual investor, but further amelioration in macroeconomic and market dynamics will increase the luster of these two currencies, broadening the choice of investment alternatives in the commodities world. Considering that the average duration of a commodity supercycle has lasted 17 years and the bulk of the present cycle began in 2001–2002, robust price action will remain part of the global economic landscape for commodities and their currencies.

CHAPTER 9

Selected Topics in Foreign Exchange

H aving tackled the bond, equity, and commodity market nuances of foreign exchange markets, we now turn to a compartmentalized approach in the book, revisiting previous themes as well as opening new ones. While the components of the chapter may seem distinct from one another, they all form part of the prevailing debate shaping currencies and the global economy.

In Chapter 6 we focused on the relationship between the U.S. yield curve, the economy, the stock market, and the U.S. dollar. The main purpose was to demonstrate the use of yield curve inversions in anticipating Fed rate cuts. In this chapter, the tables are reversed as we explore the use of steepening yield curves in order to predict interest rate hikes. We then move to the theme of dollar stability, tackling the advantages of a robust dollar as well as the repercussions of persistent declines in the value of the currency. Commodities and equities are also revisited, but this time the focus is placed on commodities as a whole rather than on gold in order to better highlight the relationship between monetary and hard assets. Finally, we venture into the world of U.S. politics, analyzing the patterns and the connection between bipartisan politics and the performance of the dollar, stocks, and the overall economy.

REVISITING YIELD CURVES

In Chapter 6, we analyzed the relationship between yield curve inversions and interest rate cuts, highlighting how this link can be used to predict future changes in interest rates and the implications for currency and equity markets. In this section we focus on how to use the yield curve—as measured by the difference between U.S. 10-year and 2-year yields—in order to signal or predict the timing of Federal Reserve interest rate increases.

Recall that Chapter 6 focused on illustrating the yield curve's effectiveness in predicting interest rate cuts by the Federal Reserve, when other indicators have pointed otherwise. Figure 9.1 starts off with summer of 1998 when the yield curve moved from normal to flat, suggesting the possibility of interest rate cuts ahead. The signal did materialize as the Fed cut rates in September, October, and November to shore up liquidity in the aftermath of the Long-Term Capital Management failure. The yield curve signal was a valuable indicator especially considering that macroeconomic figures were pointing to persistent strength; non-farm payrolls stood above their historical average; and GDP growth was above the Fed's trend growth rate of 2.5 percent.

The yield curve again proved effective when it signaled the peak of the 1990s tech bubble with a two-month lead, which was later followed by a three-year bear market and a recession in 2001–2002. Eleven months after the inversion of the yield curve, the Fed began cutting interest rates, prompting a two-and-a-half-year easing campaign and dragging the funds rate from 6.5 percent to 1 percent.

In January 2006, short-term yields rose above their longer-term counterpart to initiate an 18-month-long yield inversion. As in 1998, the inversion was accompanied by contradictory market signals from record-breaking highs in stocks and escalating liquidity. As the housing market slowdown turned into an outright recession, the repercussions became increasingly prominent in the economy and the financial markets. Once again, the Fed was forced to slash interest rates, less than two months

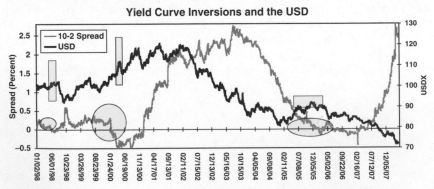

FIGURE 9.1 Inversions in the U.S. yield curve have often preceded Fed rate cuts and USD declines.

after it had warned of inflationary pressures. The central bank slashed rates from 5.25 percent to 2 percent in a matter of eight months. Stocks descended into a bear market and the dollar prolonged its own seven-year bear market.

Yield Curves Patterns Ahead of Fed Hikes

While the preceding dynamics explained the yield curve's effectiveness in predicting interest rate cuts, how could the yield curve be used in predicting interest rate *hikes*? Recall that the period of time elapsed between the beginning of yield curve inversions and the beginning of the Fed cuts ranged from as little as 3 months during the June–July 1998 inversion to 19 months during the January 2006–June 2007 inversion. The duration depended on the length of the inversion, with more prolonged inversions taking longer to signal rate cuts; the converse is also true.

So can we predict interest rate hikes with the opposite of yield curve inversions—that is, yield curve normalization? Figure 9.2 shows the relationship between the Fed funds rate and the yield curve as measured by the spread between the yields on the 10- and 2-year Treasury notes. The chart focuses on the past four tightening cycles, namely February 1994 through February 1995; March 1997; June 1999 through May 2000; and June 2004 through June 2006, with each of the cycles marked by a rectangular box in the chart. Note how all four interest rate hike cycles were preceded by peaks in the 10-2 yield spread, each of which is marked by a circle. Peaking yield spreads are explained by a reduction in the extent to which 10-year yields are gaining over 2-year yields, which is often reflected in a faster increase in 2-year yields. Rising 2-year yields occur when bond traders

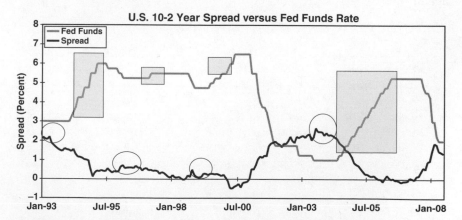

FIGURE 9.2 Peaking formations in U.S. 10-2 yield spread have often preceded periods of Fed rate hikes as short-term yields rose relative to longer-term yields.

begin to anticipate an increase in the Fed funds rate benchmark, prompting the short end of the yield curve higher. As this takes place, rising 2-year yields begin to narrow the difference between 10- and 2-year yields and the preceding increase in the spread begins to lose steam—hence the peak.

In order to better understand the peaking formation of the yield spread, we observe how the chart shows interest rate cutting cycles being accompanied by rising yield spreads (positively sloping curves), which reflect falling 2-year yields relative to their 10-year counterparts. Once the Fed concludes its easing cycle and makes the transition toward a policy of steady interest rates, the post-easing decrease in 2-year yields begins to wane, followed by a gradual turnaround that narrows the difference with 10-year yields. The result is a peak in the 10-2 yield spread. As 2-year yields gain further, the peaking 10-2 yield spread turns gradually lower, at which point is the timing of the interest rate hike.

For each of the past four rate hike cycles, the duration between the peak of the respective 10-2 yield spread and the start of each rate hike were as follows: The February 1994 through February 1995 cycle took place 10 months after the 10-2 yield spread had peaked; the March 1997 rate hike took place 13 months after the peak of the spread; the June 1999 through May 2000 hikes started 8 months after the peak; and the June 2004 through June 2006 started 11 months after its spread. Determining the peak of the 10-2 yield spread may prove challenging in its use to predict the first rate hike. But as each of the four examples illustrates, the peak has either occurred in the midst of a period of steady Fed funds rates (April 1993 and June 2003) or has coincided with the bottoming of the Fed funds rate—in other words, at the same time as the last rate cut (February 1996 and October 1998).

Can USD/JPY Help Anticipate Rate Hikes?

The preceding examples illustrated how investors could use the relationship between 10- and 2-year Treasury yields to anticipate the timing of Federal Reserve interest rate hikes. In order to help improve the accuracy of this anticipation, one more tool is added. Figure 9.3 illustrates the relationship between the Fed Funds and the USD/JPY exchange rate. The chart revisits the past four interest rate hike phases of February 1994–February 1995, March 1997, June 1999–May 2000, and June 2004–June 2006, with each of the phases marked by a rectangular box around the Fed funds rate graph. The Fed funds rate is overlaid against the USD/JPY exchange rate, which represents the number of yen per U.S. dollar.

Note how the beginning of each interest rate hike was preceded by a bottoming in the USD/JPY rate (highlighted by circles) due to the

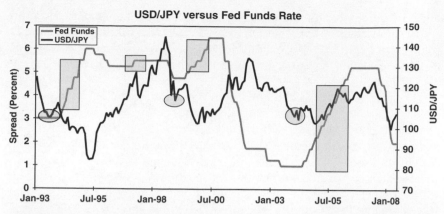

FIGURE 9.3 Bottoming formations in USD/JPY rate have preceded tightening cycles from the Federal Reserve.

anticipatory nature of currency markets. Over the years, Federal Reserve policy has grown more transparent to the public to the extent that shifts in monetary policy are increasingly being telegraphed. Thus, as economic figures show marked improvement across the broad sectors and policy makers shift toward a hawkish rhetoric emphasizing inflationary risks, bond yields begin to push higher and the dollar starts to strengthen. The bottoming process in USD/JPY is best used as a signal for higher U.S. rates as traders rush in to take advantage of anticipated carry trade opportunities, selling low-yielding yen and investing the proceeds in higher-yielding U.S. dollar investments.

Table 9.1 summarizes the various time durations elapsing between peaks in yield spreads and interest rate hikes, as well as the duration between bottoms in USD/JPY and Fed hikes. As mentioned earlier with the relationship between the 10-2 spread and Fed hikes, the four most recent rate hikes were preceded by a signal in the yield spread with time lags ranging from 8 to 11 months. The duration is fairly comparable and effective for figuring out future Fed hikes. But it is important to note that the effectiveness of the 10-2 spread signal serves best when it occurs during extended periods of steady interest rates.

The last column of Table 9.1 summarizes the duration between the lows in USD/JPY and the beginning of interest rate hikes. The effectiveness has grown stronger over time as currency markets have become more responsive to the increasingly transparent Federal Reserve. Aside from the interest rate hike of March 1997, where the bottom in USD/JPY preceded it by as long as 21 months, the other three tightening cycles saw a lag of only two to six months between the bottoming dollar and the rate hike.

TABLE 9.1 Bottoming Formations in USD/JPY Rate Preceded Tightening Cycles from the Federal Reserve

10-2 Yield Spread Peak	Interest Rate Hike Period	Time Elapsed Between Spread Peak and Rate Hike	Time Elapsed Between USD/JPY Bottom and Rate Hike
April 1993	February 1994 to February 1995	10 months	6 months
February 1996	March 1997	13 months	21 months
October 1998	June 1999 to May 2000	8 months	6 months
July 2003	June 2004 to June 2006	11 months	2 months

The prolonged 21-month period between the 1995 bottom in USD/JPY and the 1997 rate hike is due to the 63 percent rally in the dollar between summer 1995 and spring 1997. This rally was caused by combination of (1) massive capital outflows from Japanese investors following the burst of the Japanese stock bubble; (2) the dollar's secular bull market driven by high U.S. growth; (3) surging U.S. equities; and (4) a "strong dollar policy" communicated by then U.S. Treasury secretary Robert Rubin.

Determining the direction of U.S. interest rates offers one of the most vital indicators in financial markets, influencing the capital markets, currencies, equities, and commodities, as well as the medium-term functioning of the U.S. and global economies. Since the relationship between short- and long-term bond yields is paramount in predicting Federal Reserve policy, it is a valuable gauge of future economic and financial market activity as well as the value of the dollar.

IS DOLLAR STABILITY A NECESSITY?

In spring 2008, financial markets witnessed the early makings of what may emerge as globally coordinated support for stabilizing the U.S. dollar. The first signs occurred at the April G8 meeting in Washington, D.C., where finance ministers and central bankers of the world's leading economies expressed concern about the economic repercussions of persistent damage in the U.S. currency. Not only had a rapidly falling dollar further deepened the emerging economic slowdown in places such as Europe, Japan, and Canada by excessively lifting their currencies and hampering their exports, but it also signaled the acceleration in the dollar price of key commodities, such as oil and food, which boosted the cost of these imports and lifted inflation at home. Never since the 1980s has the United States and its trading partners experienced such a deep and protracted loss in the value of the dollar, and not since the Louvre Accord of 1987 have the world's leading economies expressed such broad concern with the falling U.S. currency. The U.S. Dollar Index lost 40 percent of its value between January 2002 and April 2008, averaging a decline of 8 percent per year.

On June 3, 2008, Fed Chairman Ben Bernanke shook the currency market by taking the unusual step of talking up the dollar in a speech at the International Monetary Conference in Barcelona, Spain. The topic of the dollar had long been the purview of the U.S. Treasury since the 1990s, when then Treasury secretary Robert Rubin shaped the so-called "strong dollar policy." But as the currency slipped into a multiyear decline between 2002 and 2007, the strong dollar policy was limited to mere rhetoric and no action.

In fact, the real currency policy of the United States had grown to be that of benign neglect as Treasury officials tacitly encouraged a depreciating dollar so as to favor U.S. exporters. Meanwhile, the Federal Reserve's actions were everything but dollar positive when policy makers engaged in aggressive easing of monetary policy by sharply slashing interest rates in two different easing cycles within less than five years. In the aforementioned speech, Bernanke said, "We are attentive to the implications of changes in the value of the dollar for inflation and inflation expectations and will continue to formulate policy to guard against risks to both parts of our dual mandate, including the risk of an erosion of longer-term inflation expectations." The speech was largely perceived as a potential sea change in the U.S. economic priorities vis-à-vis the value of the dollar.

Further signs of the U.S. administration's worries over its currency appeared when Treasury Secretary Hank Paulson practically urged leaders of the Gulf States not to depeg their currency regimes from the U.S. dollar. Those oil-rich nations had tied their currency to the dollar for as long as the past 20 years in order to gain currency stability, but the dollar's intensifying decline since 2002 had meant higher costs of imports and soaring inflation. The dollar peg has also required these countries to follow the Federal Reserve's monetary policy of cutting interest rates, which only exacerbated soaring prices of food and commodities for their citizens.

Despite the economic costs of such currency regimes, Washington has pleaded with its Gulf allies to maintain the status quo, claiming that inflation was caused by the global commodities phenomena as well as rising home rents in those countries. A more serious reason for Washington's reluctance is that breaking away from such a long-held dollar-based regime would herald a major phase in the dollar's corroding cycle, and may accelerate selling of the currency by speculators as well as longer-term asset managers.

Eurozone politicians at the June 2008 G8 meeting also sought to stabilize the dollar decline and cap the excessive appreciation of their single currency by noting that preserving dollar confidence is a prerequisite for attaining some calm in oil prices and tempering global inflationary pressures. Having lost control of monetary policy since the creation of the European Central Bank, Eurozone governments are left with the authority to set fiscal policy and balance their budgets.

So why all the preoccupation with attaining stability in a currency whose fundamentals have been on the wane for more than seven years? The reasons are outlined in the following sections.

Stability In Oil and Other Commodities

Although oil has proven to be driven by its own supply and demand dynamics, the falling dollar has certainly discouraged OPEC from lowering prices. In fact, USD weakness has given OPEC a pretext to hold production unchanged despite rising prices, not only due to the depreciating value from USD-denominated oil receipts, but also from the already slowing global demand environment.

OPEC is loath to repeat the great miscalculation of 1997 when it made its first output increase in four years, raising its production ceiling by 2.5 million barrels per day. The 10 percent production increase drove up total world output by 3.1 percent in 1997, the highest annual increase in 10 years. The decision was a result of soaring prices into the second half of the year, caused by Iraq's refusal to grant admission to United Nations weapons inspectors that summer. But the price impact of OPEC's supply increase was accelerated by plummeting Asian demand in the midst of the Asian currency crisis, causing oil prices to drop by more than 60 percent from their 1996 high to $9.40 per barrel in December 1998. The experience remains vivid in OPEC's memory and the cartel will make sure it remains just a memory.

Tackling Global Inflation

Continued erosion in the USD triggers further escalation in oil prices and amplifies inflationary pressures throughout oil-importing nations. It also broadens the overall commodities boom into food and agricultural raw materials as higher natural gas prices boost the cost of nitrogen fertilizers. Other agricultural inputs running on high fuel prices, such as trucks, also contribute to rising prices in the sector. And finally, the resulting increase in metals prices from overall inflation drives the cost of industrial applications emerging from copper and aluminum.

Reducing Fed Policy Dilemma

Since a stable dollar is instrumental in capping energy prices, it reduces inflationary pressures generated from the import pass-through. Consequently, this prevents the Fed from having to raise interest rates at the risk of triggering fresh disruption in housing and labor markets.

The first six months of 2008 worsened central banks' policy dilemmas between rising inflation and slowing economic growth. The European Central Bank and the Bank of England have seen inflation surge by more than a full percentage point above their mandated maximum annual rates of 2 percent, while at the same time growth slowed to near contraction territory. In the United States, although the Federal Reserve is not bound by an explicit inflation target or ceiling, surging inflationary pressures have shifted the central bank's focus away from slowing growth to that of rising prices. With financial markets feeling the strains of the subprime crisis and unemployment not having topped out, the Fed's anti-inflation crusade runs the risk of further undermining the downside risks to growth and driving the economy well into recession. Failure to steer the ship carefully may drive the country into a 1970s style stagflation, with soaring inflation prices, accelerating unemployment rates, and subpar to negative growth.

Relieving Pressure on ECB Policy

Oil price stability alleviates the second-round inflation effects of energy prices and eases the pressure on the European Central Bank to meet its price stability mandate by tightening monetary policy or talking tough on inflation. Such measures would only provoke further euro appreciation and risk jeopardizing the slowdown across the 15-nation region. Cognizant of the fact that a firm euro helps absorb the inflationary pass-through of USD-denominated oil imports, currency markets have increasingly bid up the euro in times of rallying oil prices. The repercussions of higher oil prices on U.S. growth have also led to the decline in the dollar.

As mentioned earlier, currency traders' most direct means of punishing the dollar is done via the EUR/USD exchange rate. Thus, if a robust dollar succeeds in bringing about stable oil prices, it would ease pressure off the ECB from having to steer monetary policy largely toward combating rising energy prices.

Reinstilling Confidence in U.S. Markets/Assets

Establishing confidence in the U.S. dollar affirms foreign interest in U.S. markets and maintains the financing of the current account and budget deficits. As a result, robust foreign demand helps increase the price of U.S. Treasury securities and caps bond yields. China's increased accumulation

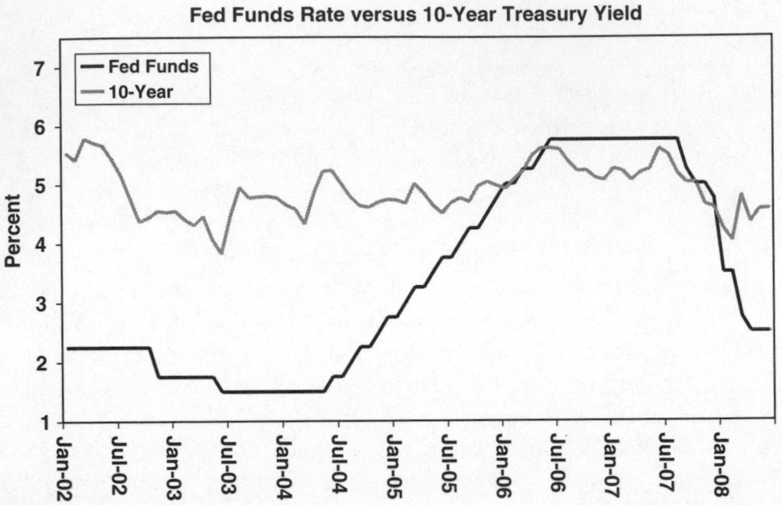

Fed Funds Rate versus 10-Year Treasury Yield

FIGURE 9.4 The Fed hikes of 2004–2007 failed to boost yields in long-term U.S. Treasuries.

of U.S. Treasuries between 2003 and 2005 had kept 10-year yields generally confined to the 3.5 percent to 4.5 percent range. Low bond yields had taken place despite the Federal Reserve's increase of interest rates during the same period. Other factors included bond traders' forcing down of bond yields as they began pricing a low inflation environment. Figure 9.4 shows the divergence between rising Fed funds rates and relatively flat 10-year yields.

But the situation began to change when foreign net purchases of U.S. Treasury notes and bonds reached a plateau in spring 2004. As the dollar extended its declines, foreign purchases continued to falter, raising questions about the long-term implications of foreign interest in U.S. assets. These doubts further resurfaced as a result of waning foreign participation in auctions of U.S. government debt, such as 2-, 5-, and 10-year Treasury securities. Figures 9.5 and 9.6 illustrate the pertinent peak and subsequent decrease in foreign demand for U.S. government auctions of 2-year and 10-year U.S. Treasury notes after 2005.

Deteriorating confidence in the U.S. currency impacts general investor perception of the value of holding U.S. assets, barring the potential for capital gains in these assets. We saw in Chapter 7 the increased role of sovereign wealth funds (SWFs) in shaping global capital flows. Sovereign wealth funds from the Gulf States, valued at nearly $800 billion, have begun diversifying away from the United States, directing focus toward Asia and Europe. When including SWFs from China and Singapore, the amounts exceed $1.5 trillion. As the bear market emerged in global equities in 2007,

FIGURE 9.5 Foreign participation in U.S. government 2-year Treasuries began to wane in 2005.

FIGURE 9.6 Foreign participation in U.S. government 10-year Treasuries descended into a notable downtrend despite occasional recoveries.

led by the domino effects of the subprime credit crisis in the United States, many of these SWFs' holdings lost as much as 15 to 20 percent within one year of their initial investments in U.S. banks and companies.

Several economists have backed the thesis that Gulf State funds will continue to direct their focus toward U.S. markets as long as they are bolstered by rising oil revenues. But one should not confuse the current environment with the late 1970s when Gulf nations' petrodollars had no other way to flow but to U.S. banks, prompting the latter to lend hastily to Latin American nations without careful credit analysis. Capital flight and faulty monitoring of those eventually led to the Latin American debt crises. Today, SWFs have a whole new world to the east side of the globe, with equity stakes in Singapore and China becoming attractive investment alternatives to U.S. investment stakes.

Tackling Inflation in Gulf States and Reducing Need of FX Depeg

Considering that the currency regimes in Arab Gulf nations are tied to the U.S. dollar, a falling dollar tends to reduce the value of these local currencies, which raises the value of imported goods and drives inflation at home. The problem is intensified by the dollar's 35 percent decline against the euro between 2003 and 2008. This has hit countries whose share of total imports from Europe has risen to as high 30 percent. A firmer dollar helps stabilize the value of these currencies against non-USD currencies and stabilize the cost of imports. It also curbs OPEC's concerns with oil pricing and reduces the need for them to consider alternative-currency pricing of their USD-denominated oil, such as in euros or a basket of currencies. Even a change toward a basket of currencies that is dominated by the dollar would have considerable psychological effect among traders, asset managers, and the media, with the main headlines announcing the "end of dollar hegemony" after nearly 40 years of USD-pricing of oil revenues.

A more stable dollar helps relieve several policy shocks in the U.S. and global economies via direct and indirect mechanisms. U.S, European, and Asian officials have recognized this fact as they witnessed the extent of prolonged dollar damage via oil, commodities, international trade, and financial market contagion. A major challenge is whether central bank and finance ministry officials can effectively steer markets into a more stable dollar via more hawkish interest rate expectations, without the risk of exacerbating the shaky U.S. labor and housing markets.

HOW FAR WILL COMMODITIES OUTSTRIP EQUITIES?

In Chapter 1 we tackled the relative growth between gold and equities in order to compare the evolution of two popular measures of value: perceived corporate market value (equities) versus real asset value (gold). We noted that between January 2002 and June 2008, gold rose by nearly 10 times as much as the S&P 500 and the Dow Jones Industrial Average. A more important finding is that throughout the twentieth century, the equities/gold ratio had peaked every 35 to 40 years, and followed by a long-drawn-out pullback toward the preceding lows, which lasted for 7 to 15 years.

At the time of this writing, the major equities/gold ratios have fallen by more than fivefold from their 1999 highs. In order for the ratios to remain persistent with the patterns of the past 100 years and reach the lows of the early 1980s, they have to lose at least another 70 percent. Such a development may entail a loss of as much as 15 percent in stocks from their levels of June 2008 in addition to the 20 percent declines that have ensued since the October 2007 highs. It would also entail a rise of at least 50 percent in gold. From a time perspective, the period 2008–2015 is likely to witness continued outperformance in gold relative to equities in order for the decline in the equity/gold ratio to remain consistent with the past 100 years.

Are Commodities Too Rich for Equities?

What about the rest of commodities? Do the equity/gold ratio patterns apply for other commodities? We start off by comparing the S&P 500 Index with the Reuters/Jefferies-Commodities Research Bureau Index (CRB), the most renowned index of commodities prices. Figure 9.7 shows that as of

FIGURE 9.7 Commodities and equities recovered during 2003–2006, but stocks later topped out, paving the way for commodities to assume the next bull trend in financial markets.

the end of June 2008, the CRB had closed at a fresh new all-time high while the S&P 500 closed at a three-month low, losing 20 percent off its record highs of October 2007. The CRB appears to have a more volatile ascent than the S&P 500 during the 27-year period, partly because it consists of 28 different commodities. Note how the 2003–2006 period showed an increase in both indexes as global economic growth extended from the usual increase in corporate market values, reaching toward an Asian-led commodities boom. The weakening dollar helped grease the wheels of the commodities boom as those items were largely priced in the greenback.

As the U.S. economy began to falter in 2007 on the heels of a severe adjustment in housing, stocks followed suit, bonds were mixed, and commodities took the mantle of the next financial bull market. Figure 9.8 highlights the increased pace in the growth of commodities relative to equities during the equities rebound of 2003–2006, before the momentum turned largely in favor of commodities and dragged the S&P 500/CRB ratio to 12-year lows. The importance of this chart is underlined by the evolving performance of corporate value (as measured by equities) against the performance of natural resources, as measured by an index of 28 commodities, ranging from energy, metals, agricultural raw materials, and food products.

Despite the 12-year lows in equity/commodity ratios, the current price trend has yet to unfold in order for the ratio to revert to the lows of the early 1980s. This is cogently illustrated in Figure 9.9, where the equity/commodity ratio is halfway toward reaching its historical lows. Although the 1980s lows are consistent with the lows seen in the equity/gold ratio, the commodity/equity ratio has a greater chance of attaining further downside due to the specific developments in individual commodities groups.

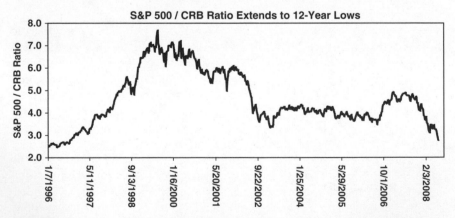

FIGURE 9.8 The S&P 500/CRB ratio dip to 12-year lows as commodities thrive across the board, while equities are hit by economic slowdown and financial market erosion.

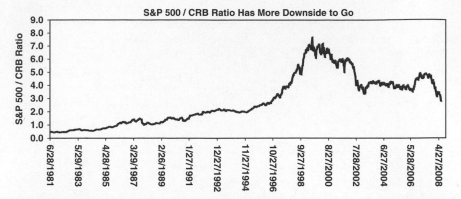

FIGURE 9.9   Past history shows commodities have yet to eclipse equity indexes, a possibility with significant implications for currencies.

Recall that in Chapter 8 the analysis of commodities was broken down into oil, gold, copper, wheat, corn, and soybeans. We found that the rally in gold had begun in 2001, followed by an intensification in oil prices in 2002, which was later joined by food and agriculture materials in 2006.

How Long Can Oil Stain Gold's Shine?

There is another emerging trend within the commodities universe that bears significant implications for the financial markets. The relationship between gold and oil has been highlighted by a complete leadership in the fuel relative to the metal and other commodities.

In Chapter 6 we explored the historical relationship of the gold/oil ratio and how protracted declines in the ratio have persistently caused recession or significant slowdown in the U.S. economy since the 1970s, as well as a cooling in the rest of the industrialized world. The rationale is that a plummeting ratio is a reflection of an excessive rise in oil prices, whose marked appreciation relative to gold signals cost and inflationary repercussions for importers and consumers. Figure 9.10 illustrates that the gold/oil ratio fell to a record low of 6.0 in June of 2008, well below its monthly average of 15.2 prevailing since 1971. Anticipating a mean-reverting rebound in the ratio, we expect an ensuing gold price recovery toward the $1,030 record high and on to the $1,500 territory that would be consistent with the aforementioned decline in the equity/gold ratio. Such a development will likely maintain pressure on the U.S. dollar via its inverse relationship with gold. Accordingly, the commodity story will remain and so will the decline in the S&P 500/CRB ratio.

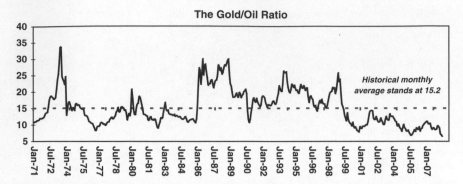

FIGURE 9.10 As the gold/oil ratio tumbles to record lows, reaching less than half of its historic average, the implications for U.S. growth remain ominous.

It could be argued that a recovery in the gold/oil ratio may also emerge on the heels of a tumble in oil prices and a more modest decline in gold, which would lift the ratio toward 9.0 or 10.0. Such an event would be accompanied by a significant rebound in the U.S. dollar as falling oil prices ease the strain off the U.S. and other oil importers. A pullback in oil prices is inevitable, but OPEC is unlikely to allow prices to drop considerably below $100 per barrel.

Chapter 8 made the case for a prolonged increase in the current commodities boom. The confluence of supply and demand factors boosting the broad commodity story suggests the bullish trend is unlikely to be reversed soon. And in looking at the commodities implications of further declines in the equity/gold ratio, it appears certain that real-asset values of tangibles such as metals, energy, and agriculture/food products will maintain their upward trajectory.

U.S. POLITICS AND THE U.S. DOLLAR

Much has been written about the relationship between the U.S. presidential elections and the performance of the stock market. A considerable amount of statistical exercise has been undertaken in dissecting the correlations and causalities involving partisan control of Congress, midterm elections, balance of power between White House and Congress, and the impact of double-term presidencies. In this section, we tackle all of these political dynamics from a currency, equity, and economy perspective.

In Table 9.2 the second column indicates partisan control in the White House; the third column shows the corresponding bipartisan control in Congress; the fourth column shows the annual performance of the U.S. Dollar Index, followed by the annual performance of the S&P 500 in the

TABLE 9.2 The Dollar, Equities, Economy, and Bipartisan Politics

Year	Political Party Controlling the White House	Partisan Control in Congress	Annual Percent Change in U.S. Dollar	Annual Percent Change in S&P 500	Economic State
1971	Republican	Democrat	−8%	11%	No recession
1972	Republican	Democrat	−1%	16%	No recession
1973	Republican	Democrat	−7%	−17%	Recession
1974	Republican	Democrat	−6%	−30%	Recession
1975	Republican	Democrat	6%	31%	No recession
1976	Republican	Democrat	1%	19%	No recession
1977	Democrat	Democrat	−7%	−12%	No recession
1978	Democrat	Democrat	−9%	1%	No recession
1979	Democrat	Democrat	−1%	12%	No recession
1980	Democrat	Democrat	6%	26%	Recession
1981	Republican	Split	16%	−10%	Recession
1982	Republican	Split	12%	15%	Recession
1983	Republican	Split	13%	17%	No recession
1984	Republican	Split	14%	1%	No recession
1985	Republican	Split	−19%	9%	No recession
1986	Republican	Split	−16%	13%	No recession
1987	Republican	Democrat	−17%	2%	No recession
1988	Republican	Democrat	8%	11%	No recession
1989	Republican	Democrat	1%	21%	No recession
1990	Republican	Democrat	−11%	−7%	Recession
1991	Republican	Democrat	2%	21%	No recession
1992	Republican	Democrat	6%	4%	No recession
1993	Democrat	Democrat	5%	7%	No recession
1994	Democrat	Democrat	−8%	−2%	No recession
1995	Democrat	Republican	−4%	25%	No recession
1996	Democrat	Republican	4%	17%	No recession
1997	Democrat	Republican	13%	24%	No recession
1998	Democrat	Republican	−6%	21%	No recession
1999	Democrat	Republican	8%	16%	No recession
2000	Democrat	Republican	9%	−12%	Recession
2001	Republican	Democrat	7%	−15%	Recession
2002	Republican	Democrat	−13%	−31%	No recession
2003	Republican	Republican	−15%	21%	No recession
2004	Republican	Republican	−7%	8%	No recession
2005	Republican	Republican	12%	3%	No recession
2006	Republican	Republican	−8%	11%	No recession
2007	Republican	Democrat	−8%	3%	No recession
2008*	Republican	Democrat	−6%	−15%	—

*As of July 3, 2008.

fifth column and the state of the economy in the sixth column. The data for 2008 are valid through July 3, 2008.

Here are some of the conclusions drawn from the patterns observed over the past 38 years. (The current year, 2008, is included even though the year has not ended at the time of this writing.)

Dollar Performance

Of the 38 years analyzed, 20 years saw negative dollar performance versus 18 years of positive performance. Seven of the 20 negative years occurred when the White House and Congress were controlled by the same party. And in all but 2 of the 20 negative dollar years, the dollar declines occurred in series of at least two consecutive years. The years 1990 and 1998 were the only negative dollar years where the decline was preceded and followed by an increase in the currency. The 1990 dollar decline occurred due to the recession caused by the savings and loans crisis and soaring oil prices resulting from Iraq's invasion of Kuwait. The subsequent Fed rate cuts dragged the dollar across the board. The 1998 dollar decline emerged from sharp unwinding of yen carry trades away from the dollar in the midst of a liquidity crisis in capital markets in the aftermath of the collapse of hedge fund Long-Term Capital Management. Similarly, all but one of the 18 years of dollar gains occurred in a string of at least two consecutive years. The year 2005 was the only year in the period 1971–2008 in which the dollar delivered stand-alone rising performance, as a result of the Fed's interest rate hikes as well as the temporary reduction of taxes on U.S. multinationals' repatriated profits.

Such patterns reinforce the notion that currencies move in trends, particularly a widely traded currency such as the dollar. As fundamental dynamics build up and are accentuated by shifts in asset managers' portfolios, traders' flows, and speculative sentiment, the trend grows increasingly established in the market.

The impact of U.S. presidential and midterm elections on currency markets was especially prominent during the controversial 2000 presidential elections and the 2006 midterm elections. In November 2000, the already tumbling euro sustained a severe blow from the dollar at the announcement of a victory for President George W. Bush. The dollar rally emerged on the tax-cutting agenda by Republicans, which was considered a boon for the markets, especially after a series of tax hikes from former Democratic president Bill Clinton. Inaccurate media reporting of the 2000 election, erroneously declaring candidate Al Gore the winner, prompted sharp but short-lived declines in the U.S. dollar. In the 2006 midterm elections, Republicans' full loss of power of both the Senate and the House of Representatives sped up the pace of an already declining greenback as the Democrats planned to phase out the Republican-led tax cuts after their expiration in 2010.

Stock Market Performance

The stock market's performance is measured by the S&P 500, which is a broad and frequently used index for benchmarking fund performance. Of the 10 years of negative stocks performance, 7 occurred during a Republican-controlled White House versus 3 under Democratic control. Of the 28 years of positive stock performance, 19 occurred during bipartisan control between the White House and Congress.

Regarding the relationship between the dollar and stocks, 7 of the 10 negative years for stocks coincided with negative years for the dollar when 2008 is included. At time of this writing, the dollar is down 6 percent and stocks are down 15 percent year-to-date. Fundamentally, the relationship between stocks and the dollar had been prominently positive during the early 1980s and the second half of the 1990s. In the early 1980s, the Fed's staunch anti-inflation war under the command of Paul Volcker boosted interest rates toward 20 percent, rendering the dollar an attractive return on foreign investors' funds, while stocks recovered as inflation was dampened and oil prices retreated. In the second part of the 1990s, U.S. equities attracted persistent growth in foreign capital flows while European economies floundered in stuttering recoveries and Japan remained in a deflationary spiral.

Economic Performance

The criteria used to determine whether the economy fell in a recession in a given year is the number of quarters showing negative GDP growth. The years 1973, 1974, 1980, 1981, 1982, and 2001 each showed two quarters of negative growth, though not necessarily consecutive quarters; 1990 and 2000 were also recession years even though they had only one negative quarter. At the time of this writing, economic reports are increasingly pointing to a recession in 2008, but the organization in charge of officially declaring U.S. recessions has not yet done so. The National Bureau of Economic Research usually announces recessions about two or three quarters after they start. Due to this formality, 2008 is excluded from the recession count, leaving us with eight recessions between 1971 and 2007. Six of these eight recessions occurred under a Republican administration versus two occurring under the Democrats, in 1980 and 2000. Regarding the sharing of power between Congress and the White House, seven of the eight recessions took place during a bipartisan split (1973, 1974, 1980, 1981, 1982, 1990) while one occurred in 1980 during dual control by the Democrats.

U.S. Elections and the Currency Effect

The preceding performances served as a reference for the historic relationship between currencies, equities, and the economy, with an added political backdrop. Going into a presidential election year in U.S. politics, financial markets fret about the potential for adverse tax consequences of a Democratic president, whereby the prevailing tax cuts will not be renewed after their 2010 expiration. The impact of the 2006 midterm elections on currency markets was also prominent as the Democrats snatched both chambers of Congress from the Republicans. The dollar, which was already under pressure as the Fed ended its rate hikes while other central banks continued tightening, accelerated its decline across the board.

There are themes other than taxes to be watched by currency traders ahead of the upcoming presidential election. Markets will closely watch the escalating rhetoric out of Washington proposing regulations by curbing speculation in commodity markets. Any measures deemed to hamper trading volumes in U.S. commodities exchanges may not only drive domestic capital out to foreign exchanges but also keep foreign capital from entering the United States.

The effect would not be too dissimilar from the delisting of several foreign companies in U.S. equity exchanges as a result of the Sarbanes-Oxley Act of 2002 (SOX), which expanded audit procedures for publicly traded companies. The Act sent the number of foreign cross-listings relative to new domestic listings to their lowest level in 16 years.[1] Non-U.S. companies choose to cross-list in the United States, using the American Depositary Receipts (ADRs), which represent an ownership interest in securities of non-U.S. companies. Accordingly, cross-listing in the United States by foreign companies allows U.S. institutional and individual investors to diversify internationally without having to trade in a foreign market and undergo the foreign exchange risk. But the SOX Act has prompted foreign companies to delist from U.S. exchanges as the costs of compliance outweigh the benefits of cross-listing. Meanwhile, U.S. companies seek other alternatives, such as going private or listing in Canada.

U.S. Treasury Secretaries and Dollar Performance

As the two-term Bush administration went through three Treasury secretaries and a 35 percent decline in the value of the dollar in a period of eight years, we reflected on the relationship between the background of U.S. Treasury secretaries and the value of the U.S. currency. The relationship is

---

[1]See http://www.nysscpa.org/cpajournal/2007/307/essentials/p32.htm.

worthy of analysis, particularly due to the Treasury's official authority to make pronouncements and conduct policy concerning the dollar.

James Baker, Treasury secretary under the second Reagan administration, led a historic intervention in the mid-1980s to drive down the overvalued dollar in coordination with the world's most powerful economies. Bill Clinton's Treasury secretary Robert Rubin coined the "strong-dollar policy" in the mid 1990s, helping to usher in multidecade highs in the value of the currency. When President George W. Bush took over the White House in 2001, none of his Treasury chiefs could stabilize the dollar. Or we could rephrase that sentence to say that none of his Treasury secretaries found it a priority to support the currency, considering the currency's excessive strength at the early stages of the presidential first term.

Table 9.3 highlights the relation between the backgrounds of former U.S. Treasury secretaries and the value of the U.S. dollar under the tenure of those secretaries since the currency became freely floating in 1971. Treasury secretaries with considerable background in banking and/or Wall Street have served during periods of mostly dollar strength. Bill Simon of Salomon Brothers (1974–1977), Donald Regan of Merrill Lynch (1981–1985), and Robert Rubin of Goldman Sachs (1995–1999) served during the best rallies for the U.S. currencies. In contrast, the dollar's worst

TABLE 9.3 U.S. Treasury Secretaries and the Value of the Dollar

Treasury Secretary	Employment Prior to U.S. Treasury	Tenure	Performance of Dollar Index
John Connally	Texas governor	Feb. 1971–June 1972	−9.7
George Schultz	Dept. of Labor secretary	June 1972–May 1974	+8.2%
William Simon	Salomon Brothers	May 1974–Jan. 1977	+5.3%
Michael Blumenthal	Bendix Corp.	Jan. 1977–Aug. 1979	−17.2%
William Miller	Textron Inc.	Aug. 1979–Jan. 1981	+9.2%
Donald Regan	Merrill Lynch	Jan. 1981–Feb. 1985	+68.2%
James Baker	Private law practice	Feb. 1985–Aug. 1988	−38.1%
Nicholas Brady	Banking, U.S. Senate	Sep. 1988–Jan. 1993	−5.4%
Lloyd Bentsen	U.S. Senate	Jan. 1993–Dec. 1994	−4.0%
Robert Rubin	Goldman Sachs	Jan. 1995–July 1999	+13.4%
Lawrence Summers	Harvard University	July 1999–Jan. 2001	+10.5%
Paul O'Neill	Alcoa Inc.	Jan. 2001–Dec. 2002	−9.2%
John Snow	CSX Corp.	Feb. 2003–June 2006	−13.6%
Henry Paulson	Goldman Sachs	July 2006–Jan. 2008	−15.3%

performances occurred under the tenure of secretaries with backgrounds other than Wall Street. Michael Blumenthal (1977–1979), James Baker (1985–1988), Paul O'Neill (2001–2002), and John Snow (2003–2006) had significant experience in policy making and industry rather than banking or financial services; their tenure as Treasury secretary saw mostly dollar weakness. This 35-year pattern broke in 2005–2008 as former Goldman Sachs CEO Hank Paulson led the Treasury during protracted dollar declines.

The underlying rationale is that secretaries with a background other than banking have generally preferred a weaker dollar in order to boost the priorities of U.S. exports, domestic industry, and employment. Treasury secretaries from the financial services industry have served during periods of general dollar strength, in line with Wall Street's priority to draw foreign capital toward U.S. financial assets and exchanges. Naturally, the performance of the dollar has largely been a function of U.S. economic growth and interest rates relative to the major economies. But the aforementioned patterns between the value of the dollar and U.S. currency policy as part of overall economic priorities have been far from coincidence when factoring in the appointment of Treasury secretaries.

The Breaking of a Pattern

Yet, just as prominent as the relationship between U.S. Treasury secretaries and the value of the dollar has proven to be over the past 40 years, so has the break in the relationship during the term of Secretary Hank Paulson, a former CEO of Goldman Sachs, arguably the world's most successful investment bank. From his nomination on May 2006 to the end of June 2008, Mr. Paulson served during one of the worst two-year periods in the history of the dollar, which fell 15 percent in trade-weighted terms, 24 percent against the euro, and 18 percent against the yen.

Paulson's nomination coincided with the end of the Fed's two-year tightening campaign and the emergence of a rare divergence between the monetary policies and growth rates of the United States and major industrialized nations. Those cyclical problems have compounded the damage in the dollar due to a prolonged slowdown in the U.S. economy, which was accompanied by deepening erosion in the capital structure of U.S. banks and continued instability in the overall financial system. Such are the prominent dynamics in the current foreign exchange market that they trigger the break in multidecade-long patterns, whether the relationship between the currency and the background of U.S. Treasury chiefs, or the gradual transition toward a multidimensional world economic order that is no longer dictated by the pace of the U.S. economy. While one cannot disregard the considerable impact of a U.S. slowdown on the world economy, the cyclical and structural advancement of emerging economies in Asia, Eastern/Central Europe, and South America has increasingly shielded capital and trade flows from the repercussions of a U.S. recession.

Earlier in this chapter we addressed the advantages for the United States and the rest of the world to be gained from attaining stability in the value of the dollar. As long as the greenback remains the world's reserve currency used for invoicing oil and other major commodities, stabilizing its value is paramount in averting a global inflationary spiral at a time of slowing world growth. Failure to secure a soft landing in the U.S. dollar could land the world economy in protracted supply and inflationary shocks, while dealing renewed corrosion in U.S. financial markets as the world loses confidence in the currency. When President Bush appointed Mr. Paulson at the helm of the U.S. Treasury in May 2006, his main priorities consisted of bolstering confidence in the U.S. economy and financial markets via preserving the tax cuts beyond 2010, expanding access for U.S. businesses in China, and pushing Beijing to bring about faster appreciation in the remninbi. From a strict currency perspective, the goal of the appointment was to further pursue a competitive dollar without compromising the world's confidence in it. But not even Mr. Paulson could avoid the currency impact of the Fed's aggressive interest rate cuts resulting from what is increasingly becoming the most penetrating credit crisis of the last sixty years.

This chapter has revisited a few themes already tackled throughout the book, while turning to a new page concerning the role of U.S. politics in shaping the long-term dynamics of the dollar and the U.S. economy. Whether evaluating the case for a Fed rate hike, questioning the relevance and importance of dollar stability, or assessing the long-term direction of commodities relative to equities, such topics are likely to comprise part of the long-term thinking in financial markets in general and currencies in particular.

CONCLUSION

The scope of this book has extended beyond listing the mechanics of foreign exchange markets or breaking down the various methods of analyzing them. The main goal has been to incorporate the flows in commodity, equity, and bond markets into currency dynamics, with a detailed look at the principal drivers of central bank policy. It is not a coincidence that the dollar has fallen below parity against the Swiss franc and Canadian dollar at the same time that gold prices have surged above $1,000 per ounce for the first time in history. Nor is it a matter of chance that the secular

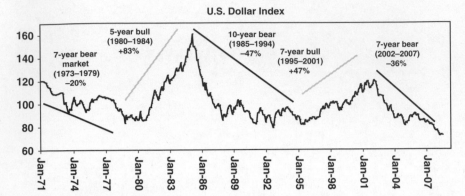

FIGURE 9.11 Has the dollar neared the end of its bear market, or will it break from past patterns and extend its sell-off?

dollar decline is accompanied by a new supercycle in commodities, which is increasingly dwarfing the relative performance of equities. Understanding the interrelationships molding these markets together is essential in grasping financial markets forces with minimal confusion and distraction from what often can be noise and corrective price patterns. Figure 9.11 summarizes the journey of the U.S. Dollar Index since 1971.

The key gauges of risk appetite have been introduced so as to better track speculative funds into low- and high-yielding assets, across currency, equity, commodity, and bond markets. And with the multitude of new currencies now becoming available for trading by retail and institutional investors, effective ranking of FX performance must go beyond comparing returns simply against the dollar or the euro. Using gold and oil as secular benchmarks helps draw important conclusions pertaining to commodity currencies and enables more profitable trading of stronger currencies versus weaker ones.

Last but not least, financial markets make little sense without understanding the price of money. Rather than focusing on each and every pronouncement by central bank officials and risk being behind the curve or, at best, in line with the rest of the pack, investors can assess future moves in interest rates by dissecting the interaction between short- and long-term interest rates, and how their co-movements interact with the general economy, the stock market, and the currency. Contrasting and comparing interest rate patterns and cross-market developments can pay major dividends in determining the next shift in central bank policy and in the price of currencies.

Bibliography

BOOKS AND ARTICLES

Blas, Javier. "Bullish on Bullion." *Financial Times*, January 4, 2008. http://us.ft.com/ftgateway/superpage.ft?news_id=fto010320081425010501&page=2.

Brice, Steve. "Kuwait Revaluation Is Not a Sign of Things to Come." *AME Info*, May 21, 2006. http://www.ameinfo.com/86603.html.

Energy Information Administration. County Analysis Briefs 2008. http://www.eia.doe.gov/cabs/Russia/NaturalGas.html.

Evans-Pritchard, Ambrose. "The Bell Rings Time for the Steel Boom." *The Daily Telegraph*, April 30, 2008. http://www.telegraph.co.uk/money/main.jhtml?view=DETAILS&grid=A1YourView&xml=/money/2008/04/28/ccview128.xml.

Falloon, Matt. "Dollar Pegs Spur Global Inflation—Bank of England." Arabian Business.com, June 26, 2008. http://www.arabianbusiness.com/523139-boes-king-dollar-pegs-add-to-inflation-pressure-?ln=en.

Greider, William. *Secrets of the Temple*. New York: Simon & Schuster, 1989.

Kaufman, Henry. *On Money and Markets*. New York: The McGraw-Hill Companies, 2000.

Kishan, Saijel, and Gavin Evans. "Metals Surge as Rationing Cuts Power at Biggest Mines." *Bloomberg*, May 5, 2008. http://www.bloomberg.com/apps/news?pid=20601103&sid=aCUU6NbjPfmM&refer=us.

Kosich, Dorothy. "Barrick Concerned about Lack of New Gold Industry Discoveries, Drop in Global Mine Production." Mineweb, May 7, 2008. Mineweb, http://www.mineweb.com/mineweb/view/mineweb/en/page34?oid=52491&sn=Detail.

Mathur, Naveen. "China to Keep Copper Shinning [*sic*]." New Delhi Television Limited, April 17, 2008. http://www.ndtvprofit.com/2008/04/17191141/China-to-keep-copper-shinning.html.

Mitsuhito, Ono. "Rising Crude Oil Prices Affect the Japanese Economy." Japan External Trade Organization (JETRO), July 2007. http://www.jetro.go.jp/en/stats/survey/pdf/2004_07_other.pdf.

Murphy, John J. *Intermarket Analysis: Profiting from Global Market Relationships*. New Jersey: Wiley Trading, 2007.

Reuters. "Saudi Inflation Tops 5% Even as UAE Sees Plunge." *Arab News*, December 25, 2007. http://www.arabnews.com/?page=6&section=0&article=104954&d=25&m=12&y=2007.

Salomon, Steven. *The Confidence Game*. New York: Simon & Schuster, 1995.

Zhu, Hong, and Ken Small. "Has Sarbanes-Oxley Led to a Chilling in the U.S. Cross-Listing Market?" *CPA Journal*, March 2007. http://www.nysscpa.org/cpajournal/2007/307/essentials/p32.htm.

GENERAL RESOURCES

The following are Internet links to central banks, government and non-government agencies as well as business-related media, serving as a useful addition to the research of the book.

Bank of International Settlements   www.bis.org

Bloomberg Financial Markets   www.bloomberg.com

Chicago Board Options Exchange   www.cbot.com

Economic Research Service, U.S. Department of Agriculture   www.ers.usda.gov

Energy Information Administration, U.S. Department of Energy   www.eia.doe.gov

Federal Reserve Bank of Atlanta   www.frbatlanta.org

Institute of Supply Management   www.ism.ws

International Monetary Fund World Economic Report   www.imf.org

Ministry of International Finance, Japan   www.mof.go.jp/english/

Organization of Petroleum Exporting Countries (OPEC)   www.opec.org

Reuters/Thompson   www.reuters.com

The Bank of Canada   www.bankofcanada.ca

The Bank of England   www.bankofengland.co.uk

The Bank of Japan   www.boj.or.jp.en

The CIA 2008 World Fact Book   www.cia.gov/library/publications/the-world-factbook/

The Economist   www.economist.com

The European Central Bank   www.ecb.int

The Financial Times   www.ft.com

The Reserve Bank of Australia   www.rba.gov.au

The Reserve Bank of New Zealand   www.rbnz.govt.nz

The Wall Street Journal   www.sj.com

U.S. Bureau of Economic Analysis   www.bea.gov

U.S. Census Bureau   www.census.gov

U.S. Commodity Futures Trading Commission   www.cftc.gov

U.S. Department of Labor   www.dol.gov

U.S. Department of the Treasury   www.ustreas.gov

U.S. Federal Reserve Board   www.federalreserve.gov

U.S. Geological Survey   www.usgs.gov

About the Author

Ashraf Laïdi is the head foreign exchange strategist at CMC Markets, where he oversees the analysis and forecasting functions of G10 currency pairs as well as decisions and trends of the major global central banks. Laïdi is also responsible for education services and informing clients on the essential dynamics underpinning FX markets. His FX analysis has received a wide following for more than a decade, centering on G10 currencies and economies.

Prior to joining CMC, Laïdi monitored the performance of a multi-FX portfolio at the United Nations, assessed sovereign and project investment risk with Hagler Bailly and the World Bank, and analyzed emerging market bonds at Reuters. Laïdi also created the first 24-hour currency web site for traders and researchers alike on the eve of the creation of the euro.

Laïdi regularly appears on CNBC TV, Bloomberg TV, CNN, PBS's *Nightly Business Report,* and BBC. His insights also appear in the *Financial Times,* the *Wall Street Journal, Barron's,* the *New York Times, Marketwatch, TheStreet.com, Futures,* and a host of other international publications. He is fluent in English, Arabic, French, and Spanish. He is the founder of *AshrafLaidi.com.*

Index